Educating the Disadvantaged Learner

Part III of *The Disadvantaged Learner*

The Disadvantaged Learner consists of three parts, which are published in two forms to respond to prepublication requests:

A single-volume edition, comprising all three parts and bound in cloth covers.

A set of three volumes in paper covers,
each volume equivalent to one part of the single-volume edition.

The titles of the three paperbound volumes are:

Knowing the Disadvantaged
Understanding the Educational Problems of the Disadvantaged Learner
Educating the Disadvantaged Learner

The page numbers in the three paperbound volumes are identical with those in the single-volume edition. The contents of the single-volume book is printed at the end of each paperbound volume.

⤙•⤚

Educating the Disadvantaged Learner

⤙•⤚

PART III of

The Disadvantaged Learner

Edited by STATEN W. WEBSTER

University of California, Berkeley

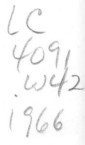
 CHANDLER PUBLISHING COMPANY

124 SPEAR STREET, SAN FRANCISCO, CALIFORNIA 94105

CONTENTS

v

PREFACE

Why This Book?

The events of recent years have begun to illustrate the situation of large numbers of American citizens who can be classified as disadvantaged. Such persons can be considered socially disadvantaged because the society has tolerated attitudes, social practices, and legal barriers which have restricted their access to equal opportunity competition and to possible full self-realization commensurate with their abilities. Within this group of people is a cross section of the ethnic fabric of the American people. However, a disproportionately large number of the disadvantaged Americans are members of the oppressed nonwhite and bilingual minority groups.

The ever-increasing concentration of socially disadvantaged persons in our major urban areas has been termed the "urban revolution." This mass movement of our population is bringing increasing numbers of individuals who are ill-equipped to cope with urban life into a highly competitive, sophisticated, automation-ridden environment. Among such persons are rural and Southern Negroes, Puerto Ricans, Mexican-Americans, poor whites, and increasingly larger numbers of American Indians.

The arrival of these newcomers has a profound effect upon cities in a variety of ways. Urban whites possessing better educational attainment, political sophistication, and leadership potential flee to the security of suburbs to escape interaction with these groups. Crime rates and levels of social dependency increase and produce additional demands for public services upon an already inadequate tax base. Schools change in ethnic composition overnight. Long conditioned to instructing eager learners, teachers find themselves helpless in their efforts to educate the generally hostile, alienated, educationally retarded, and uninterested new students.

So massive is this problem in its present and potential dimensions that in 1960, as cited by Riessman, one out of every three students in the schools of our fourteen largest cities could be classified as disadvantaged. It is predicted that by 1970 the ratio may increase to one out of every two students in such cities.[1]

---

[1] Riessman, Frank, *The Culturally Deprived Child* (New York: Harper & Row 1962), p. 1.

The problems of the big urban centers are further complicated by the fact that the average age of the nonwhite and other ethnic minority in-migrants tends to be significantly younger than that of the white population. These newcomers enjoy a decided advantage in potential reproductive years. Even now, a major proportion of the total nonwhite population lives in large cities.

No social institution feels the effects of the urban revolution as directly as the schools of these cities. Also, no other social institution can effectively assume the function of the schools in this aspect of social change.

Why this book? As indicated by the title, this collection seeks to assist the reader in getting to know the disadvantaged groups of this country and their millions of learners. Second, it aims to increase the reader's awareness and understanding of the problems associated with teaching the disadvantaged student. Finally, it is hoped that this book will introduce to the reader some of the exciting and fruitful approaches used by educators in attempting to educate the disadvantaged student more effectively.

Organization

The Disadvantaged Learner is divided into three parts. This book contains Part III. Each is prefaced with an introduction and followed by the presentation of several general articles which set the stage for an understanding and appreciation of the more specific selections following.

In essence, this book makes use of the sociocultural approach to increased understanding of and effectiveness with the disadvantaged learner. It is based upon the premise that one must know something about the learner, his subculture, and his sociophysical environment before one can realistically see his problems and help him to learn in an effective manner.

Uses of the Book

It is hoped that this book will be of value to the individual reader (be he an educator or not) who seeks to know and understand better the problems of socially disadvantaged groups and learners. Another possible use is as a text in classes dealing with problems of urban education. Finally, a book such as this could be used effectively as a reference source or text for in-service workshops and institutes dealing with problems of disadvantaged learners. With these groups in mind then, an effort has been made to effect a proper blending of the factual, theoretical, and practical.

ACKNOWLEDGMENTS

I am indebted to those numerous authors and publishers who so willingly permitted the use of their work in this volume. Special appreciation is given to Miss Linda Shlep and to Mrs. Lou Bernhardt, who assisted with the preparation of the final manuscript, and to Mrs. Gertrude Funkhouser who encouraged me throughout the preparation of this publication.

Special appreciation is also given to the students whose original poems are presented at the beginning of each section of the book. These adolescents are students in the Special Opportunity Scholarship Program at the University of California, Berkeley, for promising high school students. The idea for this program originated with Dr. Owen Chamberlain, Nobel laureate in physics.

Enrolled in the program are large numbers of ethnic-minority-group students from disadvantaged backgrounds. Those pupils represented in this text were enrolled in a social science class which I taught during the summer of 1965. The poems cited were the products of a homework assignment in which the students were asked to write from the perspective of a person from the lower socioeconomic class.

Educating the Disadvantaged Learner

THE GIFT OF KNOWLEDGE

The gift of knowledge
Does not come easily.
Do your homework,
Learn! Arise!
I can't!
Young children fighting, crying,
Screaming.
Mother comforting,
Sometimes
Screaming back at the young children
Under my feet.
Late to bed, I can't sleep.
I hear them arguing,
Mother crying
In the next room
And I know, to rise
Out of this hole,
I must KNOW,
I must overcome.

DEBBIE WINSTON

Foreword

Public education is faced with what is perhaps its greatest challenge—
the effective education of the socially alienated, often unmotivated,
and retarded disadvantaged learner. It may well be that the continued
development of America as a democratic and open class society will be
influenced by the ways in which we cope with this massive problem.

A new form of education is needed. Methods and curriculum patterns which have been directed toward learners from the more favored,
motivated, middle segment of American life are largely unsuccessful
with disadvantaged learners. Ideas being advanced in the literature
suggest that education for these students must be more cognizant of the
learner and his problems. It must be more dynamic and impactful in
its methodology, and its curriculum must be carefully designed to emphasize the sequential and integrated learning of essential content.

It is possible that the increased attention being devoted to the learning problems of the disadvantaged may be productive of an educational revolution which will bear fruit for students not falling in this category. The increased emphasis on student involvement, discovery of
knowledge and solutions to problems, and creativity can very well
change the course of American education.

This possible revolution in education is in its initial stage, since little
attention appears to have been devoted to these problems of educating
disadvantaged learners prior to the sixties. Much remains to be discovered, much remains to be tried, and much remains to be learned.

Educating the Disadvantaged Learner

Part III of *The Disadvantaged Learner* is subdivided into two sections. Articles dealing with school, teacher, and community problems
related to the education of disadvantaged students are found in the
first section, titled "Problems in the Education of the Disadvantaged."

The initial selection, by Niemeyer, deals with the elementary school,
but has much to say to those educators at the secondary level as well.
While Niemeyer's attention is devoted to matters of instruction or curriculum, he also strongly suggests that the basic structure and organization of the school in disadvantaged areas may need changing.

Throughout this entire section, emphasis is placed on school-community relations problems, the problems of administrators and counselors, and of those teachers facing the demanding task of educating disadvantaged and alienated pupils. Bettelheim's selection about these teachers clearly illustrates the interpersonal and instructional problems involved.

Section I serves as background to the second section, "The Process of Educating the Disadvantaged Learner." Presented initially are selections by Ausubel, Webster, and Bloom which contain both theoretical and practical strategies aimed at the related problems of motivation and learning of the disadvantaged. These articles are followed by published articles and original selections written by teachers and other educators. In addition to discussing problems associated with educating the disadvantaged learner, these articles, representing a variety of subject areas and all grade levels, present specific approaches to education, and will hopefully challenge as well as inform the reader.

This material does not represent all of the possible ways in which the disadvantaged can be more effectively educated. Thousands of good ideas and approaches are being used presently which will never find their way into the literature. This book will serve its purposes if it stimulates new ideas and creative approaches to the solution of this vital educational problem.

Section One:

PROBLEMS IN THE EDUCATION OF THE DISADVANTAGED

﹈•﹈

Some Guidelines to Desirable Elementary School Reorganization

﹈•﹈

JOHN NIEMEYER

Some of the experimental projects and research which Bank Street College has recently been conducting will be briefly described here, because they seem particularly pertinent to the topic before this conference and because they may suggest various lines of new action and thought.

Although Bank Street, from its inception in 1916 as the Bureau of Educational Experiments, has been conducting multiple-discipline research in the area of schools and learning for children up to adolescence, it has in the past 5 years been working particularly on the question of how the elementary schools in New York City, and presumably in other large urban centers, can raise the learning level of the children of lower social class families, especially those of minority groups.

Since 1943, Bank Street has worked cooperatively with the Board of Education of New York to improve a number of elementary schools, many located in crowded, low socioeconomic neighborhoods in the city. In 1957 the superintendent of schools invited Bank Street to try to help a cluster of three integrated elementary schools to strengthen their programs in various ways so as to (1) check the drift away from these schools of white middle-class families; (2) attract to the nearby middle-income housing development then under construction middle-class families with children who would, hopefully, enroll their children in these public schools.

The field action team for this project consisted of a sociologist, a social psychologist, and an educator working fulltime, as well as four

Reprinted with permission of the Department of Health, Education, and Welfare, from *Programs for the Educationally Disadvantaged*. John Niemeyer is at Bank Street College of Education, New York.

classroom consultants who worked in these three schools part-time. These teacher consultants were public school teachers, selected by Bank Street and then assigned by the superintendent to this particular project. They worked directly with classroom teachers in the three schools to help them strengthen their classroom programs. The other Bank Street team members worked with the principals, the district superintendent, the parents, and certain community agencies. Other aspects of the project included a writing workshop for teachers who wished to prepare materials meaningful to their pupils; a preliminary sociological study of a school and the school system; seminars for the 30 principals in that school district; and the beginning of the Parent-Teacher Communication Project.

The most important outcome of this project for Bank Street was the development of our hypothesis as to the cause of low achievement in schools of this kind and a general conclusion about what needs to be done to correct the situation.

Our hypothesis is that the chief cause of the low achievement of the children of alienated groups is the fact that too many teachers and principals honestly believe that these children are educable only to an extremely limited extent. And when teachers have a low expectation level for their children's learning, the children seldom exceed that expectation, which is a self-fulfilling prophecy. A logical concomitant to this hypothesis is the conclusion that the problems of these schools will not be solved simply through "more services" or "changing family backgrounds" but through a functional, and probably structural, reorganization of the schools themselves.

The following areas should be scrutinized for needed reorganization:

1. The Child, His Teacher, and the Teaching-Learning Program

An effective way to start would be for a school to take a hard look at everything it does and every aspect of the curriculum. It cannot do this productively without looking at the children and asking the question: "What are the interests and needs, the motivational forces for learning, the learn-pattern with which these children come to school?" Is it not possible that these children have resources for the educational program which do not depend upon books, or the arts, or intellectual conversation in the home? May it not be that these children have a deep foundation for educational growth in their day-to-day social experience in urban life? And how can the school, without relinquishing its long-range goals, change its approach so as to take advantage of the true educational potential of these children?

A few of the projects which Bank Street is engaged in at this moment seem particularly relevant to this first area of reorganization:

Multiculture "Readers" Project. One specific way in which schools have unconsciously augmented feelings of alienation is by introducing children to the world of reading and books through readers which hold up as an exclusive model the culture pattern of the white middle-class suburban family. The child knows in his heart that the school gives the highest prestige value to books, and yet everything that is familiar to him is excluded from the image of life presented in the books which the school provides. Consequently, Bank Street has a team of writers working to produce readers which will use stories and illustrations to reflect back to children the positive aspects of the variety of community and cultural settings which constitute American society. These will not be books written specifically for minority or low-income groups, but will be books for and about all children. Important, too, is the fact that these books will be published by one of the well-established textbook publishers who have previously been afraid of economic repercussions from the production of books like these. This should help to break down some of the stereotypes which have characterized all instructional materials published for our schools.

School Entry Study. This is a research project studying the relationships among such factors as home background, method of entry into kindergarten, the type of kindergarten program, and apparent success of adjustment to the school world on the part of the child. Both middle and lower social class children are involved, and the public school kindergartens which served as locations are very different in character. From this study should come helpful hints for curriculum changes at the kindergarten level.

Classroom Processes Study. In four public schools offering contrasts in racial and socioeconomic settings, the classroom life of four second grades and four fifth grades has been examined to clarify mental health implications for children. The report from this study is expected early in 1963 and should reveal possibilities for beneficial changes in school practices. It will also probably provide a new procedure by which schools can analyze a classroom in terms of its learning climate.

2. The School's Role Vis-a-vis Parents and Community

This is the second area for reorganization. Because Bank Street feels that the schools's first job is to cast out the mote from its own educational eye instead of concentrating upon the eye of family background, it does not follow that the school should not do everything possible to help parents help their children learn in school. Neither does it follow that the school can think of itself as a community agency operating in isolation from all other community agencies. Each school operating in a deprived neighborhood needs to work cooperatively with all of the agencies in that neighborhood. Further, certain schools will need to take on some of the responsibilities which usually are thought of as belonging to social agencies and not the school. One elementary school in Philadelphia, for example, has won the cooperation of police and milkmen to the extent that the school learns early in the morning of any child who has been locked out of his home for the night. Such a child is greeted by the principal, given a hot shower and breakfast, and put to bed for several hours. This may seem a far cry from the usual role of the school, but children of this type in this particular school had proved to be drastic disrupting forces and obviously learned nothing during the schoolday.

All persons speaking at this conference have reported somewhat the same findings that Bank Street has gained: namely, that nearly all parents, even those who are severely alienated or defeated, look upon the school as the one source of hope that their children will have better lives than they have had. Nevertheless, the problem of how the school can help parents help their children in school is not an easy one to solve.

Even though these parents look to the school with hope, many of them are fearful and confused in relation to the school. Furthermore, the school has difficulty in communicating with these parents. Sometimes there is an actual language barrier, but more often the chief barrier is stereotyped thinking on the part of both teachers and parents. There is also the communications barrier which separates different social classes. One mother, speaking of a previous Parents Association meeting, said, "In that there meeting the principal and all the teachers called us dopes—poor slobs that don't know what our kids are getting from school." To which the principal immediately countered, "Why, Mrs. ——, you know very well that no one said anything of the kind in that meeting," and the mother in question replied, "Maybe you didn't say it, but that's what the atmosphere said." However correct or incorrect this parent was in her perception, it is clear that communication between her and the professional staff would be difficult. Two of Bank Street's present projects may be of interest here.

The Teacher-Parent Communication Study. In this project a Bank Street team consisting of a social psychologist and an educator has been working with a school in a depressed area to try to improve the communication between school and parents. In the first phase of the project, most of the kindergarten and first-grade teachers, faced with the necessity for holding periodic conferences with their pupils' parents, worked with the Bank Street team to try to understand the obstacles to effective communication. They evaluated all contacts between the school and parents (a copy of their report is available from Bank Street on request), and the Bank Street team attempted to affect the attitude of the teachers by broadening their cross-cultural understandings. In the second phase of the program, which is now in progress, the attention of the Bank Street team was turned more to the total school situation. Depth interviews have been held with 44 parents. An effort has been made to study the implications of pupil turnover and all the subtle and overt ways in which the school deals with parents.

The plan for the coming year will also include experimentation with a research educator and licensed teacher in the role of assistant to the principal in improving the communications between the school and the parents of the school's children.

Study of a parent's association in relation to the total system of a school. In one of the projects located in a school within a low socioeconomic neighborhood, the attempt is to facilitate change by working with classroom teachers, the principal, and the parents. A research educator with much experience in schools has been assigned to work with the very active Parents Association. The leadership of the association, mostly Negro, is troubled, as is the school principal, about the fact that only a small proportion of the parents participate in the activities of the association. The researcher has assisted the parent committee and, having won its confidence, is now interviewing other parents to ascertain their attitudes toward the school and the Parents Association. In 1962-63 the researcher's findings will be reported in appropriate ways to the parent leadership and the principal as the basis for new practices. One of the purposes of the total project is, of course, to devise better ways for the school to stimulate the kind of participation which gives positive support to the learning of the children in school.

3. The Internal Organization of the School as an Entity and as a Part of a System

The third area calls for scrutiny. The school in its efforts to educate the "disadvantaged" must begin to study itself as a social system. An individual school is a small culture in and of itself; as such, it may operate in certain ways which prevent many of its pupils from realizing their true learning potential. Here is one very practical example: Many schools unconsciously seem to put out an "unwelcome mat" to parents. A parent who comes to one of these schools enters the school office and is faced with a long counter, behind which are three or four secretaries. No one is set up as a receptionist. No names are in evidence. The parent may stand for a long time, shifting from foot to foot, before anyone comes to inquire as to his or her mission, let alone to extend a welcoming hand and smile. Yet the secretaries in question are friendly, warm people, devoted to the school and their work. What has happened is that somehow, subtly, there has been built into the system of the school a deep impersonality in terms of relationships between the school and the parents. Another example, much more serious perhaps, is the condition which exists in most school systems by which each lower rung on the bureaucratic ladder is led to believe that its purpose is to serve the rung immediately above. Somehow, down at the very foot of the ladder is the child in the classroom.

Of help in facing this entire problem should be the sociological studies which have been in process at Bank Street. A number of mental hospitals and one large industry have been studied as social systems, but the American school apparently has not. At the moment Bank Street's chief sociologist, Dr. Donald Horton, and his associates are conducting such a study. The study was begun in some of the schools of New York City but is now being carried out in the town of Brookview in a neighboring State. One particular school in the system is being studied while at the same time the entire school system in a community of 30,000 population is being examined as a whole. The reports on these studies should be published by 1965.

Equally important to knowing what changes should take place within our schools is knowing how change can be brought about in the schools and particularly in the school systems of our large cities. We are all familiar with many of the ways in which educators have traditionally worked to bring about change. Among these methods are in-service courses, the study of children and children's behavior by small groups of teachers, conferences and workshops, assistance to teachers, demonstration schools and classes, bulletins of curriculum bureaus, dicta issued by the superintendent, and so forth. A recent report done for the Commissioner of Education in New York State takes the position that change can be brought about in a school system only if those in high authority require the change and if they simultaneously provide teachers with demonstration units which offer proof that all of the teachers can do what the demonstration unit is doing. This is not a new approach to the process of change in education, even though the author of this particular report would have the goals for change established through research. The prevailing method being used in the programs attempting to upgrade schools in the economically depressed neighborhoods of our big cities is to saturate these schools with all kinds of "special services." It remains to be seen whether the chief change which will result will be upgrading of children's learning or the elimination of the responsibility of the classroom teacher for the learning of each pupil.

The truth is that the process of change in our large school systems is baffling. This process is one which Bank Street is studying intensively. Our hypothesis is that the most productive kind of change process is that which involves intervention at many points in the social system called a school. This calls for actual experimentation. In the school mentioned above in relation to our study of the Parents Association, Bank Street is quite obviously attempting "to intervene," as the researchers say, at all levels of this particular school. Principals in schools like these who wish to bring about change are often baffled by what seems to them to be teacher indifference, if not opposition. The teachers, on the other hand, frequently feel that the principal is interested in his pet projects but does not pay attention to the changes which they, usually as individuals, wish. The parents, or at least the active parents, finally feel obligated to participate in the school but usually do not know why they are participating, and unless they are middle-class parents, for whom having an organization in itself is a satisfying aim, they do not know how to proceed vis-a-vis the principal and the teachers. In a school such as this it is quite apparent that the traditional procedures for attempting to bring about change or to introduce innovations may not be effective. The Bank Street effort to work for change in all phases of the school simultaneously, therefore, may well open up productive new approaches to the problem.

The entire project team meets regularly at Bank Street College with the principal of the school. By the end of the first year the principal has begun to involve more and more teachers. An increasing number of parents are thinking about why they should participate in the school. Also, the principal has seemed increasingly receptive to parent action; rather than regarding it as obstructive, he has come to see it as an opportunity for the school to educate parents about their supportive role. It is not yet certain whether the teachers by and large have begun to lose the suspicion which they seemed to feel at the beginning of the project. (In many of our other efforts to bring about change in schools, work had been done only with teachers who volunteer for the project. It is made very clear to teachers and principal that only those things will be reported about any teacher which the teacher herself decides shall be reported.) . . .

༔•༔

The Role of Parents and Family Life

༔•༔

GORDON P. LIDDLE AND ROBERT E. ROCKWELL

To what extent is it reasonable to expect help from the parents of disadvantaged children? In the past we have expected little from the disadvantaged child and even less from his parents, and perhaps because of these expectations, our experiences have not caused us to change our views. Recently, however, a number of people have been suggesting that many parents of the disadvantaged can play a constructive role in the education of their children if the school will modify its methods of working with parents. This chapter will examine some of these suggested modifications.

A number of person share the view recently expressed in the *Washington Post* by Eve Edstrom:

A Harlem child's learning potential and verbal skill are about normal when he enters school—and dip sharply between the third and sixth grades. Consequently, Haryou's planners conclude that the real knockout blow to Harlem children is dealt by "inefficient and inferior" schools and not by woefully deficient homes which, they state, have only a "minimal" effect on school achievement rates.

The authors of this chapter disagree with this view. They have been working with disadvantaged four to nine-year-old Negro and white children. Their testing and observations have led them to conclude that a majority of children in disadvantaged communities come to school very unprepared to succeed in the traditional elementary school

From *Journal of Negro Education*, Summer, 1964. Reprinted by permission of the publisher and the authors. Gordon P. Liddle is director of the Interprofessional Research Commission on Pupil Services, College of Education, University of Maryland; Robert E. Rockwell is chief consultant, Quincy Youth Development Commission, Quincy, Illinois. This research was supported by the National Institute of Mental Health, Grant No. OM-633.

curriculum; they come to school already seriously retarded, particularly in their verbal skills.

Nevertheless, in most communities the schools are doing little to enlist the aid of parents in helping disadvantaged children find ways of becoming successful. When school programs have the interest, enthusiasm, and encouragement of parents behind them, they usually do a reasonably good job of educating children; when the schools "go it alone," their batting average is very poor.

✳ The most important learnings in life begin in the family. It is here that children learn the extent to which people can be expected to help or hurt you, the extent to which you can trust others, and the extent to which the world is going to be a pleasant or painful experience. In the home children learn to communicate. They pick up the words, the intonations, and the actions which establish or inhibit communication with others. They learn when it is important to listen carefully, and when it is best to withdraw into yourself. In the family the child learns who he is and how he is valued by others.

It is difficult to know whether or not, on the average, all groups of children are created equal at the time of conception, but we do know that by the time children are born, diet and prenatal care have begun to make their influences felt. The preschool years accentuate intergroup differences. If meals are little more than individual raids on the icebox, children don't get a balanced diet. If vision and hearing difficulties are not diagnosed and treated, the child is partially cut off from his world. High fevers, if untreated, often result in brain damage.

Usually the disadvantaged child has a sufficient quantity of stimulation. His home is crowded and the TV is blaring, but the stimulation lacks variety and meaningfulness, and the language he hears is unlike that he will be expected to use at school. What he sees on television is not interpreted to him so its educational usefulness is limited. Viewing the late show, quite common among disdvantaged children, inhibits learning the next day. The disadvantaged child has too few toys and books, and too little opportunity to be read to or to engage adults in conversation.

Adults do not have to be well-educated to be intellectually stimulating to young children. Skeels and Dye found that a group of infants who were raised by a group of institutionalized mentally retarded young women during the first three years of life and then were placed in foster homes came to have, on the average, slightly above-average intelligence. The parents of the disadvantaged can learn to play the important functions of showing, telling, and listening for their children.

Unfortunately, disadvantaged children often arrive at school deficient in tender loving care. Their emotional relationships with adults have lacked depth and consistency. School-related learning, such as learning to read, is difficult, frustrating, and only distantly related to children's primary needs. Unless children have had relatively good relationships with adults, it is difficult to engage them in the learning situation—as teachers put it, "they don't try."

In their own personal lives the parents of disadvantaged children are usually discouraged and often bitter. They experience more defeat than success. They did poorly in school and, as adults, do little reading. They have dull routine jobs with low status and are frequently laid off in slack periods. When income is low and unsure and children come too soon and too often, everyone suffers, including the children. Many children come from homes which suffer from too much drinking, sickness, and fighting, and too little privacy. If the mother has a serial relationship with a number of men, most of whom have little interest in her children, children come to feel that they are not badly wanted; that they are of little value.

Nevertheless, most children cling tenaciously to their family loyalties and values. Human beings have a strong need to belong somewhere, and children are especially dependent. The child soon learns that even though his parents are not all that he would like them to be, they do feed him when he is hungry, take care of him when he is hurt, and stay with him through the years, while most well-intentioned peripheral adults such as teachers and scout leaders move in and out of his life like serial fathers. Also, within the family the disadvantaged child is thought to be normal or even "smarter than I was at his age," while at school he is often thought to be stupid. We cannot separate the child from his family even if we would like to do so, and the school can make little headway if the home is reinforcing inappropriate attitudes and habits. In most instances, if we are to have a significant effect on a child's motivations and values we must strengthen and change the family's interaction with its children.

Before we can modify the family's educational atmosphere, we must learn to communicate with these parents in a meaningful way. In order to communicate, we must first understand; we must attempt to see the world, including ourselves, from the parents' point of view. We must learn to listen empathically.

The civil rights movement may profoundly change this view, but at present the parents of disadvantaged children feel powerless in a world governed by power. They see the world as being governed by influence and luck rather than by cause and effect relationships. "It is who you know, not what you know that counts." Middle-class parents and teachers teach children that life is a series of hurdles which must be jumped, but these parents teach their children that life is a series of difficult situations which should be avoided if possible. Unfortunately, avoiding the difficult is incompatible with learning.

To a degree the parents' views are reality-oriented. For example, a high school education often does not result in a better job for Negroes. Nevertheless, if disadvantaged children are to be engaged in the educational process, they must come to see that what goes on in school is meaningfully related to jobs and to happiness. This is why programs for the disadvantaged often emphasize parent meetings which bring successful graduates of the school back to give testimonials.

The families of disadvantaged children vary greatly. Some are vitally interested in their children's education, but are inexperienced in knowing how to help. Others love their children but do little with them educationally because they fail to understand the importance of education. Still others have only a shallow relationship with their children.

Often the parents of the disadvantaged view the school with suspicion and pessimism. Their own experience at school was painful and didn't pay off. They don't believe that they can effect any significant changes in the school experiences of their children and don't really expect their children to gain much from the time they spend there. While teachers think of teaching as a demanding, poorly paid job, these parents think of it as a clean, easy job, that pays well.

This does not mean that most of the parents are hostile toward the school. Particularly when the children are young and have not yet failed, parents hope that somehow their child will achieve some success in school. They know that it is difficult to get a decent job unless you've gone "all the way," that is, through high school. They want the teacher to discipline their child into learning, although they don't want him belittled. They want their child to sit still, be quiet, obey the teacher, and keep out of trouble, but they do not communicate a sense of excitement or urgency about school to their children. If we want to modify the communication which takes place between parent and child about school, we must communicate with the parents.

We try to communicate now, but we are often ineffective. We send home health histories and pupil questionnaires which only sophisticated parents can complete. If parents don't fill these out, we label them "uncooperative" but if they fill them out poorly, we laugh at their inadequacies. If we really need this type of information, let's find other ways of getting it. Let's look at the reading level of our notices and forms.

Complicated parent-teacher organizations with officers, by-laws, committees, and money-raising projects are also barriers to communication. Instead we need more opportunities for parents and teachers to sit around over coffee to get to know each other as persons, and more school personnel who are interested in making the school a community center which attempts to bring about needed changes in the neighborhood. In our project we found that informal grade level meetings of parents and teachers built around topics such as children's activities in reading, family field trips, or how to use the public library, frequently brought more parents to school than did school-wide PTA meetings. We made a concerted effort to help parents see how our materials, experiences, and methods contributed to what we were trying to accomplish in class.

We asked parents to participate directly in their child's school experiences whenever possible. Some of the fathers contributed by building a playhouse, a merry-go-round, and painting classroom furniture. Others who had jobs such as firemen and policemen were asked to visit the school to talk about their job with the children. With the aid of advanced planning with the fathers we were able to make this a successful experience for the parent as well as the children. A number of mothers joined us in working with their children in a garden project or in going on field trips and came to school one morning a week to serve as teacher aides. Since parents' aspirations for their children usually reflect their own views of themselves, changing the parents' views of themselves through success experiences in school-related activities is one means of raising children's aspirations.

The parents of the disadvantaged are not organized into community betterment groups, social groups, and a multitude of special interest groups. Except for the store-front churches, they are almost totally unorganized. Going to meetings on a regular basis or serving on committees are not a part of their life. Like the rest of us, they don't want to go where they are not wanted or where they will feel out of place. We are faced with the job of convincing them that they are wanted at school. Do we greet them at the school with an attractive parent lounge or parent-teacher lounge where they can wait in comfort to pick up their children? Or, are they first greeted with a sign saying, "Register at the Office" and then with an irritated, "What do you want?" from the school secretary?

Since many of these parents are reluctant to come to school until they know and trust the people there, we are faced with the necessity of going to them. Going to them in their homes not only gives us an opportunity to see the child in his home setting, but lets the parents know that we are interested in getting to know them and in learning to work with them in helping their child. The children see that parents and teachers know one another, that they are on the same team. This enhances the child's feelings of importance and makes it less likely that he will attempt to play one adult against another. The first visit should be made early in the year. If we wait until we have a backlog of problems, parents are apt to think that we are trying to push our problems off onto them.

Why, then, are there so many schools in underprivileged areas in which home visits almost never take place? Teachers say that they don't have the time, but since, in our view, we must find a way, let's look at some of the alternatives.

In the Banneker district in St. Louis, each school compiles a list of the families sending children to the school. Then each family is visited by a teacher who has one of its children. Since many families have four or five children in the schools, each teacher has only about ten interviews each fall. In other districts, children are dismissed at 2:00 or 3:00 on several afternoons so teachers can visit parents in their homes. Of course, if parents should prefer to come to the school, they should be able to choose that option. Teachers write a note home suggesting an afternoon or evening time and ask the parents to suggest an alternative time from among those available. There will be times when the parents aren't home at the appointed time. When this happens, the parents should be given an opportunity to keep another appointment without resentment being shown.

In part, teachers don't make home calls because they are afraid that they will not be received courteously, but this fear is unfounded. A statement such as, "I'm going to be working with Bob this year, so I'd like to get to know you and to know him better," will open almost any door.

Another reason is more serious. Teachers need to know how to make the interviews productive. A workshop session of an hour or two can be helpful. School counselors, nurses, or teachers who have made home visits can lead the group through discussion and role playing to see what a first home visit can be like. Teachers shouldn't try to accomplish too much in one interview. Usually they should try to get across only one main point. The first task is to get acquainted. Later, the teacher or home visitor will usually want to leave the parent with some learning-related activity which the parents can undertake with their child. This activity should not be complicated, nor should it be of long duration, but by some means the parent needs to be able to report back on the success or failure of the project to the teacher.

Teachers sometimes feel safer if they carry with them a short form to be filled out by the teacher as she interviews the parents. This form might elicit information on the child's past experiences of an enrichment nature, his interests, his feelings about school, and the parent's ambitions for the child, but long involved questionnaires which emphasize parental inadequacies are not a good way to give parents a feeling of oneness with the teacher.

In making home calls or in attending parent meetings status differences should be de-emphasized. Teachers should dress appropriately. This is not the time to wear high heels, a hat, the new spring dress, and the latest hairdo, nor is it the time to discuss a European trip.

In school with large numbers of disadvantaged children, there is probably more need for parent education than any teacher has time for. In these schools, unless class size is lowered, the school should hire a home-school liaison person. This might be a school social worker, or it might be a high school graduate from the neighborhood. In either case the home visitor is not primarily a case history taker, nor is she a therapist. Rather, the home visitor is a bearer of information. She talks to the teacher about the children. She finds out how each child is doing in class, and what the teacher thinks the parents can do to help the child develop his or her interests or overcome a learning difficulty. The visitor should be prepared to give the parents *specific* suggestions. The visitor can also talk to the parents about units that are being studied, trips that are going to be taken, etc., to urge the parents to talk with their children about the trips, read stories on certain topics, watch certain TV shows, etc.

In visiting with the parent the home-school visitor asks about children's evaluations of their school experiences. "What does he seem to enjoy that we are doing in school?; or, "What is he having difficulty with?"; "Has he told you about our trip to the hatchery?" Parents who are not in the habit of asking their children, "What went on in school today?"; "What are you learning?"; "What is causing you trouble?"; etc., can learn to do this if we can convince them that this is important in motivating their child and in helping the teacher to individualize her instruction of their child. If parents would start talking to their children about their learning, would ask their children to read to them, etc., learning rates would increase.

Unfortunately teachers have often been guilty of telling parents that they, the parents, are at fault for their children's failure, without offering any remedies for the situation. When parents ask for concrete suggestions, instead of giving actual demonstrations of how the parent can help with school work, we too often say, "Well, he's a little slow, but he may pick up in time," or, "The proper teaching of reading requires professional techniques, and I've found that parents without proper training frequently cause permanent damage." In effect we tell parents not to meddle with their child's difficulties and to adjust to a life of frustration. The communication of this attitude reinforces parent negativism toward the school.

Until a good relationship has been established, visitors to the home should give the parents plenty of forewarning. Many of these parents feel on the defensive and have been investigated by various governmental and social agencies. Advanced notice helps to alleviate the feeling of being spied upon, and demonstrates that we appreciate the fact that parents are usually busy people too.

Any aid or suggestions offered should be made in a nonpunishing manner, and care must be taken not to try to improve Junior in every area of life at once. Be liberal with praise and encouragement, and help them to be comfortable enough to voice their complaints. Be more interested in understanding the parents than in justifying the school's position.

Home visitors do however interpret school policies, talk about and urge attendance at forthcoming parent meetings, pave the way for possible unpleasant realities such as retention, and steer parents to agencies who can help them with health, relief, and other problems with which we are not equipped to work.

Detroit, New Haven, and other cities are expanding their efforts to involve parents in the planning and evaluation of parent meetings aimed at educating children. They are also surveying the parental needs for adult education in areas such as sewing and how to buy foods wisely, and are giving refresher courses in typing or other skill areas for parents who need a salable skill. Unfortunately many of these parents have needs for employment or problems with older or younger children that are so strong that it is difficult to get them interested in the child we are interested in until they have gotten some help with the more immediate problem. School based people who are wise in the ways of agencies and have the status the parents don't have, can often prepare the agency for the problems they might encounter with these parents. Their interest, sponsorship, and follow-through will often get a reluctant parent to the help he needs.

In summary, no school program will achieve marked success unless the interest, enthusiasm, and encouragement of the parents is present. From the day he enters school the lower-class child is faced with the obstacle of understanding what education is all about and why he is there; when his parents understand he will understand. Parents must be taught how to implement their aspirations for their child. In order to do this school personnel must reach out to the parents, establish meaningful communication with them, and then give parents something concrete to do. Increased communication will give teachers greater insight into the home environment and its effect on the child, information that will open new avenues of working successfully with the child; will let the parents know firsthand what the teacher and children are doing in school and why; and will enable parents to gain a greater sense of accomplishment from watching their children grow. Many parents who now avoid the school because their children are neither happy nor successful there, can be enlisted if we reduce our criticism, look for places where they can help, and build on the rather limited efforts they are now willing to make in their children's behalf. No one wants to work hard in a hopeless cause, but if we set reachable limited short-term goals and then help parents reach them, we will have fewer disadvantaged adults in the next generation.

When Schools and Parents in a Disadvantaged Community Clash: A Proposal

STATEN W. WEBSTER

The Problem

Too often conflict situations involving the staffs and parents of students within disadvantaged schools[1] are problems produced by a poor human-relations situation. In the heat of such battles—be they over the curriculum, the qualifications of the school staff, or the counseling program—the factors which have created such a situation are often overlooked by both sides.

When a disadvantaged school and sizeable elements of its community are engaged in a major conflict, one can almost always conclude that little prior attention had been devoted to the realization of the following human relations essentials:

1. Mutual respect and positive expectations for harmonious relations by both sides.

2. Understanding by both groups of each other's anxieties, concerns, problems, and aspirations.

The author, editor of this compilation, is a supervisor of teacher education in the School of Education, University of California, Berkeley. He has served as a research specialist with the Richmond Youth Project which is concerned with the problems of socially disadvantaged youth and is a member of the Human Relations Commission of the city of Richmond, California.

[1] Disadvantaged schools are held to be those institutions populated by large numbers of representatives from the lower-class stratum of society, among which are numerous representatives of ethnic minority groups.

3. Considerable interaction between the members of the two groups.
4. Open, two-way communication between the involved parties.

The consequences of a failure to seek and achieve good school-community relations based upon the above principles can perhaps best be illustrated by the following hypothetical statements of an educator and a disadvantaged parent regarding their feelings and perceptions in a conflict situation.

Educator: "What right have these people to charge down to the school and accuse us of keeping their children out of the college prep courses? They don't give a hoot about education. They never have supported us. They are only raising hell now, because protesting has become fashionable. Do you think they usually care enough about their kids to join the PTA? I'm tired of hearing everybody yell that all of the problems of communities such as this are the school's. We do the best we can and with too little help from parents or their kids. We hold meetings to explain what we do here, but they don't care enough to take advantage of them. If a kid cuts up and you have to send for them, they come in all pushed out of shape and looking for trouble. You try to explain the problem and whose side do they take? They side with their children of course."

Parent: "Those school people don't give a damn about us or our kids. Hell, they don't even live around here, so how can they tell me what I want, or what I want for my kid? The only time they want to see you is when your kid has got them all shook up. Rest of the time they don't care if you are dead. I don't like to even talk to those people. Their big ten-dollar psychology words bug me. They really don't want you to know what they are talking about. My kid is just as good as those other kids. They use all of those big science words to try and con me that he is dumb. I work too damn hard for too damn little money, and pay too damn much taxes to take that crap off those people."

In addition to the four already listed, there are other factors operating to further alienate the disadvantaged school's staff and the parents of its community. Since most urban disadvantaged schools are populated largely by ethnic minority groups, the personnel of such schools constantly fear (a) charges of prejudice and discrimination and (b) the activities of civil rights groups. The slightest protest or threat of such is viewed with great alarm and defensiveness. Disadvantaged persons sense these fears and anxieties and exploit them, in the absence of a good human-relations climate, by accusations or prejudice and discrimination on the part of the school and administration.

In the absence of interaction and communication between the school and its disadvantaged community, unrealistic assumptions and expectations arise which incite any confrontation. While the school building is a physical part of the disadvantaged community, few if any members of its staff are. Thus the school is generally viewed and feared as an outside agency with great powers and considerable control over the lives of the inhabitants. Seldom is a comfortable feeling of unity with the school established.

There are factors relating to the parents themselves, however, which inhibit the efforts of the sincere school staff to be of assistance to them and their children. Because of his generally handicapped circumstances, the disadvantaged parent tends to be excessively diffident when interacting with educators. While school personnel may not believe this, such parents do respect, if sometimes begrudgingly, the knowledge and formal English of the educator. Considering language alone, for example, from the first word of their conversations with school people, the disadvantaged people are placed on the defensive. The life of the poor is generally a hard one. It leaves little energy for night meetings at the school. The rewards of the work of the disadvantaged leave little for dress, personal grooming, or furnishings for the home of which they can be proud. Other factors cause parents to view themselves as outsiders. Consequently it is no wonder that oftentimes they behave and respond as outsiders.

The Approach

The approach to the resolution of school-parent conflicts to be described is not original with this author. It was devised by a settlement house in the San Francisco Bay Area in attempting to help the local high school and parents of its community resolve a conflict existing between them.

In this, readers should note the effort to establish those essentials of a good human-relations situation discussed earlier. Specific steps included the following:

1. Once the existence of a potential conflict was realized—in this instance counseling practices—the representative of the settlement house sought to avoid an immediate confrontation between the school and parents involved.

2. Instead, the parents were contacted and asked to discuss grievances with a representative from the settlement house who was then to convey parental feelings to the school counselors.

3. After being informed of these complaints, a discussion by the school counselors was held, after which the representative arbitrator conveyed back to the involved parents the reactions and questions of the counselors.

4. Questions from the parents were then returned to the school personnel.

5. A meeting of both groups in the community was finally arranged, after due consideration of all statements and questions involved. At this meeting, questions and feelings of both parties were discussed.

6. The issue was settled to the mutual satisfaction of both parties.

Key factors contributing to the success of this problem-solving approach include the acknowledgment by the settlement house worker that the essentials of a good human relations situation did not exist at the time of the crisis. Also, because it was apparent that the feelings of both parties were too aggravated for meaningful communication, the bringing together of the groups was delayed. Third, each group's cathartic reaction was isolated from the other up to the point where grievances and concerns could be shared and discussed. Fourth, indirect communication was established, allowing for the generally uninhibited flow of feelings, complaints, and concerns. It was during this communication that the mediator was able to interpret to each group the concerns and point of view of the other. Fifth, it was only after each group had clarified its own position and had acknowledged the position of the other that a joint meeting between the two took place. Also of importance—when this meeting did occur, it was scheduled at a nonschool, and therefore nonthreatening, facility.

This approach to resolving school-parent conflicts and misunderstandings clearly illustrates the all-too-frequent lack of understanding and communication that exists between parents and administrators and teachers in disadvantaged-area schools. In addition, however, it illustrates some of the techniques capable of being used in promoting better human relations that are so important between parents and teachers if effective education is to be achieved.

This effective education of the disadvantaged learner is an exceptionally difficult task when one considers the negative social forces bearing down on such children and their parents. It is one which nonetheless must be undertaken. Hopefully, through the emphasizing and recognition of adequate human relations, the education process will be facilitated and improved. To ignore human relations and, more specifically, the parents of disadvantaged learners, is to fail to use a vital resource, and to invite attacks upon the school when issues arise.

Included within the following selections are additional comments and descriptive human-relations techniques that have been undertaken.

꒦•꒦

An Anthropologist Looks at
School Counseling

꒦•꒦

RUTH LANDES

[Abstract.] This article relates counseling to the total cultural indoctrination whereby the child, or culture novice, matures into a culture adept. Concepts of learning, motivation, normality and deviation are discussed as keyed to particular traditional standards operating in social relationships. American minorities, immigrant and native, learn under customary and formal duress, which are now complicated by official decisions to undo the duress by desegregation and integration. Minorities learn the family subculture and local versions of the dominant culture, but only incompletely. Resulting conflicts and confusions often enter school, police and other official reports as serious violations or failures. Nine suggestions relate proposed counseling practise to cultural factors.

The social anthropologist's sphere of study is the entire culture of any given society, and analytic comparison of it with others to deduce generalizations about social behavior and development of the human race. In this perspective, formal education in the United States is one institution and set of traditions that mesh into the whole patterned civilization of American society; and counseling is a special mode of education.

Then, how does an anthropologist view a school counselor's job of

From *Journal of Counseling Psychology*, Volume 10, No. 1, 1963. Reprinted by permission of the publisher and the author. Dr. Landes has been Visiting Professor of Anthropology at Claremont Graduate School, MacMaster University, Toronto, Canada, and Director of the Education and Anthropology Project since 1959. This study, made in conjunction with the Education Faculty at Claremont, is described in a forth-coming book, *Cultures in American Education*, University of Washington Press, 1964. It is summarized in a chapter of *Foundations of Education*, George F. Kneller (Ed.) , Wiley & Sons, 1963.

fostering pupils' "normal development"? What is this normality? What goals are the proper pursuit of school guidance?

To social anthropology it is logically improper to conceptualize a "normal person" but it is proper to conceptualize traditional or prevailing standards of normality and of deviation in particular societies, which are carried by members of these societies. Members carry them upon being taught to do so by authoritative persons, with the knowledge and the responsibility defined by the parent culture. In anthropological theory, personality is shaped by the dynamics of a particular culture interacting with genetic potentials of the newborn, the whole mediated by indoctrinated adepts called parents, teachers, clergy, police, friends.

This means that the "child," conceptually, is a novice in culture who progresses toward adeptness or maturity as specified by the culture, meaning, by the determinations of parents and other teachers. By this system of thought, only adepts or adults are responsible for "normality," not the child as is suggested by phrases about "normal and abnormal children."

According to these concepts, children may learn well or ill. Since learning is shaped preeminently by the culture or social environment (viewed both as external and as internalized in thoughts, emotions and habits), it is possible to hypothecate that much bad learning results from improper exposure to particular standards of normality. Learning, in the comprehensive sense of acquiring a culture, is measured by established norms of channeling success and failure, by the achievement and maintenance of status and by its loss, by neurosis, physical disease and creativity. Normative emphases and appearances vary around the globe. The theoretical position is expressed classically in Ruth Benedict's *Patterns of Culture* and in Alfred L. Kroeber's *Configurations of Culture Growth*. These studies argue that each people's tradition evolves upon a limited base of selected human potentialities in temperament and talent, inferred from analytic comparisons of many human societies; and that each selection follows a particular culture's bent that integrates aspects of the total life into a characteristic "pattern" (in Benedict's term) or "style" (in Kroeber's term). Kroeber goes on to reason that not more than 2 or 3 per cent of human creative potential is given opportunity by any culture; but that without culture there would be no realization of human gifts at all.

Supported by biological and behavioral sciences generally, anthropologists hypothesize that human potentials for learning are practically limitless, if learning conditions are suitable. To the anthropologist, learning conditions include all of life's circumstances in a given society, around the clock, education in formal public schools being only one set of circumstances.

Studies of school performance, initiated in the classic work of Otto Klineberg and continued by Allison Davis and others, show that Negro and Indian pupils fall below American "middle-class" norms in discriminatory surroundings, like the Jim Crow South and the tribal reservation, but improve markedly in favorable surroundings, as after moving from rural to urban schools and from southern to northern schools. Similar reasoning can be applied to learning by women. Women resemble a minority in our society because demands of our traditional equality conflict with other values and practices in women's lives and reduce women's incentives for public achievements. Yet now the equality principle affects ever more profoundly the lives of females so that more girls and women must foster appropriate ambitions, though the only choices of prestige are in men's careers.

Suggestions on School Counseling

Practical suggestions for school counseling programs flow from assumptions of cultural anthropology.

1. Since norms of conduct are taught a child first by his parents, who continue to teach through daily living, the school must develop active associations with parents, on school grounds and *out* in their neighborhoods and homes, through teachers, counselors and school social workers. California and New York schools find that, for instance, Spanish-speaking children can be taught more readily when their parents are school-taught, though this has nothing essential to do with so-called "bilingualism." It has to do with the fact that the school world is already familiar to the elders, though usually under conditions of segregation. California teachers, who complained of Mexican-American pupils generally, made the point that the satisfactory ones were children of former pupils, who thus had a head start in the school culture. New York City's Board of Education releases school personnel as field coordinators for work with Puerto Ricans and American Negroes in their home areas. The writer completed 2 years of training educators, under one California school system, in how to reach Mexican-American parents; the fortunate results included parents' soaring participation in school conferences, PTA programs and school bond issues. When school activities reach beyond buildings and grounds, all parties learn about opportunities, responsibilities and needs; and the gains mount among pupils and teachers.

2. Counselors and teachers must learn carefully the subcultures and perhaps the languages of the groups they counsel and teach. Even the

English spoken at home by low-status groups, like rural Negroes and Okies, is in great part a foreign language. It voices an alienated subculture that must be understood before it can be led to support educational communication. Details of each family must be known, regarding education, occupations, marital status, religion, regional origins, for these determine a child's responses to school.

3. Individual counselors and other educators should each learn his own cultural background and family antecedents in systematic detail, in order to understand his own behavior with those of other origins. The writer has worked with many educators and social workers in this connection—all parties observed that such knowledge clarified disturbed exchanges with pupils and parents when the disturbances rested on differences of cultural origin. Thus, "apathy," for example, gets understood as a *creative* social mechanism in *particular* situations of prejudice rather than as personal insolence or stupidity. This training requires access to a cultural specialist, especially in sections of sociocultural variety, high transiency, desegregation and integration. Schools in southern California, for example, may have annual pupil turnovers of up to 70 per cent, showing different ethnic strains, and teacher turnovers of 30 per cent or more.

4. The interest of the child *and* of his parents should be observed carefully in school recommendations, whether the proposals concern study programs or something else. "Observed" includes literal watching, even silently. People tell a great deal apart from or despite words. Words that come from authority can be alarming to any group. What is communicated through such observation marks useful guide-lines. For example, a high school counselor complained of his distress that a Mexican-American girl refused to transfer to the enrichment program he recommended. He had directed her to get the approval of her father, an unschooled man with a flourishing taco stand. When she failed to report, the counselor asked the girl why and she answered. "My father says he doesn't know and that I don't have to transfer anyway." A house visit revealed that neither the parents nor the girl welcomed the emotional isolation that the scholastic advance would create; parents and juvenile peers felt they would be unable to talk with the girl afterwards, and she felt the same.

This does not mean that school standards should not prevail. It does mean that fresh tactics are demanded for showing all parties the extent to which the recommendation is of general benefit.

5. School staff should be clear about boundaries and modes of evincing responsibility as these are defined by the group from which the pupil comes. The frequent counseling device of asking a child, "Now,

what shall we do?" to correct some wrong, falls flat with a Mexican, Negro or Okie boy. These children are accustomed to sharp demarcations of authority by generation, sex and status. In none of these groups does an adult ask a *child* to make a decision, though such a query may be proper among some American Indians in particular connections. To the receiving group of low or minority status, such school action is suspect and irresponsible. It arouses confused behavior which is recognized at school under rubrics like "hostile . . . apathetic . . . ," etc. Knowing the boundaries of authority and responsibility, and the modes of enacting their ranges in particular cultural groups, are vital for these cultures differ so significantly in details as to determine success or failure in school relationships.

6. Provide or demonstrate models of work and action for the desired ends offered to pupils, parents and school staff. Limitations of time and staff mean heavy reliance on printed materials; these should include novels, poems and reproductions of fine works in arts, sciences and other humanities. Such models stir emotionally charged convictions that inspire counselors and teachers to carry on. One integrated California junior high school trained its Mexican-American pupils (in a traditionally segregated town) to teach conversational Spanish to classmates, who were almost entirely Anglo-American whites. This provided so effective a model of competence, decency, and respect that parental and adolescent gang hostilities vanished, local newspapers carried unprecedented stories of appreciation, and the school won a national award.

7. The conceptual "normal curve of distribution" should be forgotten in counseling pupils of backgrounds unfamiliar to the particular counselor. This is because the curve sets a negative frame that cues counselors' expectations, and the expectations inevitably reach pupils and parents. New York City's "higher horizons" programs among Puerto Rican pupils, originally scored very low on standard tests and curves, report the superior achievements of the pupils under judiciously enriched guidance of these pupils and their parents.

8. Counselors must attempt to personalize and individualize the educational relationship. Teaching is more than putting information into a brain or machine and waiting to see the outcome. Teaching, like loving, must nurture the desire to carry on. This is what educators call motivation. Our mass industrial society and our massive professionalization carry grave liabilities of depersonalization and anonymity. The human creature does not flower without strong specific social orientations and recognition; the pupil of minority or alien status is often confused anyway as to what school and he can do together. Responsi-

ble personalizing elicits surprising responses in teacher and pupil, which carry enthusiastic and creative solutions to questions like what job or study course should be advised or to questions about how delinquent symptoms can be re-directed.

If we consult simpler societies, including 19th century pre-industrial ones, we find that personalizing was extended responsibly and fruitfully to treating even such divergent and eccentric personalities as we now consider neurotic and psychotic. Innumerable independent reports over centuries document how American Indians kept their berdaches (respectable male homosexuals or male transvestites) and their extreme visionaries in the community, putting on them responsibilities of their divergencies, and so permitting them to be useful, content, and "adjusted." Berdaches cultivated arts and other male visionaries cultivated war and hunts. Russians provided similarly for the so-called village idiots, as recorded in novels of Tolstoi, Dostoievsky, Turgenev. All persons hunger for respect and status, and this is what honorable social usefulness allows.

9. A final suggestion is that counselors and teachers be trained to assume responsibility towards pupils and to manifest this without expressing hostility. As the adolescent approaches the adult generation, at high school and junior college, many counselors and teachers show him strong competitiveness. Teachers and counselors so driven are often unaware of their actions, but pupils are amply aware of the sexual and sadistic overtones. Doctrines of permissiveness in child-rearing have questioned firm assumption and disciplines of responsibility by adults. The counselor's or teacher's uncertainty about his own responsibility does not advance teenagers learning and motivation but actually injures the trust needed to advance learning and ambition. Dependence on a competent teacher, at any age, characterizes man's genius. Want of this responsibility wastes school facilities and destroys the goal of education.

Educating the Socially Disadvantaged— A Challenge to Administrators

BETTY LACY

For several semesters I have led seminar groups of teachers concerned with teaching their unmotivated, low-achieving, hard-to-handle students more effectively, and taken classes on this same subject. I have constantly listened to teachers express the feeling that a teacher might have the desire and ability to reach these largely nonwhite, nonmiddle-class students, but that administrators are the stumbling block. "How do we get around the administrators?" has been repeated over and over.

Is this feeling justified? Are the teachers passing the buck? Do administrators give teachers this feeling without meaning to? Are they actually slow in allowing teachers to try new, different, experimental methods? I personally have been encouraged by fine administrators and hampered by petty ones. I have worked with fine creative teachers and have seen many teachers who just didn't care. I find it hard to make this assumption about administrators, but because so many teachers are expressing it, perhaps administrators should examine what is involved. We recognize that for effective teaching we must begin where the child is. This applies to working with adults as well; if teachers believe an educational policy is valid and worthwhile, their administrators should understand and work with them at that level.

I have several specific ideas to suggest to school administrators, based on assumptions that should be stated at the outset. For example, I am talking here about the approximately one-third of our school population within large urban areas which is not learning because home and

Printed with permission of the author, who is an elementary counselor at the Nystrom and Verde Elementary Schools in Richmond, California.

community subcultures are at variance with the white middle-class standards and methods traditionally espoused by the school. While the cultures of the Mexican-American, Puerto Rican, or Appalachian white might be considered in relation to this situation, within this paper I shall speak predominantly of the Negro.

Administrators from white, middle-class schools need to be just as concerned with the problems of students culturally divergent from our predominant society as do those administrators dealing directly with these disadvantaged students. Also, if the white, middle-class child is to learn about his country and to make a realistic adjustment to life later on, Negroes must cease to be "invisible" in his education. Some specific ideas directed to administrators concerned with the education of the socially disadvantaged follow.

1. Many school personnel resent what they feel to be unfair blame for the problems which exist in teaching our culturally divergent children. In considering such accusations, it is advisable not to respond to "blame" and to "problems." Instead, illuminate the potentially creative opportunity to be found in teaching the disadvantaged. Society is faced with a vicious cycle of low motivation, poor education and jobs, unemployment, low income, broken homes, poor housing, de facto segregation, increased low self-esteem, poor school performance, and so around again. Too often agencies involved place the responsibility for breaking the cycle on other agencies. Educators have the unique chance of breaking it, because schools have the potential of reaching everyone and interacting with individuals who are still young. Other agencies reach only splinters of the total population and see them only after this problem cycle has been established. Finding more effective ways of working with these children can and should be challenging and exhilarating, rather than depressing and hopeless.

2. Recognize that divergence in cultures is not a matter of right or wrong, inferiority or superiority. Also, do not always assume the school system to be right. School personnel should be familiar with students and their families—their way of life and values. To the extent that you can understand another's frame of reference, his behavior will become more understandable. All too often students have been made to choose between school and home values so that if they accept one they must reject the other. It is seldom realized that values can be introduced to children without being imposed upon them. Fighting, for instance, can be prohibited because it is impossible to teach and learn while students are fighting—not because fighting is morally "bad." Likewise, standard English will be more readily accepted and practiced if the beauty and

creativity of the students' own speech—not the incorrect grammar involved in their dialect—is recognized.

3. Give parents status. Sincerely welcome parents into the school; let them know that they are important and that their help is needed. Also, make contacts with parents on a total basis, not just when their child is in trouble. Ask parents about their child, about what you can do, rather than tell them what they should do. Most important, recognize that not coming to school does not indicate a lack of interest on the part of parents. They may be afraid and feel that their lack of education will put them at too great a disadvantage with school personnel. They may be hostile, feeling that the school is part of an alien culture which rejects them. They may be exhausted, physically and emotionally. They may have realistic problems of baby-sitting and transportation. It is often worth the effort to go to parents, to make home visits, and to let them know that *you* care. Also, because of the frequent resentment in many disadvantaged communities of the commuting professional, who works there and then hurries out of the area, it is also important and beneficial for teachers and administrators to take part in community activities. However, pity and patronization is not what is needed or advocated here.

4. Distinguish between feelings and behavior. Efforts seeking to solve the problems of the culturally disadvantaged child do not necessitate the lowering of those standards held by the school. Part of respecting a person is letting him know that you expect him to perform up to ability and to meet rules of conduct. There must be definite, firm, consistent limits; a structured situation with room for opening up, discussion, disagreement, and warmth in the relationship. Educators who consider the socially disadvantaged inferior and incapable of learning soon exhibit this feeling whether they express it openly or not, and soon lessen the student's belief in himself. As a result, motivation and achievement diminish. Any administrator who lets his faculty know that he will be satisfied if they keep their classes quiet and under control can expect poor performance unless he stresses and aims for higher goals.

5. Give teachers the freedom to be creative. This freedom applies to teaching all children but especially the student who is not responding to traditional methods of instruction. Let the teacher discard recommended books, if necessary, since new techniques and methods of reaching nonachievers generally cannot be developed within constricted rules of organization. The administrator who can say to an innovator, "Give it a try; you may fall on your face but I'm with you," may find some highly useful results emerging. This applies equally, of

course, to the central office administration in its attitude toward the field administrator. The teacher who has discipline problems with children should not be readily categorized as a "failure" if he has warmth and interest and really cares about teaching. Given time and support, methods of control will usually follow. Many of the best teachers of the disadvantaged have had great difficulty at first.

It is not my intent to discount the importance of discipline. However, it should be realized that it takes time for a middle-class teacher to learn the methods which are effective in instructing children who have a different value system.

6. Set the tone in your school or district. Let the teachers know that the school and its staff are part of the community and that the students and parents are part of the school. Set the tone in talking with teachers so that the biased or unaware, who often tend to be the most verbal and discouraging, do not handicap the new or potentially creative teacher. Teachers should be encouraged by in-service training and faculty seminars which include films, speakers, and the discussion of feelings. Likewise, parent-teacher contact should be encouraged in the various ways already mentioned. Staff selection is a vitally important function of administrators in setting the tone of the school. The child from a subculture different from that of the school and society as a whole has special needs, so that the school personnel who will deal with him must be chosen for sincerity, concern, ability, potential, consistency of discipline, and warmth. They must be people who want to work with the child for positive reasons.

7. Realize and admit to yourself and others that race is important. Too many educators feel that to admit an awareness of racial difference is an evidence of prejudice. It is, rather, facing up to a fact. Society had made race important and it cannot now be ignored. Oriental children are helped to face prejudice by the possession of a proud heritage of centuries of tradition. Negro children and their parents, on the other hand, are generally unaware of their heritage and worth. For years society has scolded them as inferior and, unfortunately, too many have come to believe this. Silence on the subject only reinforces this sense of inferiority. As with sex, silence and artificial cover-ups indicate that there is something "bad" about a subject which cannot be spoken of. The Negro has often had to cover up, too, and put on his front. But race must be handled directly in the schools if this feeling of worthlessness is to be broken down. An initial discomfort and awkwardness may exist, but if the educator is sincere, open, and honest in his handling of racial discussion, it can be successful.

8. Make the school both interracial and intercultural rather than an

extension of the white world. Available or class-made interracial readers, supplemented by text and library books, should be used with the good bibliographies available for all grade levels. Subscribe to Negro magazines. Display interracial material on the bulletin boards as an everyday part of the school, not just during Negro History Week—in all schools, not just those in Negro neighborhoods. See that your staff teaches Negro history, culture, and the contributions to our society by home and community helpers and figures from state and American history. Books are available, not yet as texts but in materials the teacher can incorporate into the curriculum. This material should be made available to the teachers, who should be encouraged in the compiling of more. "Not knowing enough" should not be used as an excuse for excluding from the curriculum the facts of the Negroes' part in our culture.

9. Don't take criticism personally by reacting to it defensively. To most Negroes of any class and most lower-class persons of any race, the school represents an alien agency, an extension of the society which has rejected them. School administrators needn't get defensive when criticized for not doing a better job for their students. This is admittedly a big problem, which has only recently been generally recognized. The schools can hardly be doing everything right. Personnel become defensive when *de facto* segregated schools are attacked, and end up defending segregation. When a community asks the school to do more, it does not want to hear what is already being done and how good it is. Schools are doing many good things and are trying to do more, but in establishing rapport with an upset community group, there is always more to be done. Your recognition of the problems is usually wanted; honest admittance of needed changes may be all that is wanted to begin with. School administrators and others in authority need to communicate with the dissatisfied members of their community and communication requires listening as well as talking. Find out why they are unhappy, what changes are wanted, and whether they have suggestions which might be helpful. We are only beginning to realize that the minority groups want to and can do for themselves more effectively than outside agencies. They need to participate in solving their problems. Telling them or even implying that "the man" knows what is best and will do it for them has always been resented and should no longer be tolerated.

10. Get personally involved. Because lack of involvement is a problem of our whole society at present, there is no better place to initiate personal involvement than in educating those students with whom the schools have so far been unsuccessful. Each individual

among you is important. Read and listen not only about the socially disadvantaged, but to them. Read what they have written for themselves—their poetry and fiction—which so often tells more than the more scholarly works. Above all, don't be ashamed of not knowing. In this society it is incredibly easy not to know. You may be considered naive and even hypocritical but the rewards of perseverence within this quest for knowledge and understanding are many. Lomax has described this period wherein the white man is trying to establish communication and is saying to the Negro, "I don't hate you," only to get the response, "Are you sure, Mr. Charlie, are you sure? We know you from way back." Our Negro students who aren't learning in our schools come to us from this skeptical background and whether educators like it or not, agree with it or not, they can only work from that fact. Educators want the Negro student to go ahead and to achieve despite what society has done to him and, consequently, educators need to be able to go ahead even while feeling misunderstood and unjustly accused.

11. Be the leaders the school system needs. When achievement is truly desired, much can be done with staffs and communities. Teachers are frequently expressing frustration about and feeling hemmed in by their administrators. If they are right, administrators should get with them; if wrong, the teachers should realize it. Look at what teachers in your school or district are doing and encourage them when they care and dare to try new ways to be innovative and creative. It is often said that the classroom teacher is the most important person in education and in many ways this is true. However, it must be realized that the number of people a teacher alone can reach is limited compared to the number that can be reached when concerned leadership is given to the entire staff.

If some of the above suggestions are followed, it is possible that a new cycle can emerge. When you become involved, new ways of life will be made clear to you and as you learn, respect will grow which will then be transmitted to all with whom you work. As students and parents feel this respect they will be with you and the school personnel will no longer be outsiders. Finally, as you believe in them, students—socially disadvantaged or not—will believe in *you,* and in themselves, and will finally be freed to learn.

Teaching the Disadvantaged

BRUNO BETTELHEIM

This article is based on meetings which I have held during the past two years with small groups of classroom teachers from schools populated mainly by Negro children from culturally deprived homes. The teachers ranged from beginners with one or two years of experience to those with a great deal of experience. Some of them were white and some were Negro, but almost all of them came from middle class backgrounds.

As the meetings proceeded, it became apparent that white and Negro teachers had similar attitudes toward their pupils and that classroom problems were not based on color but grew out of the clash between the teachers' middle class attitudes and their pupils' lower class attitudes.

At the first meeting of each group, I explained that I could not possibly tell a teacher how to handle a particular child in a particular school situation. Instead, my purpose was to help members of the group to develop a certain way of thinking about these children and the problems they encountered with them; in short, to help them develop an approach that might be called clinical. This, I told them, I would try to do by helping them think through any situation they encountered in daily teaching which they cared to discuss. I then let the

From *NEA Journal*, September, 1965. Reprinted by permission of the publisher and the author. Bruno Bettelheim is Rowley Professor of Education and principal, Sonia Shankman Orthogenic School, University of Chicago. This paper reports on one part of a series of studies being coordinated by Morris Janowitz, Division of the Social Sciences, University of Chicago, which deals with the application of social science concepts to youth problems. These studies are sponsored by a training grant from the Office of Juvenile Delinquency and Youth Development, Welfare Administration, U.S. Department of Health, Education, and Welfare in cooperation with the President's Committee on Juvenile Delinquency and Youth Crime.

teachers decide where they needed help in understanding, handling, and teaching the culturally deprived child.

One recurrent problem was the teachers' anxiety that if they were to take time away from the teaching of the subject matter of the three R's, they would be falling down on their job. Indeed, it was apparent that they became anxious and resistant whenever it came to letting the momentary learning task ride for a while to follow the emotional or social needs of these children. Although they paid elaborate lip service to the fact that these children need socialization more than anything else, it took considerable discussion before they could begin to act in line with their stated convictions.

The most frequent objection was that it would not be fair to the other students in the class. Or, as one teacher said: "If you have one pupil that's causing trouble, how can you consistently take time away from the rest?" I asked her to give an example, and she said, "Well, I have one show-off in my class. I found at first that talking to him and giving him a lot of attention quieted him down. But the rest of the class was suffering because I was giving this boy so much attention, so I stopped doing it."

I asked how she knew they were suffering. "Well," she said, "I was taking time out from teaching."

"True," I said, "but didn't they learn anything from it—how to deal with a show-off, for example—which might be useful knowledge later on in life?" The teacher allowed that this was possible, but still felt that it didn't seem fair.

I remarked that we all agreed on the great need to teach these children socialized behavior and yet she felt guilty when she took time away from her subject matter teaching to do it. I pointed out that the middle class child can usually learn good manners by observing his parents, whereas about the only way the underprivileged child can learn them is by observing his teachers.

Three weeks later the problem of socialization came up in a different form. A teacher said she was irritated by the children who shout out answers when they haven't been called on.

"Why is it so irritating?" I asked.

"First of all, because it's usually the wrong answer," she said. "I guess that's really what is most galling." I then asked her for an example of a question she had asked and the wrong answers she got.

"Well, for instance," she said, "the other day I pointed to the word 'the' on the board and someone shouted 'my.' " I asked her what reaction she had to that. She said her reaction was that the children hadn't learned the word—that they weren't being thoughtful and attentive.

I now asked her to speculate with me about why anyone would shout out "my" when the word she asked for was "the."

"Because they're both on the board," she said, "and the children don't know either one. They just want to say something." I said I doubted the latter, because I was sure that none of them shouted words like "horse" or "moon" in reply.

"The children are just dying for attention," the teacher suggested, "and so they holler out of turn."

"Exactly," I said, and wondered what was wrong with that.

"We just can't tolerate kids shouting out constantly and having the room in a turmoil," I was told.

Then another teacher spoke up: "Within limits, I like this kind of response in my classroom, even if it does make things noisy."

"How about when they don't know and still shout?" asked the teacher who had raised the problem. And the other teacher replied, "I think this is good and I'll tell you why: They're contributing, they're part of it, and this is what they want. But even the children that don't know get the chance of contributing. And to the children who give the correct answer I can say, 'That's right,' and everybody has had his say."

A teacher who had previously remained silent said she wished she could arouse any kind of enthusiasm—even the wrong kind. "By the time I get them," she said, "they've been so beaten down in the lower grades about 'Keep still, fold your hands,' that I don't get any response from them at all."

I now suggested that we try to understand what goes on in the mind of the children while the teacher is writing the word "the" on the board. "Let's suppose," I said, "that somebody writes something on the blackboard in Greek letters. You're trying to read it, but you don't quite know the letters. What will your reactions be? You're not going to shout out the wrong answer. You might even be afraid to say the right answer if you're not sure. What are you going to think as you look up there, trying to figure it out?"

Teachers began to answer, to say, "Why should I learn it?" "What's in it for me?" or, "I don't know this; I'll have to go home and study it."

"That's right," I said. "Some of us would feel this way or else, 'Why don't I know this? What's wrong with me?' But most of us would think, 'My God, what can that be?'

"Now all of these are rather uncomfortable feelings, but all of us have learned to handle moderate emotional discomfort. The children, though, haven't learned to do that as yet. What I'm trying to suggest is that we make the mistake of viewing these children's reaction to learning or to not knowing as though it were the same as ours.

"When children in general are uncomfortable, they begin to holler and yell. I'm afraid you overlook the discomfort you project the children into by putting something on the blackboard they cannot read."

Next I turned to another aspect of the same "my" and "the" situation. I asked the teachers, "What did this child who shouted out 'my' want to learn?" and one teacher said that she didn't understand what I meant. "Well," I asked, "where was his interest?" And the teacher said, "With himself."

"Of course," I said, "because he shouted 'my.' Now let's think for a moment about what's more important to a kid: to have a boat, or that there is a boat somewhere?" To which the teachers answered in chorus, "To have a boat."

"So actually," I said, "this boy gave us a very important clue about how to teach these children: namely, that we have got to personalize the whole thing—that 'my' should be taught before 'the.' While they are not ready yet for abstract learning, they may be ready for personalized learning. In his own fashion this boy told you how he ought to be taught, as most children will tell us how they ought to be taught, if we will only listen to them. It's another example," I said, "of how we use teaching that is geared to the middle class child even with underprivileged children who come to us from primitive environments, with a relatively primitive language.

"I can't rewrite the curriculum, or your textbooks, but I can help you understand what motivates this boy who says, 'I can learn only if a thing is very personal to me,' who by implication tells us, 'I might be interested in "my" boat, but I'm not interested in "the" boat.'

"All these weeks you have complained here that these children cannot distinguish very clearly between what's theirs and what is other people's—quite a difficult thing to learn. All I'm trying to suggest is that here we're up against exactly the same problem."

This was a lengthy example, but I have taken time for it because it deals with two questions: What's more important to teach to these children than reading? But also, how do we teach children the difference between what's theirs and what's not theirs? My next example deals explicitly with this second problem.

"We have a teacher," I was told, "who's working with a particular group of lower class children and we all admired her tremendously for how much she was able to do with them. Then two of those children were picked up for purse snatching. When they came back, the teacher, who had had an excellent relationship with them said 'If you needed money why did you have to steal? You know I always have money in my desk.' The following day her desk was cleaned out of money."

"Well she asked for it," I said, and the teacher nodded. "That's just the problem," she said. "None of us realized this. When the money was stolen, we were all stunned."

But things were more complicated than that. "The teacher meant well," I said. "I'm sure she was ready to give these kids some money if they needed it. The trouble is she didn't realize how the children would interpret her remark. Only recently have the sociologists and anthropologists begun to recognize what they call 'the culture of poverty.' In our example, it might be better to say 'the morals of poverty'—morals very different from ours.

"Within this culture of poverty it is perfectly all right to take things from the out-group as long as you never take from the in-group. If you take from the in-group, then you're really a low-down bastard; if you take from the out-group and get away with it, you're smart.

"Now these children snatched purses because they wanted money, but it never occurred to them to take money from the teacher because they considered her to be a good friend. But lo and behold, she says it would have been better to take the money from her. That is, she tells them to do something which, in terms of their morality, is the worst thing a human being can do. When this teacher says, 'I expect you to come and take from me,' it means to them that she, whom they trusted, thinks they're no damn good. This makes her a stranger, if not an enemy. In my opinion this teacher's desk was rifled as a punishment; out of anger that she held them in such a low opinion, that she thought them the kind of so-and-sos who take money from friends."

This example shows that these middle class teachers, despite their desire to be helpful to the culturally deprived child, and despite their best intentions, often get bogged down because they cannot transcend their own value system to meet that of the children.

When teachers like these teach disadvantaged youngsters, they need a clinician's help in going beyond their own middle class mores, a task they find difficult at best, despite their conscious desires. They also need help with their feeling of obligation to push the subject matter, a feeling intensified by all the public clamor of white and Negro citizens that everyone needs more education. Pressured by this sentiment, they concentrate on academic learning and ignore those emotional problems which, when not handled, prevent learning altogether.

Perhaps a final example will illustrate.

"I have a little girl," said one teacher, "who's been troubling me. She alternates between extremely aggressive and extremely dependent behavior. She'll understand an assignment, but she'll ask me specifically to help her with it, so I'll sit down and help her even though it's obvious that she doesn't need the help. Sometimes she'll accept this help, and sometimes she'll just get angry instead. And if I'm not looking at her for five minutes, she'll make a nasty comment."

"Like what?" I asked.

"Well, she makes allusions to my race all the time by saying, 'You ugly old white woman,' or something like that. Or she'll try to hit me."

"And what do you do when she says you're an ugly old white woman?" I asked

"Well," said the teacher, "I think I try to get her to sit down, or something like that, and actually ignore the problem. I never take her comments personally."

"Now that's hard for me to believe," I said, "that somebody says you have an ugly white face, and you don't take it personally. How do you take it, if you don't take it personally?"

"I mean I'm not insulted by the comments, really," she said.

"But why not?" I wondered. "I've been a student of human emotions for more years than I care to remember. And people are always trying to teach me new things, but I'm an old dog and I don't learn new tricks any more. One of the new tricks people are trying to teach me is that if somebody tells somebody, 'You have an ugly face,' they don't take it personally. Because if that's really so, then the Negro group hasn't a thing to complain about. If all the remarks made about them don't hurt, then what's all the screaming about? But I think they have a right to scream, because I believe these remarks do hurt."

"Well, let me put it this way," said the teacher. "She says enough good things to offset the bad things."

"All right," I replied, "so your husband, who usually says many good things to you, says that the dinner you cooked is awful. Doesn't that faze you even though he said some nice things two days ago? In spite of good things, bad things still hurt.

"If a child says to you, 'I hate your ugly white face,' you are certainly going to be bothered unless you don't take the child seriously, and this is what I'm driving at. If we don't take a person's nasty remarks seriously, that means that we really don't take him seriously. It implies, 'You're irresponsible, no good, of no account.' Because if a person is of any account, then it seems to me that we must take seriously what he says."

"But don't children sometimes say something just for shock value?" asked a teacher.

"Of course," I said, "but if someone says something to shock you and you don't get shocked, then he's terribly deflated."

"But if they continually do this kind of thing, do you have to be shocked each time they say it?" she persisted.

"That's right," I said. "In a situation like that, I'm shocked each time they do it. And the more shocked I am, the sooner they stop. If you pay no attention to a remark like this, the child will be driven to keep up or try harder all year long: She says it to make you angry, or hurt you, and if you're not hurt, then she's a nincompoop.

"If, on the other hand, she can hurt you, then she might think, 'Do I really want to hurt my teacher?' And that's what we're striving for."

What it comes down to, as I tell groups of teachers I work with, is that we must have very clearly in our minds what educational goals we have for these children. Should our goal be that these youngsters learn the important things in life; not to steal, not to hit people over the head, to be able to stand some small frustration and still go on with the task? Or should our goal be that they learn, like Lee Harvey Oswald, to read and write, no matter what?

An Urban Teacher Speaks Out

ஃ•ஃ

BETTY LEVY

Here are specific details on my work: I am teaching a fourth grade class in a public school in Central Harlem. Our school is part of New York City's More Effective Schools program that has just been initiated this past September. This pilot program is an attempt to improve schools in depressed areas, so it might be relevant to you in your work in Boston. Basically, the program involves smaller classes, heterogeneous grouping, a team-teaching approach, and a variety of increased teaching and guidance services. My own feeling about this program is that it involves some small reforms (e.g., it is easier to teach 20 than 35) but does not involve any of the basic and needed changes in orientation and curriculum.

As to my own experiences and reactions to Harlem teaching, let me say that I was initially totally unprepared and totally at a loss. My experiences at Harvard were centered mainly around curriculum improvements (or "How to get College Level Concepts down into the Elementary Schools") and around middle-class suburban children. Harvard's assumptions, methods, and approaches simply did not prepare me at all and are totally irrelevant to the lower-class urban Negro children I am teaching.

What impressed me most was the fact that my children (9-10 years old) are already cynical and disillusioned about school, themselves, and life-in-general. They are hostile, rebellious, and bitter. Some belong to

From *Harvard Graduate School of Education Association Bulletin,* Vol. X, Summer, 1965, No. 2. Reprinted by permission of the publisher and the author. Betty Bollinger Levy, Ed.M. '64, is a native of New York City and a Queens College graduate. Mrs. Levy studied Elementary Education at Harvard and did student teaching as an apprentice at Lexington. This article was written as a letter to Dr. Rose E. Sabaroff, Director of Elementary Internship and Apprentice Teaching at H.G.S.E., in reply to her request for information about Mrs. Levy's teaching experiences in Harlem.

gangs, some sniff glue, and some even have police records. They are hyperactive and are constantly in motion. In many ways they can be compared to wild horses that are suddenly fenced in. The problem is: How can you tame them without completely breaking their spirit?

Unfortunately, the school usually fails and the children retain their rebellious I-hate-the-world attitude, while having had knocked out of them the more positive aspects of their rebellious spirit.

Their physical and intellectual worlds are quite limited: many have never been more than a few blocks away from home; many do not own a single book, nor do their parents. Almost all come from broken homes. Many live with a grandmother or a guardian who is burdened with more children than she can take care of. A few literally take care of themselves with no adult at all present in the home. The home environment has not, does not, and in many ways can not prepare the children for school or encourage them to do well in school. The school is seen as remote and alien to their lives. They have very low self-images, most have experienced failure throughout their school careers, and they are frustrated and defeated easily. They live difficult, chaotic lives and do not come to school with the curiosity, interests, and controls that the middle-class-oriented school expects, demands, and uses as an assumption for much of its curriculum.

Need for Relevance

A most basic problem, then, is that of motivation. To motivate slum children to want to learn goes far beyond finding cute gimmicks to catch their attention. Rather, it is a constant striving for relevance, an attempt to show that school has a meaningful connection with their lives. Considering the present school curriculum and methods, this can often be a difficult and even absurd task. In mathematics, for example, one cannot offer a challenging problem and then say, "All right, children, open your books to page 43 and you will discover how to solve this problem." To slum children, this offer of a "challenging problem" is a portent of another frustrating experience, not to be again endured, and chaos will reign in the classroom. End of math lesson! Instead, the children must be cajoled into learning, and it must not seem like "learning." A whole series of "informal" lessons involving money transactions during milk and cookie time, figuring out amounts of material to be shared during an art lesson, working out daily attendance, etc., may be necessary before the children will accept a more formal textbook lesson. The new math concepts are very difficult to teach, whereas approaching the children through representative materials and concrete problems from their own lives is more successful.

In social studies, too, it might be necessary to find a more rounda-bout way of reaching the children. For example, I scrapped the entire ridiculous curriculum for many months and dealt only with civil rights and Negro history. Starting off from a situation where saying the word "Negro" in class created embarrassment and shame and where the words "black" and "colored" were used as curse words among the children themselves, we are now at a point where the children are open and eager for discussions on discrimination and prejudice, and where many of the children carefully follow daily events in the civil rights movement. Interest in Selma, Alabama, has created an interest in studying the map of the United States. Their knowledge of what Ne-groes in the South are enduring to try to vote has enabled me to moti-vate them into learning about the structure and function of govern-ment. Discussion of conditions in their homes leads into lessons on city services (e.g., Whom would you go to to complain about rats? no hot water? etc.) Much of what I have said seems to be no more than the idea of "beginning where the children are." However, it is somewhat different in that I am attempting to make the children feel that "where they are"—their problems, interests, etc.—is acceptable and relevant to their school work, rather than divorced from it, which is what they have learned in the past.

The children are far behind in reading, and this presents the most difficult challenge to the teacher. The reasons for this retardation are many. Most of the children come from homes where education is not valued. Many had no kindergarten experience, were pushed into read-ing in the first grade before they were ready for it, had to repeat first grade, and thus were frustrated from the start. The books fed to them had very little motivational value as they were all about little white suburban boys and girls leading sterile, blissful, and unreal lives. Rare-ly did these children experience success in reading and rarely did they experience the relevance of reading to their own lives. It is often neces-sary to backtrack almost to reading readiness types of activities to try to recapture the initial enthusiasm and interest that was lost so early. Reading to the children, especially reading humorous stories and sto-ries about Negroes and city children, is important (*The Snowy Day* and *Whistle for Willie* by Ezra John Keats are excellent, but there are not enough books like this.) Having labels and written instructions and sign-up sheets for activities is also helpful. Supplementing or even superceding the basal reader with things like the Reader's Digest Skill Builder, trade books, comic books, and other reading material that can be completed in one session and that is interesting, is more successful. Individualized reading can be very effective once it is started. The use of experience stories helps to bridge the gap between "reading" (school subject, remote, alien) and "my life" (real, close, relevant.)

Much of what is neded to help these children to read goes far beyond what any single classroom teacher can do. There is a crying need for a good multi-ethnic series of basal readers, with stories involving real emotions, real conflicts, and real people. There is a need for graded trade books based around city children and urban life. We must begin to start much earlier with these children—perhaps institute kindergarten and even pre-kindergarten as a requirement. The idea of an ungraded primary is also particularly relevant to slum children, so that they move on when they are ready, rather than move on every year, ready or not, and experience failure and frustration as they move.

Toward Self Respect

I would like to emphasize a point alluded to earlier—building the children's self-images. Feelings of worthlessness and self-denigration are often so ingrained in slum children that it is quite a difficult and persistent task to try to overcome them. The importance of teaching Negro history cannot be stressed enough. These children need proof that Negroes really can do worthwhile things; moralizing about brotherhood and equality does nothing to change their attitudes. It is important to teach not just about the Jackie Robinsons and the Ralph Bunches, but about the Nat Turners, Harriet Tubmans, Frederick Douglasses, Robert Smalls, and current civil rights leaders who are more attainable role-models for slum children. In another area, having a mirror in the room helps the children to literally "see themselves." Taking and displaying photographs of the children has an amazing effect. Using a tape recorder is also valuable. Any and all ways that can devised to help the children to think better of themselves are prerequisite to helping them to learn.

A few words about classroom order, control, and discipline are in order. Growing up in a disorganized and chaotic environment, these children are understandably very difficult to control in school. A firm, structured, and highly regulated class environment is not only necessary in order to teach, but is also, as I am finding, desirable for the children's own growth. For example, insisting almost to the point of fanaticism on neat notebooks and desks, a standard school heading on every paper, bringing two pencils every day, and other definite routines, schedules, and procedures to follow drives me crazy but I find that it really helps the children to bring some order and predictability into their disordered and unpredictable lives. It is essential to establish clear rules and definite limits and to insist that they are obeyed. Give an inch, and the children take a mile. Most of the children simply do not have the self-direction or the controls to handle even the smallest amount of freedom without turning it into an explosive situation. Unlike middle-class children who are used to being told by their parents to "go read a book" or "do a puzzle," etc., these children spend much of their free time "hanging around" on the streets. Thus, they have to be taught how to use free time acceptably in school. Independent activities have to be carefully planned and explained. It cannot be assumed that they will "find something [acceptable!] to do" when they have finished their work.

On Foreign Ground

I would like to make some final remarks which I think accentuate the already mentioned problems. Most teachers, and Harvard graduates in particular, grow up in and are trained to work in a middle-class environment. Working in a Negro slum school is in many ways like going to a foreign country. The values, interests, goals, experiences, and even language of the children are quite different and often in conflict with the middle-class-oriented school and its teachers. Unfortunately, the school usually attempts to transplant itself unchanged into this different environment, without taking any of the differences into account. The barriers to understanding on both sides are great. For example, academic competition and doing well in school are not highly valued by slum children. Thus, the children cannot understand the teacher when she holds these (her own) values up to the children to try to motivate them. The teacher, in turn, cannot understand why the children are so "stupid, lazy, and unresponsive." As a further example, it is not respect for authority but rather rebelliousness and resentment against all authority that is the norm among these children. Picture, for example, the absurdity of trying to teach "The Policeman is Your Friend" part of a "Community Helpers" unit to slum children. Slum children know a great deal about "the fuzz," but "friendship" with them is in conflict with their experiences.

The administration in slum schools also seems to share the pervasive "middle-class bias." For example, a recent administrative announcement in my school concerning the free lunch program read as follows: "Although we do not wish to deny free lunch to any child needing it, neither do we wish to encourage children to eat in school when it is not necessary. . . . There are numerous benefits to be obtained when he goes home to lunch and discusses the day's events with his mother. Similarly, the parent can learn about her child's activities in school and can establish stronger family bonds." This is a fine ideal and one which might be relevant and acceptable in a middle-class setting. In a slum environment, however, I doubt its relevance. Most of these children cannot go home for lunch simply because no-one is at home. In other situations, the home is so crowded and the mother so harassed by family, financial, and other worries, that she has little time or energy to sit down and discuss one child's school activities. And in some situations the home environment is so unpleasant that the child would prefer to remain in school. Rather than the child eating lunch at home to "establish stronger family bonds," the following situation is more typical. In the case of one boy, a known "troublemaker," the father had left the family, leaving them with no funds and no means of support. In order to get money to buy food so that the family could eat supper one night, the boy, aged ten, worked that afternoon in a grocery store. He came home with $1.50 and said to his mother, "Here, Mom, buy us some food." When I contrast this real situation with the administrative announcement I wonder whether educators are naive or simply afraid to face up to the situation they are dealing with.

To Train for Slums

I have talked a great deal about the need for more relevant and meaningful teaching methods and curricula. I would like to emphasize now the even greater need to train teachers to be able to deal with and attempt to overcome their own "culture shock" and "culture bias." Most middle-class teachers, for example, have little experience, training, or understanding to be able to deal with parole officers, truant officers, social workers, and welfare investigators. Teachers who work in slum schools need to be prepared to work also with these people. They need to be told beforehand that they might have children in their classes who have police records. They need to be *prepared* so that they can understand and deal with these problems, rather than to go in unprepared and be shocked, frightened, or resentful of them. They need to be prepared to deal with parents who may be illiterate or partly literate, concerned but helpless, or hostile and abusive. More than anything else, I think that teachers who work in slum schools must be helped to become more community-minded. They must be made aware of the social and economic backgrounds of the community. They must know the community values, interests, and problems. It is necessary to stress this training because the slum environment is usually quite different from what the teacher has experienced as a child or as an adult. Once a teacher begins to understand and to appreciate the slum community, she is closer to understanding and appreciating why her children "are the way they are" and is less likely to condemn and reject them because they are not what she, in her middle-class framework, thinks they "ought to be." She is then in a much better position to be able to reach and to teach them.

Attempting to bridge these cultural gaps is prerequisite for success in teaching slum children. Blaming and condemning them because they don't fit into the middle-class-oriented school system or attempting to mold them along middle-class lines is not only unfair to the children but will fail as it has done in the past. It is necessary for teachers to really listen to these children, to truly accept their values and their experiences, and to learn from them. If I can make a suggestion and a plea to you in your work in Boston—please don't try to adapt a suburbs school to the Boston slums. It won't work. What is needed is a thoroughly new approach and new curriculum ideas oriented specifically to lower-class Negro children. Their values, their interests, their experiences, and their entire culture demand and need this. A specific blueprint I cannot offer. I only hope that you and other educators who realize the need for basic change will be able to come up with some radically new solutions.

Teaching and Students: The Views of Negro and White Teachers

DAVID GOTTLIEB

[Abstract.] The research reported here deals with the results of a study pertaining to differences in the attitudes of 89 Negro and white elementary school teachers, toward Negro and white pupils from low income families in a midwestern urban community. The results indicate that the Negro teachers were more likely than the whites to come from urban areas; from low income families and from homes where there was no father. The Negro teachers tended to be younger and to have less experience in teaching than did the white group. The Negro teachers were more satisfied with their current teaching positions than were the white teachers. The Negro teachers tended to see the children as "happy," "energetic," and "fun-loving," while the white teachers were likely to see the same children as "talkative," "lazy," and "rebellious." Among reasons for job dissatisfaction, Negro teachers listed large classes, poor equipment, inadequate supplies and the lack of proper curriculum, while white teachers emphasized the lack of ability of students, their poor motivation, discipline problems and parents who were not concerned with the education of their children.

The continued shifting of urban populations, the occupational mobility of Negroes, and an actively expressed desire on the part of Negroes for equal educational opportunities have had a dramatic and frequently disturbing effect on many urban school systems. For some communities the actual integration of schools and talk of "bussing in students" have played a part in the rejection of funds needed for the operation of local public schools. In these instances school bond proposals have

From *Sociology of Education*, Summer, 1964. Reprinted by permission of the publisher, the American Sociological Association, and the author. David Gottlieb is at Michigan State University.

been defeated by both Negro and white citizens. The rationale behind the voting patterns appears to be a form of racial reasoning in which white voters reject an increase in school taxes because they do not wish to support additional integrated schools, while Negroes reject the same proposals because they feel that added funds will be used to maintain a segregated school system.

At the school staff level other dilemmas are apparent. Negro teachers resent what they see as selective placement by school administrators in the assignment of both teachers and students. Frequently, as Negro teachers perceive it, race and not skill is the salient variable in teacher placement. Although little empirical information is available as to the actual processes of teacher placement, impressionistic observation indicates that there is a tendency to place Negro teachers in schools with a Negro student majority and white teachers in schools with a predominantly white student population. In part this racial homogeneity in school composition may be explained by a prevailing assumption that both Negro and white teachers prefer to "teach their own." On the other hand, it may well be that teachers seek to minimize travel and hence teach in schools close to their own homes. Residential segregation then becomes the factor which accounts for placement segregation. Whatever the explanation, it is apparent that there is some unrest among teachers, students and parents.

Within the classroom setting we see other consequences of school integration. Studies comparing Negro and white students indicate that in a number of academic areas Negro youth lag behind white students.[1] Numerous explanations have been offered for these findings. Some suggest that differences in "cultural" background account for the academic inadequacies of Negro students.[2] Others propose that the school culture represents the middle class and that lower income children, lacking both the social cues and verbal skills of the middle class, are unable to compete with their more affluent peers. Still others take the position that tests currently being used to measure motivational and behavioral differences are not really adequate in that they fail to tap salient factors and are usually structured in a manner which does not allow the lower income student to express his real talents and interests.[3] Finally,

---

[1] See G. Ferrel, "A Comparative Study of Sex Differences in School Achievement of White and Negro Children," *Journal of Educational Research*, 43:116-121, 1959. Bernard C. Rosen, "Race, Ethnicity and the Achievement Syndrome," *American Sociological Review*, 24:47-60, 1959.

[2] Frank Riessman, *The Culturally Deprived Child*, Harper and Brothers: New York, 1962.

[3] Burton R. Clark, *Educating the Expert Society*, Chandler Publishing Company, San Francisco, 1962.

some maintain that Negro students, even more than other minority group members, are not highly motivated to achieve in the academic setting since they fail to see the relationship between the classroom situation and their own post-school expectations. In other words, Negro youth are less likely than white youth to believe that they will be judged on ability and past performance when they enter the occupational market.[4] Whether all or any of these factors are really crucial to the performance of the Negro student is not known at the present time. Surprisingly enough despite the attention given to the problems of racial integration in our schools, little is known of the values, attitudes and expectations of Negro students and teachers. We know even less about differences and similarities between Negro and white students who find themselves in schools where there are variations in the racial composition of students and teachers.

The purpose of the research reported here is to look at but one part of the problem. We are concerned with identifying differences and similarities in how Negro and white elementary school teachers view their work and the students they teach.

Sample and Methods

A total of 89 elementary school teachers, from six public schools of a medium-sized industrial community in the midwest, were the subjects of this research. These six schools differ from others in this community in that they are located in the "inner-city" and have a majority of students who are low-income Negroes. Fifty-three of the teachers were white and thirty-six were Negro.

The author, while acting as consultant to the school system of this community, had an opportunity to conduct personal interviews with many of the teachers and to distribute a paper and pencil questionnaire which was completed by 83% of the teachers from these schools. The seventeen per cent who did not reply included both Negro and white teachers. There appear to be no differences in background among teachers who did and did not respond to the questionnaire.

Background Characteristics of Teachers. There are a number of interesting differences in the backgrounds of Negro and white teachers. While the proportion of males to females is the same for both racial groups—less than 20%—the Negro teachers are: (1) younger, with 47% being less than thirty-five years of age as compared to the white teachers among whom fewer than 30% were under thirty-five years of age; and

---

[4] David Gottlieb and Warren Ten Houten, "Social Alienation: The Case of Negro Youth," Michigan State University, 1963 (unpublished preliminary report).

TABLE 1.

TEACHERS' RACE AND COMMUNITY OF ORIGIN

Community of Origin	White Per Cent	Negro Per Cent
Farm	10	—
Small town (less than 25,000)	14	10
Medium-sized town (25,000–99,000)	53	22
Other (including suburbs and metropolitan areas of 100,000 or more)	23	68
	(100%)	(100%)
N =	53	36

$\chi^2 = 18.897$ $P < .01$
3df

(2) more likely to be married, with age perhaps accounting for the smaller numbers of divorcees and widows among the Negro group.

Table 1 deals with community of origin and indicates that there are differences in the residential backgrounds of these teachers.

The Negro teachers are more likely to have come from large communities than are the white teachers. This distribution is not surprising since we would expect that the Negro with a higher education is very much more likely to be urban than rural. A comparison of institutions where the BA degree was obtained by the subjects of this research shows that the Negro teachers are twice as likely as the whites to have received this degree from a public, urban university. No doubt both lower educational costs and more liberal admission policies contribute to the greater enrollment of Negroes in public, urban educational institutions.

Differences are also to be found in the socio-economic backgrounds of the teachers. Using father's occupation as a measure of social status, we see that Negro fathers were most heavily concentrated in the manual occupations while the largest single group of white teachers come from families where the father was either a professional or in some managerial occupation. In addition, Table 2 indicates that over a fourth of the Negro teachers were raised in families where a woman was the head of the household as compared to only 4% of the whites. These differences may help to explain, in part at least, differences in the attitudes and perceptions of the two groups of teachers.

Teaching History and Job Satisfaction

Since age is related to teaching experience we find that the white teachers, being older, have had the longer experience. While 79% of the white teachers in our sample have been employed in the profession for

TABLE 2.
TEACHERS' RACE AND FATHER'S OCCUPATION

Father's Occupation	White Per Cent	Negro Per Cent
Professional, proprietor, manager	40	14
Sales	10	10
Clerical, skilled, semi-skilled	20	32
Service	4	3
Unskilled	4	6
Farm-owner or worker	18	6
Woman was head of house	4	29
	(100%)	(100%)
N =	51	35

$\chi^2 = 17.814$ P < .01
6df

six or more years, the same is true for only 57% of the Negro teachers.

Job satisfaction is related both to years of teaching experience and to race. As can be seen in Table 3, Negroes express the greater satisfaction with their current position but for both groups, satisfaction decreases with increased years of employment.

The findings pertaining to job satisfaction raise a number of questions. First, how do we account for the impact of race and experience on job satisfaction? Second, what are the factors that teachers see as contributing to job dissatisfaction?

In response to the first question we would propose that younger teachers frequently enter the field with a certain missionary zeal and dedication to the ideal of "helping children." Over time, expectations as to the role of the teacher in the educational process undergo some modification. Teachers soon come to learn that the professional role

TABLE 3.
TEACHERS' RACE, TEACHING EXPERIENCE AND JOB SATISFACTION
"Per Cent Who Like The Job Very Well and Would Not Consider Leaving Present Location."

Years in Teaching	White		Negro	
	Per Cent	N	Per Cent	N
Four years or fewer	60	(5)	83	(6)
Five years to nine years	44	(9)	67	(18)
Ten years or more	36	(39)	50	(12)
Total N =		(53)		(36)

$\chi^2 = 14.749$ P < .01
2df

may include problems of student discipline, clerical work, involvement with parents, committee meetings, inadequate materials, and teaching large groups of children who differ greatly in ability as well as motivation. In all probability the gap between pre-job expectations and job experience varies greatly among teachers.

The individual whose own educational experience included being part of a middle class culture where children were "well behaved" and sophisticated in the handling of educational tasks, and whose parents played an active role in the school and saw to it that their children did their school work, no doubt experiences a feeling of "cultural shock" when placed in the setting of the inner city school. When such an individual's expectations are not modified by what is taught in schools of education, there is little reason to believe that they will be realistic. The fact that Negro teachers are more likely than white teachers to come from backgrounds similar to those of the children of the inner city probably tends to make them more realistic in their expectations, and hence less likely to be dissatisfied with their current teaching roles.

Some empirical evidence to support the observation that white teachers are less prepared than Negro teachers for the inner city school system comes from responses to a question dealing with changes that these teachers feel should be made in current training of school teachers. From Table 4 it can be seen that almost two thirds of the white teachers suggest revisions that would make the training program more realistic. Among the Negro teachers there is a greater dispersion of responses, with only 26% of the group expressing a need for more realistic types of educational preparation. [Table 4] indicates in addition that the Negro teachers are more likely than the white to see a need for "greater selectivity" of education majors and for more thorough training in substantive areas such as reading and arithmetic.

TABLE 4.

TEACHERS' RACE AND SUGGESTED CHANGES IN EDUCATIONAL TRAINING

Types of Changes	White Per Cent	Negro Per Cent
More realistic teacher training	62	26
Greater selectivity of education majors	4	28
More thorough training in substantive areas such as reading, arithmetic, etc.	34	46
	(100%)	(100%)
N =	(52)	(33)

$\chi^2 = 15.330 \ P < .01$
2df

There are, of course, other possible explanations of the differences in satisfaction. There may be a greater sympathy with the Negro child and his problems on the part of the Negro teacher. In a later section of this report, data will be presented which indicate that there are significant differences in how Negro and white teachers perceive the children they teach. Negro and white teachers in this sample give different reasons for *dis*-satisfaction. Negro teachers tend to emphasize problems related to the physical setting of the school while white teachers are more likely to stress problems pertaining to the shortcomings of the students. Finally, Negro teachers may be less likely than white teachers to express a desire for job re-assignment because they feel that opportunities for placement in a different kind of school setting are unlikely for the Negro teacher.

For both groups of teachers, as was shown in Table 4, dissatisfaction increases with years of teaching experience. Without a comparison group of teachers from other kinds of schools, however, it is impossible to determine whether continued teaching experience will inevitably lead to job disenchantment among most teachers in most places or whether this relationship is most likely to occur in specific types of school systems with particular kinds of teachers.

Factors Contributing to Job Dissatisfaction

A variety of factors seem to contribute to the job dissatisfaction of the teachers in the school studied. These factors can be divided into those related to the institutional aspect of the school and those pertaining to the clientele.

TABLE 5.

TEACHERS' RACE AND REASONS FOR JOB DISSATISFACTION

Reasons	White: Per Cent of Total Responses	Negro: Per Cent of Total Responses
Inadequate materials and poor facilities	6	33
Crowded classrooms	13	38
Lack of parental interest	25	6
Behavior—discipline problems	46	19
Other	10	4
	100%	100%
N =	(48)	(32)

$\chi^2 = 23.40$ P < .01
3df

Table 5 shows several differences between Negro and white teachers in reasons for job dissatisfaction. The items mentioned by white teachers tend to fall within the category we have designated as "clientele" factors whereas the items expressed by Negro teachers are more likely to fit within the "institutional" grouping. The two items most frequently mentioned by white teachers are "lack of parental interest" and "student behavior or discipline problems." Although some Negro teachers do express concern over these same problems, they tend to place the greater emphasis on factors such as "lack of proper equipment" and "overcrowded conditions."

An explanation of these differences can be only speculative at this time. We suggest that Negro teachers, because of their greater personal identification with these children, tend to look for factors external to the student to explain the problems that arise within the school. A similar phenomenon can certainly be observed among members of other minority groups where the reaction to deviant or undesirable behavior on the part of a group member is met either by hostility or by an attempt on the part of the group to explain the individual's actions in terms of factors in the social system as opposed to the unique characteristics of the minority group.[5] In the case of the Negro teachers in this sample the tendency is toward holding the system responsible for problems on the job and not this particular group of children.

The white teachers, on the other hand, with less personal identification with this group of children, are more critical than Negro teachers of students and parents.

Further evidence to support the proposition that race does play some part in how teachers react to these children can be seen in Table 6. In this table we deal with the relationship between teachers' race and their perceptions of students.

Each teacher was given a list containing thirty-three adjectives and asked to check those adjectives which came closest to describing the outstanding characteristics of the children with whom she was working.[6] Subjects were told that while they could choose as many adjectives as they felt were applicable, most people chose between five and six. Of the thirty-three adjectives there are fifteen in which Negro and white teachers differ by at least ten per cent in frequency of choice. The five items that are most frequently selected by white teachers in order of frequency are: "Talkative," "Lazy," "Fun Loving," "High Strung," and "Rebellious." The five items most frequently selected by Negro teachers in order of frequency are: "Fun Loving," "Happy," "Cooperative," "Energetic," and "Ambitious." The only item men-

[5] See among others: E. Frazier, *The Negro in the United States.* The Macmillan Co., 1949; Arnold M. Rose, ed., *Race Prejudice and Discrimination,* New York: Alfred A. Knopf, Inc., 1951.

[6] The adjective check list used here was adapted from an instrument developed by the National Opinion Research Center, University of Chicago, 1961.

TABLE 6.

TEACHERS' RACE AND THEIR PERCEPTIONS OF STUDENTS

Adjectives	White Per Cent	Negro Per Cent	Per Cent Differences
Ambitious	20	36	16
Athletic	25	13	12
Calm	8	19	11
Cautious	10	6	4
Cooperative	35	61	26
Cultured	2	10	8
Dominant	2	—	2
Easy going	35	29	6
Energetic	33	48	15
Forceful	8	3	5
Fun loving	45	74	29
Good looking	16	16	—
Happy	31	65	34
Hard driving	6	10	4
High strung	39	3	36
Idealistic	6	10	4
Impetuous	33	13	20
Intellectual	2	3	1
Lazy	53	19	34
High brow	14	6	8
Methodical	—	6	6
Middle brow	4	19	15
Moody	33	13	20
Obliging	37	26	11
Outgoing	33	19	14
Poised	6	6	—
Quiet	8	13	5
Rebellious	35	13	22
Reserved	6	3	3
Shy	12	21	9
Sophisticated	—	3	3
Talkative	59	6	53
Witty	—	8	8
N =	(51)	(35)	

tioned among the top five by both groups of teachers is "Fun Loving." The greatest discrepancy between the two groups of teachers with respect to these items are found in the adjectives "Talkative" (a difference of 53%); "High Strung" (a difference of 36%); "Happy" and "Lazy" (a difference of 34% for both items); and "Fun Loving" (a difference of 29%). Most teachers are in agreement that these children do not possess those qualities usually associated with middle class children.

They are not "Cultured," "Dominant," "Forceful," "Poised," "Witty," or "Sophisticated."

Generally white teachers tend to avoid those adjectives which reflect stability and the types of qualities one would desire of children in the formal classroom setting. Negro teachers on the other hand select items which seem to be universal attributes of children (i.e., energetic, fun loving, and happy) in addition to those which appear to go hand-in-hand with a successful learning experience (i.e., ambitious and cooperative).

Again, it would appear that the Negro teachers are less critical and less pessimistic in their evaluations of these students than the white, probably because many of them have themselves come from backgrounds similar to that of their students and yet have managed to overcome social barriers to attain positions of responsibility and status.

The Teacher and the Negro Child: "Invisibility" in the School

Maxine Greene

In a fundamental sense, the civil rights struggle is a struggle for dignity, for what Martin Luther King calls "somebodiness." The goal may not be so defined by the rank and file of activists; nor may the mass of Negro people articulate it in such terms. But this is the note sounded most often in literature by and about the Negro since the Civil War. It is one of the aspects of the Negro Revolt with which teachers must be concerned.

The acknowledged purpose of the public school today is to teach all children to think as intelligently as they can, to conceptualize, to form their worlds. No classroom teacher, however, can ignore the difficulties due to the "degenerating sense of 'nobodiness' " which, we are told by Dr. King,[1] afflicts every Negro, adult as well as child. To feel, in James Baldwin's language, "faceless" is often to feel indifferent to the demands made by the world. In the classroom, this may result in failure to master elementary skills; it may affect an individual's attitude towards any sort of work and make him "play it cool" when asked to feel responsible for what he does or does not do. If this happens, the effects of early impoverishment are confirmed. The disabilities most obvious to employers—unreliability, poor work habits, lack of skills[2]—

From *The Educational Forum*, March, 1965. Reprinted by permission of Kappa Delta Pi, an Honor Society in Education, owners of the copyright.

---

[1] "Letter from a Birmingham Jail," in *Why We Can't Wait* (New York: Harper and Row), p. 84.

[2] Abram L. Harris, "Education and the Economic Status of the Negro," in Robert A. Goldwin, ed., *100 Years of Emancipation* (Chicago: Rand McNally & Co. 1964), pp. 152-3.

are built into character and style. And the vicious circle that supports so much discrimination is tightened once again.

This is not, of course, to say that the predicament of the Negro is the "fault" of those who have taught him in the school. It is to suggest that one of the contributing factors may be dealt with in the school if teachers can be brought to see the meaning and somehow feel the pain of "facelessness." As the widow of Willy Loman says in *Death of a Salesman*, "Attention must be paid."

One way to see and to feel is through imaginative engagement in presentations like Ralph Ellison's exemplary novel, entitled—all too relevantly—*Invisible Man*. The nameless hero of that work suffers from what he call "invisibility," a condition not of his own making but due to a "peculiar disposition in the eyes"[3] of others. Those others are white people; and it makes little difference if they are benevolent or malign. The disposition in their eyes enables them *not* to see the Negro as a living human being, a creature of "substance, of flesh and bone, fibre and liquids,'"—of mind. They see him, rather, as an object, an abstraction: "Negro," "member of a subculture," "culturally deprived."

Ironically, it is the humanitarian concern for the poor and underprivileged that has led to teaching teachers terms and categories like these. They are obviously useful if linked to understanding of special circumstances influencing learning in the school. But they are also potentially dangerous. They may lead some teachers to regard their pupils as "cases," even "causes,"—to forget that they are individuals, to impose on them (with the best of intentions) a new invisibility.

This is important because of the duality of the work the classroom teacher is asked to perform. The teaching act is, on the one hand, a behavioral affair, rationally conducted, and guided (hopefully) by theory. On the other hand, it is an affair of face-to-face encounters, dependent for their validity on the teacher's own authenticity, on his ability to identify imaginatively.

If he has been recently educated in the art of teaching, he is likely to be familiar with the structure of his subject matter. He is probably equipped to organize the materials of his teaching in accord with the logic of the subject and, at once, with the conceptual level of the learners concerned. There is no question but that he *knows* more and communicates more effectively than some of those who were taught to teach "not the subject, but the child."

If the teacher is a fairly recent graduate, he is also likely to be committed to a subject matter specialty which he finds exciting, complex, "real." He may be exposed, therefore, to a frustration unknown to

[3] Ellison, *Invisible Man* (Signet edition), p. 7.

some of his older colleagues; and this may make it even harder for him to engage in encounters with youngsters innocent of the joys of learning, pupils who "couldn't care less."

When we link such frustration and estrangement to the increasing professionalism and precision of instruction in the schools, we can easily envisage the consequences for the nurture of identity. Yet neutrality and, perhaps, impersonality may be a function of the cognitive orientation becoming characteristic of the schools.

This orientation has been accounted for by Sputnik I and the subsequent panic over "mediocrity." More significant, however, is the general acknowledgement that it is the only appropriate educational response to a society growing more organized, automated, and intricate each day. The person adequately prepared for the jobs to be done requires more than rudimentary literacy. The citizen equipped to make a choice in an election or in a local controversy must be able to conceptualize, to form the world about him in a variety of cognitive ways. We have only to recall some of the recent battles over school desegregation or housing exclusion laws, or the issues raised in the Presidential campaign. Far more than factual information is needed in each case. The individual asked to take a stand must know how to reason, how to visualize alternatives, how to evaluate—how to think. The recent innovations in the fields of curriculum construction and subject matter organization have been responses to these necessities.

Further research, further experience in programming teaching machines, for instance, may increase our understanding of the slow learner and his requirements; but the special problem of the Negro child in the slum school may still remain. This is in part because of the ineradicable effects of deprivation in early life. It is also because of the larger problem of the Negro in America, and the uncertainty regarding his identity. Although—theoretically—every child can be taught any subject, the actuality of the Negro child's expectations is not yet fully understood.

There is a growing consensus that severe impoverishment in early childhood makes "normal" concept development impossible.[4] If a child is deprived of a range of sensory stimulations, of linguistic experiences, individualized care, security, and continuities, he is likely to be doomed to perpetual "underachievement" when measured against the cultural norms. The only hope is said to be compensatory pre-kindergarten education as in the experimental programs developed by Mar-

---

[4] See, for example, Bruno Bettelheim's review of Benjamin Bloom, *Stability and Change in Human Characteristics* in *The New York Review of Books*, September 10, 1964.

tin Deutsch and his associates at the Institute for Development Studies in New York. The focus there is on pre-school enrichment, "to reduce the attenuating influence of the socially marginal environment."[5] Because the pupils are three- and four-year olds, the teachers can devote themselves to cultivating the sense of individual personhood, enriching sensory experiences, cultivating curiosity, teaching the children to know their names. The work done already gives evidence of releasing some children from the limitations of impoverishment, of enabling them to learn to learn.

But there are thousands of equally impoverished youngsters moving through the grades and into high schools. If not helped before the age of six, we are told, the influence of the early environment cannot be reduced. In any case, the Deutsch program—*qua* program—can scarcely be adapted to grades where skills and subject matter must be taught. It holds clues, nonetheless. Something must be done to nurture child identity, even if it is too late for him to be "saved."

The teacher, then, confronts ambiguities and perplexities of all sorts when he takes the responsibility for a Negro child. He realizes that he will be hard put to motivate and teach if there is little feeling of self-regard or worth. He may realize, too, that there is little hope of the child's becoming cognitively excellent if he has not been helped when very young. To complicate his task, he may find that his own view of worth—because of his commitment to subject matter and to learning in general—is linked to his prime regard for capacity to learn.

The very terminology of his trade, "cultural deprivation" and the rest, may intensify this difficulty. A majority or middle-class bias is implied; and, although it may be pragmatically warranted, it is potentially hurtful as far as certain patterns of individuality are concerned. The bias may be reinforced by the teacher's own middle-class values, which often interact with commitment to his discipline to form a kind of screen in front of him. And the screen, once again, obscures his vision of the Negro child as creature "of substance, of flesh and bone. . . ."

He no longer is made to feel guilty about being middle class, as he might have been ten or fifteen years ago. With the exception of those public school people who romanticize the working class and the values they ascribe to it (lack of hypocrisy, delinquent "chivalry"), most teachers tend now to acknowledge at least the expediency of middle-class restraints, aspirations, codes.

---

[5] Martin Deutsch, "The Disadvantaged Child and the Learning Process," in A. Harry Passow, ed., *Education in Depressed Areas* (New York: Teachers College 1962), pp. 163-179.

Even if he has no feeling of guilt or shame at being middle class and intellectual too, the teacher must still break through the barrier his loyalties tend to raise. If he does not, he will not succeed in "fascinating" children, as Frank Riessman puts it,[6] with what there is to be known. If he cannot reach his pupils, he will be unable to discern the variety of "learning styles" that may be used. If he is unable to individualize the members of his class, he will be unable to adapt the strategies at hand, the techniques that might involve them, *as* individuals, in the struggle to learn. Clearly, he must do all he can to promote the cause of rationality—using flexible time schemes, allowing for alternative ways of framing material and responding to it, being permissive with some children and structured with others. But as he attempts to promote the cause in diverse ways, he must also try to enlarge his own conception of worth. He cannot exclude the life styles which seem to him to be non-rational, frivolous, shallow, "low"; because, if he does, he excludes individuals from his category of the worthy—and, perhaps, from his category of the human. And he cannot teach those he excludes.

If he succeeds in diversifying, in enlarging his conception of worth, if he succeeds in distinguishing among individual youngsters—his task has only begun. He cannot be "color-blind" when he considers his pupils; since this is often to become unintentionally discriminatory. He cannot treat his Negro pupils and his middle-class white pupils equally; since that would lead to thrusting the children of the poor into fixed positions of inequality. He needs to make distinctions and to be non-discriminatory as well. He needs to find a way of permitting every child to express his own uniqueness visibly, to "become" in his own authentic way.

What is authenticity for a Negro child? And how is the white teacher to know? If he cannot know, if he cannot empathize, it will be difficult to move a child to trust—to trust in a way that builds what Erik Erikson calls "fidelity," one of the building stones of personal identity. How can the white teacher find out how it is with his Negro pupils, what it is like to yearn (as a Single One who is deprived and Negro) to become someone—to *be?*

He is told by some articulate Negroes that he can never know, not if he is the Man, "Mister Charlie," white. Le Roi Jones, in his play called *Dutchman,* suggests that no white man can conceivably know, that no white man can even comprehend Negro jazz or Negro blues. When Robert Kennedy met with Dr. Kenneth Clark and James Bald-

---

[6] *The Culturally Deprived Child* (New York: Harper and Row 1962), p. 94.

win, the estrangement between Negro and well-meaning white was dramatized in the public eye. Kennedy, taken unaware, was told that he could not possibly understand. John Oliver Killens, the novelist, explains this with talk of a difference in "psyche"[7] and in emotional chemistries. Yet all stress the importance of respect and regard; all speak of integration; all give voice to the need for a recognition of identity.

The teacher, with his unique responsibility, cannot expect clear directives from the side of his profession or from the Negro people themselves. Day after day—unless he chooses to remain "scientific" and impersonal—he will find himself asked to make particular choices, urgent choices; and no one, in or outside his school, will be able to tell him with certainty that his choices are right or wrong. If he is fortunate, he will have contact with the parents or with other people from his students' neighborhood. It may be that some of them will be equipped to mediate, somehow, between his professional function and the particularities of life on the streets and in tenement rooms. It may be that he will come in touch with the fabric of puzzlements on which his Negro pupils are trying to work with their new cognitive skills. Or he may become acquainted with the jobs that are open—and the jobs that are not. He may learn to help them develop a conception of work for work's own sake, for the sake of meanings in their lives.

It is important for him to try. It is important for his professional effectiveness to consider the significance of encounters, of what Martin Buber (and Martin Luther King) called the "I-Thou." His own humanity may deepen if he reaches out and tries to see; since he could not even begin to reach without becoming open to himself.

Again, literature may play a part. There is not only the possibility of vicarious participation when he reads; there is also engagement on his own terms, engagement in a fundamental human quest for meaning, identity, "somebodiness." He will find no final answers, certainly not to questions about the crippled and the illiterate and the poor; but he will, among all the ambiguities in what he reads, experience the power of possibility.

In *Invisible Man,* there is the question: "Yes, but what *is* the next phase?" There is the perception of diversity and oneness in America; there is the fruitful decision "to put it down," to refuse to "file and forget." And there is, just before the end:

---

[7] Killens, "Explanation of the 'Black Psyche'," *The New York Times Magazine,* June 7, 1964.

I denounce because though implicated and partially responsible, I have been hurt to the point of abysmal pain, hurt to the point of invisibility. And I defend because in spite of all I find that I love. In order to get some of it down I *have* to love. I sell you no phony forgiveness, I'm a desperate man—but too much of your life will be lost, its meaning lost, unless you approach it as much through love as through hate.

Through encounter, through the search for meaning—the forms can be imposed and the children can be taught to make sense of it too, to try to learn in their own terms, "to put it down."

The teacher can do no more than explore and pay heed and try to see. He can act *as if* understanding were possible, *as if* youngsters will become visible once he chooses to open his eyes. And he is likely, after a time, to discover that nothing is lost where mastery is concerned—that he has it in him to be a Teacher when he becomes a man.

꒰ • ꒱

The Teacher as an Alien: Some Theoretical Considerations Regarding Teachers for Disadvantaged Schools

꒰ • ꒱

STATEN W. WEBSTER

When a citizen of one country visits for the first time another country whose culture is quite different, he often experiences the phenomenon of "culture-shock." Social amenities, the uses of language, mealtimes, and the general schedule of living may be quite different from what the alien visitor has known. For a while the newcomer may experience feelings of anxiety, frustration, and even hostility.

Middle-class teachers, or even those from lower-class origins, who have been encapsulated in the academic community for a number of years, are in a similar situation to that of the alien when assigned initially to a disadvantaged school.[1]

Despite the growing severity of the problem of educating disadvantaged learners, little specific research has been devoted to discovering those factors which are related to a teacher's ability to cope with the difficulties encountered in the problem-laden, urban school.

This paper presents a series of theoretical formulations and related hypotheses which consider possible answers to the question of why some teachers are able to persist in disadvantaged schools while others

---

An original unpublished paper by the editor, who is Research Director of NIMH project MH 10916-01. A note concerning him appears with his article "When Schools and Parents in a Disadvantaged Community Clash."

---

[1] Disadvantaged schools are held to be those institutions populated by large numbers of representatives from the lower-class stratum of society, among which are numerous representatives of ethnic minority groups.

are forced to defect to more favorable educational settings.[2] It is hoped that these ideas and propositions will be of interest to researchers and others concerned with the problem.

Theoretical Framework and Hypotheses

BASIC ASSUMPTIONS

The basic problem facing the average teacher going into a socially disadvantaged school and community is that of encountering a subculture with which he has had little experience. With the current urban revolution changing the very face and composition of our cities and their schools, this problem will become an increasingly severe one.

It is common knowledge that much of public education is in the hands of educators who come from various strata of the middle-class segment of society. We believe that this fact poses a problem for the process of education in socially disadvantaged areas. These differences between the prior subcultural experiences of the teacher and those of his students serve to produce conflicts in the areas of attitudes, values, and desired social and academic behaviors.

SUBCULTURES AND SOCIALIZATION

The total culture of a people is the product of their efforts to solve two major problems: The first relates to the necessity of people comprising a society to regulate their *human interrelationships*,[3] and the second, to their need to master and control essential *physical aspects*[4] of their environment.

Within the total society various unique groups (socioeconomic, ethnic, and the like) not only participate in the adjustments that the total society must make, but also must make somewhat unique adjustments of their own to the two above culture-producing factors, which are symbiotically related.

As is shown in Figure 1, social and physical factors combine to produce the environment within which the *socialization process*[5] takes place. It is within the context of such an environmental setting that

---

[2] The hypotheses contained herein are presently being studied in a project which is partially supported by the National Institute of Mental Health (Project MH 1096-01) and is being conducted at the University of California, Berkeley, during 1965 to 1967.

[3] The nonmaterial aspects of culture, including institutions, mores, taboos, and the like.

[4] The material aspects of culture, including tools, artifacts (housing, power sources, sanitary facilities, and the like), and technology.

[5] The process by which the most commonly shared behaviors of the human group are inculcated in the child.

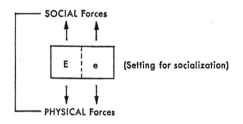

E = Total social environment

e = Environment of sub-culture

FIGURE 1

the *personalities*[6] and *personal systems*[7] of both the teacher and his students are developed. Because of social class and, often, ethnic differences between most teachers and disadvantaged youngsters, it is possible that the differing environments in which their socialization has taken or is taking place can be productive of factors which inhibit learning in the classroom and make such teaching situations intolerable to some teachers.

PERSONAL SYSTEMS OF TEACHERS

The sociophysical environments and types of socialization experienced by an individual are productive of what will be called a *personal system*. It is this system which influences both our *perceptions* of others and *behaviors* toward them.

The personal system is a two-part system, the first part of which is one's cognitive structure (Lewin, 1948). This construct is two-dimensional. Its first segment involves the cognitive aspects of an individual, which include his storehouse of facts, ideas, concepts, and generalizations about the world. The second segment involves the values, feelings, and sentiments which are related to these cognitive aspects.

The second part of the personal system consists of a cluster of three personality variables: (1) The first involves the *self-concept* of the individual, which is (as used here) a composite of two sets of self-evaluations (social competency and intellectual esteem). (2) The second variable involves the *interpersonal relations needs* of the individual (Schutz, 1958), which will be discussed in detail later. (3) The final per-

---

[6] A body of learned attitudes coupled with a set of behavioral traits that are unique for a particular individual.

[7] Defined in the next section.

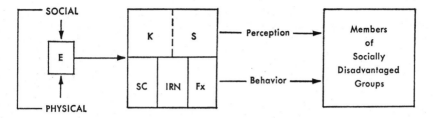

E = Environment   SC = Self-concept
K = Knowledge   IRN = Interpersonal relations need
S = Sentiments, values, attitudes   Fx = Flexibility or inflexibility

FIGURE 2

sonality variable involves the general manner of an individual when he confronts new tasks, ideas, and beliefs. Rokeach (1960) has defined such behavior as being typical of either *"the open or closed mind."*

The particular significance of all of the above variables will be discussed in detail as specific hypotheses and other related research are presented. However, it is essential to summarize the foregoing at this point (see Figure 2).

The particular environment in which a person is socialized provides the setting in which the personal system of an individual is developed. It is the manner in which this system operates that determines to a large extent a person's perceptions of others and of life in general, and which governs the particular behavioral responses that he makes to either.

The basic assumptions underlying the hypotheses which follow are (a) that the teacher and the socially disadvantaged student represent different subcultures, and (b) that certain aspects of the teacher's prior experiences (social and physical) and his developed personal system will tend to make him more or less capable of interacting in a satisfying way with those persons who are significantly different from himself.

ENVIRONMENTAL FACTORS

Physical environment. The socioeconomic status (SES) of a person determines indirectly certain key aspects of his physical environment. The more favorable the SES of a teacher's family was during his period of growing up, the greater is the possibility that he enjoyed the advantages of living in a neighborhood with fewer undesirable social influences. Also, his family's residence would provide its members with adequate space for privacy and personal autonomy. This type of an environment is the antithesis of that afforded the socially disadvantaged person.

While there appear to be no data on the following point, it is inferred that the greater the discrepancy between the prior physical environment of the teacher (up until he was age 20) and that of his socially disadvantaged students, the less capable will he be of persisting in a teaching situation populated by such learners.

The following hypothesis will be tested:

Hypothesis 1: Teachers who persist in socially disadvantaged schools will evidence significantly less discrepancy between the SES of their families with whom they lived up to age 20 and the SES of the students' families, than do those teachers who leave such disadvantaged schools.

Social Environment. The key element in the socialization process is the interactions between the growing child and those persons and groups in his immediate environment. An individual's immediate family is the most salient socializing agent, followed perhaps in importance by peer groups, individuals in his immediate community, and finally the total social group.

It is through his interaction with his immediate human environment that a person develops many of his attitudes, values, and sentiments. The more homogeneous is the nature of this human community as to its ethnic composition, the fewer are the chances that the child undergoing socialization therein will encounter divergent attitudes, values, and behaviors. It is hypothesized that the greater a teacher's exposure has been to divergent ethnic groups, cultures, and socioeconomic groups, the greater will be his capability of understanding and working with socially disadvantaged pupils. Thus,

Hypothesis 2: Teachers who persist in socially disadvantaged schools will display significantly higher scores on a measure of exposure to divergent ethnic, cultural, and SES groups than will those teachers who leave.

COGNITIVE STRUCTURE

Knowledge of the disadvantaged. It is likely that a teacher cannot understand or be satisfied in his interactions with representatives from a subculture that is different from his own unless he possesses certain essential knowledge about them.

This type of knowledge constitutes, as stated earlier, the first dimension of Lewin's *cognitive style* construct. The following hypothesis will be tested:

Hypothesis 3: When teachers who persist in socially disadvantaged schools are matched, as to age, sex, and tenure, with teachers who leave such settings, the former group will evidence significantly more knowledge about the subculture of disadvantaged persons.

Attitudes, values. The second dimension of the teacher's cognitive structure is that which involves his feelings, sentiments, and values that are related to the above knowledge component. Four types of attitudes, or inferred values, seem applicable in this study:

1. *Attitudes toward school's potential* for success in socially disadvantaged communities (pessimistic vs. *optimistic).*
2. *Attitudes toward students (student-centered* vs. subject-centered).
3. *Attitudes toward the disciplinary role of the teacher (restrictive* vs. permissive).
4. *Attitudes toward the subculture* of the lower class *(favorable,* accepting vs. negative, rejecting).

A large number of attitudes, values, and the like, could be measured here. However, we would restrict our attention to those attitudes or values which seem most relevant. The attitudes which a teacher has about the possibility of the school's really being effective in helping socially disadvantaged children would appear to be essential. It is inferred here that if a teacher feels that there is little that the school can do, his level of motivation and efforts to teach disadvantaged learners will be lower.

Another essential set of values or feelings are those which relate to whether the teacher views the students and their problems and needs to be his central concern in the learning situation, as contrasted with the presentation of his subject. While attention to both factors is essential, the problems of such learners could require that the teacher be more student-centered than subject-centered.

Students from socially disadvantaged groups appear to require, more than their middle-class peers, a more structured learning situation (Riessman, 1962), at least initially. Excessively permissive teachers working with deprived students encounter far more behavioral problems and disruptions of the learning situation than do those instructors who set standards of behavior and performance and consistently adhere to these. Thus, the teacher who perceives his role as a disciplinarian to be more restrictive than permissive should find teaching disadvantaged learners less disturbing and frustrating.

Finally, an essential body of attitudes includes those which relate to the teacher's feelings about the values, behaviors, and attitudes of the socially disadvantaged child as compared with those of the middle class. The teacher of the former group should evidence attitudes that are more accepting of the characteristics of the lower-class child. Thus,

Hypothesis 4: Teachers who persist in socially disadvantaged schools will display significantly higher scores on measures reflecting (a) an optimistic view of the school's possibility of helping disadvantaged learners, (b) a child-centered orientation, (c) the disposition to favor a more restrictive climate in the classroom, and (d) greater acceptance of lower-class values, attitudes, and behaviors than those who defect to more favorable settings.

Each attitudinal variable would be considered separately and in combination with the other variables as a composite attitudinal measure.

PERSONALITY VARIABLES

As stated previously, the personal system of the teacher was held to also contain three significant personality variables which appeared to be of importance. These personal attributes now follow.

Self-Concept. Data from studies of the self-concept by Wylie (1957), Bossom and Maslow (1957), Henry (1956), and others indicate that persons who entertain favorable pictures of themselves also display greater acceptance of others. It appears that such persons with favorable self-concepts feel (a) less threatened by others, and/or (b) have less necessity to project their own inadequacies onto others.

Other self-concept studies [see Rokeach and Fruchter (1956) and Brodbeck and Perlmutter (1954)] indicate that there is a negative relationship between favorable self-concept reports and levels of ethnocentrism.

Here it is inferred that the task of teaching socially disadvantaged students is a most demanding thing and one which cannot be done well by a person who feels himself to be inadequate.

Two types of self-perceptions appear to be significant. The first body of self-feelings has to do with a teacher's verbalized estimates of his confidence as an interactor with others in social situations. The teacher who perceives himself to be a socially competent person and who is confident of himself in interpersonal relations should feel less threatened and be less affected by the possible hostile and/or negative reactions that he may receive from disadvantaged learners. Thus, a high level of social confidence should enhance a teacher's chances of being an effective worker with such children.

Second, feelings of *intellectual competency* would appear to be an essential requisite for the effective teaching of disadvantaged students. The communication of ideas and information to such students requires that the teacher not only possess adequate mastery of that which is to be learned but that he also possess the intellectual capacity and ability to present it in a variety of both concrete and abstract ways. A teacher who doubts his abilities to function effectively in the above manner would be a less effective producer of learning in his students and would seek to leave so unrewarding a setting.

The above assumptions are combined in the following hypothesis.

Hypothesis 5: Persisting teachers in disadvantaged schools will report significantly higher levels of social competency and intellectual esteem for themselves than will those who leave such schools.

Each of these self-perception variables would be used separately in the analysis as well as a composite measure of the self-concept.

Interpersonal Relations Needs. In his *FIRO Theory* (Fundamental Interpersonal Relations Orientations) Schutz (1958) postulates that all interpersonal relations behavior can be attributed to three basic related needs. Each of Schutz' needs is two-dimensional in that there is an expressed (E) dimension (I toward others) and the wanted (W) dimension (others toward me). Examples of the needs, stated behaviorally, follow:

Inclusion	Expressed	(E^I)	"I try to be with people."
	Wanted	(W^I)	"I like people to invite me to things."
Control	Expressed	(E^C)	"I try to influence strongly other people's actions."
	Wanted	(W^C)	"I let other people strongly influence my actions."
Affection	Expressed	(E^A)	"I try to be friendly to people."
	Wanted	(W^A)	"I like people to act friendly toward me."

A comprehensive review of related research which supports the validity of the theory and of these dimensions is presented in Schutz' book.

Much of the teaching-learning act involves interpersonal behavior. If serious interpersonal relations problems exist between students and their teachers, very little efficient learning can take place. Schutz' theory suggests that attention should be given to both the interpersonal-relations needs and behaviors of both teachers and socially disadvantaged learners as a group.

Sociological studies (see Riessman, 1962; Davis, 1948; and others), have indicated that membership in the subculture of the socially disadvantaged is productive of certain general interpersonal-relations behaviors. In the area of inclusion behavior, socially disadvantaged people are described as preferring a high level of interaction with others in a warm and informal manner. The behaviors are examples of Schutz' $(E + W)$ inclusion and $(E + W)$ affection dimensions. Such people are also described as worshipping strength and preferring strong leaders, authoritarian behavior, and strict limitations on personal behavior in certain intimate areas of human conduct. These behaviors are indicative of that author's $(E + W)$ control dimension.

Knowledge of the physical and social environments of the disadvantaged (for example, encapsulated communities, extended families, crowded homes, and a general alienation from the mainstream of life) helps one to see why these groups develop these particular interpersonal behavior patterns.

As to the teacher in the socially disadvantaged community, it must be remembered that he is an "outsider," who possesses also his own unique system of interpersonal relations needs and related behaviors. To the extent that the preferred (E) behaviors of the teacher complement the (W) behaviors of the socially disadvantaged students in his class, the more satisfying will be his interactions with them, and the more harmonious.

Because of the superordinate status of the teacher and social class differences between him and his students, certain wanted behaviors on his part would appear to inhibit his possibilities for harmonious interpersonal relations with his students, and these are high levels of W^I, W^C, and W^A.

Two hypotheses regarding the interpersonal relations of the teachers would be tested:

Hypothesis 6: Persisting teachers in disadvantaged schools will display significantly greater $E^I + E^C + E^A$ scores than will teachers who defect from such schools.

Hypothesis 7: Persisting teachers in disadvantaged schools will display significantly lower $W^I + W^C + W^A$ scores than will teachers who defect from such schools.

Open vs. Closed Mindedness. The middle-class-oriented teacher working in a school composed largely of socially disadvantaged students encounters a subculture whose attributes are usually at consider-able variance with those of this own segment of the general culture. This confrontation poses a problem-solving situation for the teacher and would seem to require that he not be rigid or dogmatic in reacting to the attitudinal and behavioral differences which exist between the subculture of his disadvantaged students and his own subcultural group.

Rokeach (1960) introduced two concepts of the "open and closed mind." That author contends that the beliefs or disbeliefs which a per-son entertains constitute a "belief" or attitude system. To the extent that a person's belief system is resistant to change, it is described as being closed. The opposite type of reaction is attributed to the open belief system. The theory assumes that closed-mindedness is a syndrome that is evidenced in common by people who rigidly adhere to extreme positions (be they of the left or right politically, for example).

The book in which Rokeach advances these ideas contains numerous research reports to support his theoretical assumptions. The essential point is that certain individuals do display the tendency to be dogmat-ic and resistant to change in the case of their belief systems.

Thus, it is here inferred that teachers who tend to be dogmatic in their defense of their belief systems would encounter difficulties in un-derstanding and working effectively with students whose environments were productive of attitudes and behaviors which were in contradic-tion with those of the typical middle-class teacher.

Hypothesis 8: Persisting teachers in disadvantaged schools will score significantly lower on a scale of dogmatism than will teachers who de-fect from such schools.

The preceding eight propositions would constitute the heart of a re-search project seeking answers to the question of teacher persistence or defection in disadvantaged schools.

Bibliography

Bossom, J., and Maslow, A. H., "Security of Judges as a Factor in Impressions of Warmth in Others," *J. of Ab. and Soc. Psy.*, 1957, 55, 147-48.

Brodbeck, A. J., and Perlmutter, H. V., "Self Dislike as a Determinant of Marked In-Group-Out-Group Preferences," *J. of Psy.*, 1954, 38, 271-80.

Davis, Allison, *Social Class Influences upon Learning* (Cambridge, Harvard University Press, 1948).

Guttman, L., "The Principal Components of Scale Analysis," in S. A. Stouffer et al., *Measurement and Prediction* (Princeton, N.J., Princeton University Press, 1950), pp. 312-61.

Lewin, K., "Resolving Social Conflicts," *Selected Papers on Group Dynamics* (New York, Harper & Bros., 1948).

Riessman, F., *The Culturally Deprived Child* (New York, Harper & Row, 1962).

Rokeach, M., *The Open and Closed Mind* (New York, Basic Books, Inc., 1960).

———— and Fruchter, B., "A Factorial Study of Dogmatism and Relate Concepts," *J. Abnorm. and Soc. Psy.*, 1956, 53, pp. 356-60.

Schutz, W. C., *FIRO: A Three-Dimensional Theory of Interpersonal Behavior* (New York, Holt, Rinehart, and Winston, Inc., 1958).

Wylie, R. C., "Some Relationships between Defensiveness and Self-Concept Discrepancies," *J. Personality*, 1957, 25, 600-16.

Section Two:

THE PROCESS OF EDUCATING THE DISADVANTAGED LEARNER

꘎•꘎

A Teaching Strategy for Culturally Deprived Pupils: Cognitive and Motivational Considerations

꘎•꘎

DAVID P. AUSUBEL

The possibility of arresting and reversing the course of intellectual retardation in the culturally deprived pupil depends largely on providing him with an optimal learning environment as early as possible
in the course of his educational career. If the limiting effects of prolonged cultural deprivation on the development of verbal intelligence
and on the acquisition of verbal knowledge are to be at least partially
overcome, better-than-average strategies of teaching are obviously necessary in terms of both general effectiveness and specific appropriateness for his particular learning situation. Yet precisely the opposite
state of affairs typically prevails: the learning environment of the culturally deprived child is both generally inferior and specifically inappropriate. His cumulative intellectual deficit, therefore, almost invariably reflects, in part, the cumulative impact of a continuing and
consistently deficient learning environment, as well as his emotional
and motivational reaction to this environment. Thus, much of the
lower-class child's alienation from the school is not so much a
reflection of discriminatory or rejecting attitudes on the part of teachers and other school personnel—although the importance of this factor
should not be underestimated; it is in greater measure a reflection of
the cumulative effects of a curriculum that is too demanding of him,

From *School Review*, Winter, 1963. Reprinted by permission of The University of
Chicago Press. Copyright 1963 by the University of Chicago. A note concerning the
author appears with his article "The Effects of Cultural Deprivation on Learning
Patterns."

and of the resulting load of frustration, confusion, demoralization, resentment, and impaired self-confidence that he must bear.

Cognitive Considerations

An effective and appropriate teaching strategy for the culturally deprived child must therefore emphasize these three considerations: (a) the selection of initial learning material geared to the learner's existing state of readiness; (b) mastery and consolidation of all ongoing learning tasks before new tasks are introduced, so as to provide the necessary foundation for successful sequential learning and to prevent unreadiness for future learning tasks; and (c) the use of structured learning materials optimally organized to facilitate efficient sequential learning. Attention to these three factors can go a long way toward insuring effective learning for the first time, and toward restoring the child's educational morale and confidence in his ability to learn. Later possible consequences are partial restoration of both intrinsic and extrinsic motivation for academic achievement, diminution of anti-intellectualism, and decreased alienation from the school to the point where his studies make sense and he sees some purpose in learning. In my opinion, of all the available teaching strategies, programmed instruction, minus the teaching-machine format, has the greatest potentialities for meeting the aforementioned three criteria of an effective and appropriate approach to the teaching of culturally deprived pupils.

Readiness. A curriculum that takes the readiness of the culturally deprived child into account always takes as its starting point his existing knowledge and sophistication in the various subject-matter areas and intellectual skills, no matter how far down the scale this happens to be. This policy demands rigid elimination of all subject matter that he cannot economically assimilate on the basis of his current level of cognitive sophistication. It presupposes emphasis on his acquisition of the basic intellectual skills before any attempt is made to teach him algebra, geometry, literature, and foreign languages. However, in many urban high schools and junior high schools today, pupils who cannot read at a third-grade level and who cannot speak or write grammatically or perform simple arithmetical computations are subjected to irregular French verbs, Shakespearean drama, and geometrical theorems. Nothing more educationally futile or better calculated to destroy educational morale could be imagined!

In the terms of readiness for a given level of school work, a child is no less ready because of a history of cultural deprivation, chronic academic failure, and exposure to an unsuitable curriculum than because of deficient intellectual endowment. Hence, realistic recognition of this fact is not undemocratic, reactionary, or evidence of social class bias, of intellectual snobbery, of a "soft," patronizing approach, or a belief in the inherent uneducability of lower-class children. Neither it is indicative of a desire to surrender to the culturally deprived child's current intellectual level, to perpetuate the status quo, or to institute a double, class-oriented standard of education. It is merely a necessary first step in preparing him to cope with more advanced subject matter, and hence in eventually reducing existing social class differentials in academic achievement. To set the same *initial* standards and expectations for the academically retarded culturally deprived child as for the non-retarded middle- or lower-class child is automatically to insure the former's failure and to widen prevailing discrepancies between social class groups.

Consolidation. By insisting on consolidation or mastery of ongoing lessons before new material is introduced, we make sure of continued readiness and success in sequentially organized learning. Abundant experimental research has confirmed the proposition that prior learnings are not transferable to new learning tasks unless they are first overlearned.[1] Overlearning, in turn, requires an adequate number of adequately spaced repetitions and reviews, sufficient intratask repetitiveness prior to intra- and intertask diversification,[2] and opportunity for differential practice of the more difficult components of a task. Frequent testing and provision of feedback, especially with test items demanding fine discrimination among alternatives varying in degrees of correctness, also enhance consolidation by confirming, clarifying, and correcting previous learnings. Lastly, in view of the fact that the culturally deprived child tends to learn more slowly than his non-deprived peers, self-pacing helps to facilitate consolidation.

Structured, Sequential Materials. The principal advantage of programmed instruction, apart from the fact that it furthers consolidation, is its careful sequential arrangement and gradation of difficulty which

---

[1] See R. W. Bruce, "Conditions of Transfer of Training," *Journal of Experimental Psychology*, XVI (1933), 343-61; C. P. Duncan, "Transfer in Motor Learning as a Function of Degree of First-task Learning and Inter-task Similarity," *Journal of Experimental Psychology*, XLV (1953), 1-11, and his "Transfer after Training with Single versus Multiple Tasks," *Journal of Experimental Psychology*, LV (1958), 63-72; L. Morrisett and C. I. Hovland, "A Comparison of Three Varieties of Training in Human Problem Solving," *Journal of Experimental Psychology*, LV (1958), 52-55; and J. M. Sassenrath, "Learning without Awareness and Transfer of Learning Sets," *Journal of Educational Psychology*, L (1959), 202-12.

[2] See Duncan, "Transfer after Training with Single versus Multiple Tasks," *op. cit.;* Morrisett and Hovland, *op. cit.;* and Sassenrath, *op. cit.*

insures that each attained increment in learning serves as an appropriate foundation and anchoring post for the learning and retention of subsequent items in the ordered sequence.[3] Adequate programming of materials also presupposes maximum attention to such matters as lucidity, organization, and the explanatory and integrative power of substantive content. It is helpful, for example, if sequential materials are so organized that they become progressively more differentiated in terms of generality and inclusiveness, and if similarities and differences between the current learning task and previous learnings are explicitly delineated.[4] Both of these aims can be accomplished by using an advance organizer or brief introductory passage before each new unit of material, which both makes available relevant explanatory principles at a high level of abstraction and increases discriminability. Programmed instruction can also be especially adapted to meet the greater needs of culturally deprived pupils for concrete-empirical props in learning relational propositions.

Although programmed instruction in general is particularly well suited to the needs of the culturally deprived child, I cannot recommend the small-frame format characteristic of teaching-machine programs and most programmed textbooks. In terms of both the logical requirements of meaningful learning and the actual size of the task that can be conveniently accommodated by the learner, the frame length typically used by teaching machines is artificially and unnecessarily abbreviated. It tends to fragment the ideas presented in the program so that their interrelationships are obscured and their logical structure is destroyed.[5] Hence it is relatively easy for less able students to master each granulated step of a given program without understanding the logical relationships and development of the concepts presented.[6] In my opinion, therefore, the traditional textbook format or oral didactic exposition that follows the programming principles outlined above, supplemented by frequent self-scoring and feedback-

[3] D. P. Ausubel and D. Fitzgerald, "Organizer, General Background, and Antecedent Learning Variables in Sequential Verbal Learning," *Journal of Educational Psychology*, LIII (1962), 243-49.

[4] D. P. Ausubel, "The Use of Advance Organizers in the Learning and Retention of Meaningful Verbal Learning," *Journal of Educational Psychology*, LI (1960), 267-72; D. P. Ausubel and D. Fitzgerald, "The Role of Discriminability in Meaningful Verbal Learning and Retention," *Journal of Educational Psychology*, LII (1961), 266-74, and their "Organizer, General Background, and Antecedent Learning Variables in Sequential Verbal Learning," *op. cit.*

[5] S. L. Pressey, "Basic Unresolved Teaching-Machine Problems," *Theory into Practice*, I (1962), 30-37.

[6] D. G. Beane, "A Comparison of Linear and Branching Techniques of Programed Instruction in Plane Geometry" ("Technical Report," No. 1 [Urbana: Training Research Laboratory, University of Illinois, July 1962]) .

giving tests, is far superior to the teaching-machine approach for the actual presentation of subject-matter content.[7]

Motivational Considerations

Thus far I have considered various environmental factors that induce retardation in the culturally deprived child's intellectual growth, as well as different cognitive techniques of counteracting and reversing such retardation. These factors and techniques, however, do not operate in a motivational vacuum. Although it is possible separately to consider cognitive and motivational aspects of learning for purposes of theoretical analysis, they are nonetheless inseparably intertwined in any real-life learning situation. For example, school failure and loss of confidence resulting from an inappropriate curriculum further depress the culturally deprived pupil's motivation to learn and thereby increase his existing learning and intellectual deficit. Similarly, although a number of practice and task variables are potentially important for effective learning in a programmed instruction context, appropriate manipulation of these variables can, in the final analysis, only insure successful long-term learning of subject matter provided that the individual is adequately motivated.

Doing without being interested in what one is doing results in relatively little permanent learning, since it is reasonable to suppose that only those materials can be meaningfully incorporated on a long-term basis into an individual's structure of knowledge that are relevant to areas of concern in his psychological field. Learners who have little need to know and understand quite naturally expend little learning effort; manifest an insufficiently meaningful learning set; fail to develop precise meanings, to reconcile new ideas with existing concepts, and to formulate new propositions in their own words; and do not devote enough time and energy to practice and review. Material is therefore never sufficiently consolidated to form an adequate foundation for sequential learning.

The problem of reversibility exists in regard to the motivational as well as in regard to the cognitive status of the culturally deprived pupil, inasmuch as his environment typically stunts not only his intellectual development, but also the development of appropriate motivations for academic achievement. Motivations for learning, like cognitive abilities, are only potential rather than inherent or endogenous capacities in human beings; their actual development is invariably dependent upon adequate environmental stimulation. Cognitive drive or intrinsic motivation to learn, for example, is probably derived in a

---

[7] Pressey, *op. cit.*

very general sense from curiosity tendencies and from related predispositions to explore, manipulate, and cope with the environment; but these tendencies and predispositions are only actualized as a result of successful exercise and the anticipation of future satisfying consequences from further exercise and as a result of internalization of the values of those significant persons in the family and subcultural community with whom the child identifies.

Intrinsic Motivation. The development of cognitive drive or of intrinsic motivation for learning, that is, the acquisition of knowledge as an end in itself or for its own sake, is, in my opinion, the most promising motivational strategy which we can adopt in relation to the culturally deprived child. It is true, of course, in view of the anti-intellectualism and pragmatic attitude toward education that is characteristic of lower-class ideology,[8] that a superficially better case can be made for the alternative strategy of appealing to the incentives to job acquisition, retention, and advancement that now apply so saliently to continuing education because of the rapid rate of technological change. Actually, however, intrinsic motivation for learning is more potent, relevant, durable, and easier to arouse than its extrinsic counterpart. Meaningful school learning, in contrast to most kinds of laboratory learning, requires relatively little effort or extrinsic incentive, and, when successful, furnishes its own reward. In most instances of school learning, cognitive drive is also the only immediately relevant motivation, since the greater part of school learning cannot be rationalized as necessary for meeting the demands of daily living. Furthermore, it does not lose its relevance or potency in later adult life when utilitarian and career advancement considerations are no longer applicable. Lastly, as we know from the high dropout rate among culturally deprived high-school youth, appeals to extrinsic motivation are not very effective. Among other reasons, the latter situation reflects a limited time perspective focused primarily on the present; a character structure that is oriented more to immediate than delayed gratification of needs; the lack of strong internalized needs for and anxiety about high academic and vocational achievement, as part of the prevailing family, peer group, and community ideology;[9] and the seeming unreality and impossibility of attaining the rewards of prolonged striving and self-denial in view of current living conditions and family circumstances, pre-

---

[8] F. Riessman, *The Culturally Deprived Child* (New York: Harper & Bros., 1962).
[9] A. Davis. "Child Training and Social Class," *Child Behavior and Development*, ed. R. G. Barker, J. S. Kounin, and H. F. Wright (New York: McGraw-Hill Book Co., 1963) , pp. 607-20.

vious lack of school success, and the discriminatory attitudes of middle-class society.[10]

If we wish to develop the cognitive drive so that it remains viable during the school years and in adult life, it is necessary to move still further away from the educational doctrine of gearing the curriculum to the spontaneously expressed interests, current concerns, and life-adjustment problems of pupils. Although it is undoubtedly unrealistic and even undesirable in our culture to eschew entirely the utilitarian, ego-enhancement, and anxiety-reduction motivations for learning, we must place increasingly greater emphasis upon the value of knowing and understanding as goals in their own right, quite apart from any practical benefits they may confer. Instead of denigrating subject-matter knowledge, we must discover more efficient methods of fostering the long-term acquisition of meaningful and usable bodies of knowledge, and of developing appropriate intrinsic motivations for such learning.

It must be conceded at the outset that culturally deprived children typically manifest little intrinsic motivation to learn. They come from family and cultural environments in which the veneration of learning for its own sake is not a conspicuous value, and in which there is little or no tradition of scholarship. Moreover, they have not been notably successful in their previous learning efforts in school. Nevertheless we need not necessarily despair of motivating them to learn for intrinsic reasons. Psychologists have been emphasizing the motivation-learning and the interest-activity sequences of cause and effect for so long that they tend to overlook their reciprocal aspects. Since motivation is not an indispensable condition for short-term and limited-quantity learning, it is not necessary to postpone learning activities until appropriate interests and motivations have been developed. Frequently the best way of motivating an unmotivated pupil is to ignore his motivational state for the time being and concentrate on teaching him as effectively as possible. Much to his suprise and to his teacher's, he will learn despite his lack of motivation; and from the satisfaction of learning he will characteristically develop the motivation to learn more.

Paradoxically, therefore, we may discover that the most effective method of developing intrinsic motivation to learn is to focus on the cognitive rather than on the motivational aspects of learning, and to rely on the motivation that is developed retroactively from successful educational achievement. This is particularly true when a teacher is able to generate contagious excitement and enthusiasm about the sub-

[10] *Ibid.*

ject he teaches, and when he is the kind of person with whom culturally deprived children can identify. Recruiting more men teachers and
dramatizing the lives and exploits of cultural, intellectual, and scientific heroes can also enhance the process of identification. At the same
time, of course, we can attempt to combat the anti-intellectualism and
lack of cultural tradition in the home through programs of adult education and cultural enrichment.

Extrinsic Motivation. The emphasis I have placed on intrinsic motivation for learning should not be interpreted to mean that I deny the
importance of developing extrinsic motivations. The need for ego enhancement, status, and prestige through achievement, the internalization of long-term vocational aspirations, and the development of such
implementing traits as responsibility, initiative, self-denial, frustration
tolerance, impulse control, and the ability to postpone immediate
hedonistic gratification are, after all, traditional hallmarks of personality maturation in our culture; and educational aspirations and
achievement are both necessary prerequisites for, and way-station pro-
totypes of, their vocational counterparts. Hence, in addition to encouraging intrinsic motivation for learning, it is also necessary to foster ego-
enhancement and career-advancement motivations for academic
achievement.

As previously pointed out, however, the current situation with respect to developing adequate motivations for higher academic and vocational achievement among culturally deprived children is not very
encouraging. But just as in the case of cognitive drive, much extrinsic
motivation for academic success can be generated retroactively from
the experience of current success in schoolwork. Intensive counseling
can also compensate greatly for the absence of appropriate home, community, and peer-group support and expectations for the development
of long-term vocational ambitions. In a sense counselors must be prepared to act *in loco parentis* in this situation. By identifying with a
mature, stable, striving, and successful male adult figure, culturally deprived boys can be encouraged to internalize long-term and realistic
aspirations, as well as to develop the mature personality traits necessary for their implementation. Hence, as a result of achieving current
ego enhancement in the school setting, obtaining positive encouragement and practical guidance in the counseling relationship, and expe-
riencing less rejection and discrimination at the hands of school personnel, higher vocational aspirations appear to lie more realistically
within their grasp. Further encouragement to strive for more ambitious academic and vocational goals can be provided by making available abundant scholarship aid to universities, to community colleges,

and to technical institutes; by eliminating the color, ethnic, and class bar in housing, education, and employment; by acquainting culturally deprived youth with examples of successful professional persons originating from their own racial, ethnic, and class backgrounds; and by involving parents sympathetically in the newly fostered ambitions of their children. The success of the Higher Horizons project indicates that an energetic program organized along the lines outlined above can do much to reverse the effects of cultural deprivation on the development of extrinsic motivations for academic and vocational achievement.

Suggested Strategy for Teaching Socially Disadvantaged Learners

Staten W. Webster

Early in 1964 fourteen student teachers were assigned to urban junior high schools comprised largely of lower class Negroes and a few Mexican Americans. This was their second teaching assignment and was planned to prepare these students to teach socially disadvantaged youth. (A term used to designate pupils whose chances for achieving their potentials are limited because of such factors as minority group status or membership in the lower-class stratum of society.) It was apparent early in this experience that instructional procedures which had been used by these student teachers during their first assignments in more favored educational settings would not be effective with these disadvantaged pupils, many of whom seemed to be educational "sit-ins" who cared little about the lessons that were being presented. The student teachers were completely frustrated!

An approach had to be devised to cope with this apathy and lack of interest if learning was to take place. An instructional sequence was developed which took into account some of the learning problems that are especially acute with this type of pupil, and which utilized effectively some of the common experiences and needs which these pupils bring with them. The strategy which was developed and is reported here appeared to be more effective than procedures and methods commonly used with middle class pupils. It rests in large measure on research about learning already well documented and reported in the lit-

Reprinted from the *California Journal for Instructional Improvement*, a quarterly publication of CASCD. Office of publication: 1705 Murchison Drive, Burlingame, California. A note concerning the author appears with his article "When Schools and Parents in a Disadvantaged Community Clash."

erature and on hypotheses emerging from recent researches and experimental programs.

Learning Problems of Socially Disadvantaged Students

Research findings dealing specifically with the learning problems of socially disadvantaged students are both limited and of recent vintage. Reports by such investigators as Ausubel (1963), Deutsch (1962), Douvan (1956), Davis (1948), and Miller and Swanson (1962) among others do indicate that the following characteristics of disadvantaged students tend to have negative effects upon learning.

Concern for the Here and Now. Individuals living in impoverished environments find that the demands of the present are pressing: little time or energy is expended in speculation about the future nor is value attached to this. Adults in such settings exhibit this "here and now" orientation in their attitudes and behaviors, and the children for whom they serve as models adopt a similar outlook on life.

If one considers that many of the rewards which the school holds up to the learner involve delays of weeks, as in the case of grades, or even years as in preparation for a vocation, it is not difficult to see why disadvantaged youth often reject the goals of the school.

Concrete and Functional Versus the Abstract. Research indicates that individuals from socially disadvantaged environments tend to possess cognitive styles which require extensive use of concrete examples in perception and in learning. This phenomenon is of importance when one considers the great emphasis that is placed upon the abstract in the curriculum of the school and in the teaching act.

Difficulties in Seeing Relationships. The child socialized in an impoverished environment does not have experiences which require classifying, relating, and integrating knowledge. Such learners, then, display gross inadequacies in their abilities to engage in these kinds of intellectual activities.

Active Learning Versus Contemplative Learning. As a child advances through the grades of the school, the learning process becomes increasingly more contemplative in nature. This factor possibly explains, in part, the growing alienation of the disadvantaged student from the school and its content. Research indicates that socially disadvantaged persons tend to be more physical and expressive in their personal styles; learning can best be accomplished when the process is involving and of an active nature.

A Suggested Strategy for Instruction

In light of some of these characteristics of the disadvantaged learner we contend that many traditional approaches to instruction fail to produce effective learning and that a different approach is needed. Many lessons are begun in a way which implies that pupils are expected to transform themselves into time machines. In a social studies class pupils may be asked to deal with persons and events which pre-date them by hundreds or even thousands of years. Students in an English class are expected to understand and become involved with characters and plots which depict a way of life that they have not known and that are alien to the era in which they live.

This teaching strategy is based on an assumption that the "World Concept"[1] of the socially disadvantaged student is a limited one. Furthermore, it is assumed that ideas and information which threaten the world concepts of such individuals are ego-alien to them and are, more often than not, rejected as being of limited value and usefulness.

A problem faced by the teacher is to bridge the gap between the "World Concepts" of disadvantaged learners and the particular subject-matter that is to be mastered. In order to do this successfully, the prior experiences of the students must be used.

The Role of Experience. Any person when confronted with a problem begins to search his storehouse of accumulated experiences for strategies, related ideas, and possible solutions. The role of prior experience in the learning process appears to be vital in that:

1. a person's own life experiences greatly color and influence the values he attributes to ideas, people, and things,

2. prior experiences color one's perceptions of reality, of the future, and determine to a large extent his levels of interest, motivation, and the values which he attributes to various goals,

3. the more removed from a learner's prior experiences is the content of a new learning experience (skills, subject-matter, concepts, facts, etc.), the lower will be his levels of interest, motivation, and learning,

4. new experiences (ideas, information, relationships) are best understood in light of a person's accumulated and recallable experiences and knowledge:

5. a person remembers new experiences and information to the extent that he has some clear-cut relation to his storehouse of accumulated experiences and information.

Some Common Experiences of Children and Youth

In order to apply effectively the following approach to instruction the teacher must be aware of the probable common experiences which

---

[1] This term is used to connote an environment of which a person is fully aware and which for him is reality. The author is indebted to one of his students, Miss Janice Paff, for the definition of this concept.

socially disadvantaged pupils have had as well as their developmental interests and needs. The following list suggests some of these experiences which the teacher may use to bridge what the pupil brings to a learning situation and the outcomes expected in terms of curriculum goals.

Institutions	home, school, families, teams
Roles and Statuses	parents, siblings, peers, relatives, adults (e.g., policemen, doctors, teachers)
Experiences Relating to People	friendships, enemies, rewards, victory, defeat, work (tasks), threats, play, death, gifts, failure, punishment, conflict, success, fighting, hurt
Feelings	love, hate, hostility, jealousy, envy, shame, pride, respect, joy, sadness, happiness, surprise, disappointment, hunger, fatigue, anger, distrust, fear, courage, faith, suspicion
Needs	personal worth, friends, respect, acceptance, success, love, admiration, independence, control (self and others)

The Instructional Sequence. The method of instruction presented here differs from approaches that are commonly used. The procedure focuses initial attention and concern upon the *learner and his experiences and problems* rather than the content, skills, or attitudes that are to be learned or developed. To illustrate the three stages of this scheme, actual examples from the work of two student teachers in the areas of social studies and English are presented.

STAGE I.

Sensitization. The first step of the process involves obtaining the attention and interests of the students through the consideration of selected aspects of their prior experiences. While the students may not be aware of it initially, they will actually be identifying key concepts or ideas which will later be applied in a study of the related subject-matter.

Example: A U.S. history teacher desired to have the students consider sectionalism and its causes as it existed prior to the Civil War. She used the concept of a neighborhood as a unit comparable to a section of the country. Students were asked to agree upon the boundaries of what they considered to be their own neighborhood initially. Second, they were asked to identify those factors which determined their definition of the area as their neighborhood. Such items included language or speech similarities, similar types of work by the adults, similar socio-economic status, membership in common institutions, etc. The class then was asked to use these elements which had been isolated to compare their neighborhood with another that seemed to be different.

Example: An English teacher desired to have an average ability class comprised entirely of Negroes engage in a creative writing experience. Great wails of protest greeted the announcement of the activity. The teacher then informed the class that they would use the theme of *death* as a common focus in their writing efforts. Some pupils were greatly interested and others protested loudly that they had never seen anyone die and knew nothing about death. Discussion led to the realization by the students that death is not restricted to people; that both animate and inanimate things can be said to die, and that a particular incident of death can elicit a variety of reactions ranging from extreme grief to supreme joy.

STAGE II.

Integration: The teacher's task is to affect an integration of the key factors which were identified during Stage I with those inherent in the subject-matter which the students would have studied earlier or would then consider as an assignment.

Example: The students in the social studies class then applied the factors or concepts which distinguished between their neighborhood and a contrasting one to the various sections of the country as they existed in the mid-1800's. They were encouraged to test the validity and usefulness of these elements isolated from their own experience in the case of the various geographical areas under study.

Example: Integration took place in the English learning situation when the factors related to the experience of death were used to structure the actual stories which were written by the students. Despite the guidelines provided by the teacher, the students still enjoyed great freedom in selecting plots and themes for their writings.

This stage of the process involves much contrasting and analysis on the part of the students and the teachers.

STAGE III.

Extension and Reinforcement. In this phase of the learning process, students are encouraged to seek other applications of the key factors identified initially in their own experiences and validated in their considerations of the subject-matter. This stage of the procedure serves to reinforce that which has been learned as well as to stimulate students to utilize information which otherwise would not have been considered.

Example: The social studies class was encouraged to apply the key elements which made for sectionalism in the 1800's to other situations as in the case of nations, institutions, or geographical areas of the world.

Example: In the English class the process of extension and reinforcement was used when the stories of the students in the learning experience were used to isolate other life themes for additional creative writing activities. Subsequent learning experiences included the use of this approach in the writing of poetry.

Several advantages of this approach to teaching socially disadvantaged students are evident.

1. the teacher's initial attention is focused on the pupils;
2. the interest, involvement, and motivation of pupils is of major concern;
3. pupils are taught to see relationships;
4. retention appears to be increased;
5. the experience of pupils is extended in ways that lead to more perceptive understanding of events, ideas and values, and in ways that exceed their own first hand experience.

Other Instructional Considerations

Current studies may yield new information that will be useful in teaching these socially disadvantaged pupils. They have already reinforced principles long accepted as sound methodology by educators. In addition to the several principles cited in this paper the following are now receiving special emphasis.

Establishing Achievement Sets. Research (see Katz, 1964) strongly indicates that individuals tend to achieve at a higher level when the expectation that they will succeed at a learning task is communicated to them. One big danger of teaching socially disadvantaged learners is that instructors too often expect limited accomplishment. Here, we suggest, that *the teacher must convey to his students the honest belief, on his part, that they can achieve.*

Repetition Within a Context of Variety. Too much of what we expect students to learn is covered once and then forgotten. Teaching must seek to make permanent the useful content that students master. Earlier learned material must be repeatedly used and *applied through a variety of approaches* or it will not be retained.

Repetition must be planned. A teacher would do well to analyze in advance the content of a particular subject for a semester or school year to locate key areas or problems which relate to each other. The common and essential concepts which should be repeated can then provide the structure of the course and lead to more effective learning and retention.

The Importance of Feedback. As already noted, socially disadvantaged persons have a greater need for more immediate gratification or reinforcement. Learning can be improved when they receive frequent confirmations of their achievements or gains. The teacher should plan learning activities so that, initially at least, short-range goals are clearly obvious to the students. Feed-back on student progress can and should take many forms; verbal recognition, written analysis of work, and individualized conferences are examples.

References

Ausubel, D. P. "Teaching Strategy for Culturally Deprived Pupils: Cognitive and Motivational Considerations," *School Review* (Winter, 1963) 71:454-463.

Davis, A. *Social Class Influences on Learning* (Cambridge, Harvard University Press, 1948).

Deutsch, M. *The Disadvantaged Child and the Learning Process: Some Social, Psychological and Developmental Considerations,* Paper delivered at "Work Conference on Curriculum and Teaching in Depressed Urban Areas," New York, Columbia University, July 10, 1962.

Douvan, Elizabeth, "Social Status and Success Striving," *Journal of Abnormal and Social Psychology,* March, 1956, 213-223.

Katz, I., "Review of Evidence Relating to Effects of Desegregation on the Intellectual Performance of Negroes," *American Psychologist,* June, 1964, 19:6, 381-399.

Miller, D. R., and Swanson, G. E., *Inner Conflict and Defense* (New York, H. Holt and Company, 1960).

Improving the Education of Culturally Deprived Children: Applying Learning Theory to Classroom Instruction

SOPHIE BLOOM

In the spring semester of 1963, twenty-five teachers from the Howland, Pope, and Lawson elementary schools, all in District 19 of the Chicago public schools, participated in a workshop course entitled "Educating the Culturally Deprived Child." The workshop was built around presentations and discussions led by experts in child development, social anthropology, curriculum, reading diagnostic procedures, and other areas of knowledge which offer insights into the special problems involved in teaching culturally deprived children.

Discussions and lectures were used as bases upon which to develop practical plans for teaching. The twenty-five classroom teachers all taught in schools which served large numbers of children who could be described as culturally deprived; as the teachers heard lectures and participated in discussions, they were able to define and re-define the day-to-day teaching problems which they were encountering and to adapt concepts and insights gained from the presentations to their own classroom situations.

One concept which seemed to the teachers to be especially valuable and promising is the set of principles of learning developed by Dollard and Miller.[1] Because cultural deprivation is often associated with or accompanied by social and intellectual deprivation, special attention

From *Chicago School Journal*, December, 1963. Reprinted by permission of the publisher.

[1] J. Dollard and N. Miller, *Personality and Psychotherapy* (New York: 1950).

to *Cues, Reinforcement,* and *Participation* is deemed to be especially significant when working with such children. Each of these terms is explained below. Following the explanation of each term is a selective listing of techniques or activities employed by the participating teachers with the aim of emphasizing the aspect of the learning process which that term emphasizes. Many, indeed most, of the techniques and activities are not *new,* either in the sense that they have never been used before or in the sense that they represent startling departure from classroom techniques employed by many teachers. What is new is the recognition of the way in which a sensitivity to the learning problems of children can produce in the teacher an awareness of the implications for learning involved in the structuring of many classroom activities.

Children Learn through Response to Cues

The term *Cues* refers to the aspects of a learning situation which determine how a child will respond, in what direction he will respond, which response he will make, and even whether he will respond. As the term "respond" implies, a cue is a stimulus, a part of the learning situation which leads the learner to respond in the desired direction and with the desired response. Every teacher has had the experience of preparing a lesson, perhaps even preparing it quite carefully, and then finding that his pupils are bewildered, that they "don't know how to begin," or don't understand what they are supposed to do. One way of explaining what has gone wrong in such a situation is to say that the children did not find in the situation enough clear cues as to what response was expected.

If an important cue is not distinctive enough, if it is obscure, it is impossible for the individual, no matter how much he may want to, to make the desired or anticipated response. Good cues are explicit and easily understandable. The cue that is salient—that "stands out"—and that is concrete is easier for a young child to understand than the one that is not salient and concrete. The more modalities or senses to which a given cue or combination of cues appeals, the greater the chance that any child will personally be able to experience and comprehend the clue; hence, the greater the chance that he will react with the desired response—solve the problem, answer the question, or point to the correct picture.

Words Important as Learning Cues

Words employed by the teacher are cues to the pupils. When one of the problems which enters into the learning situation is the problem of a need in the child for acculturation, special attention must be paid to using words which the child understands. A study made in Detroit involving children with similar backgrounds to those of the pupils at the Howland school, for example, indicated that the children did not understand clearly from 20 to 50 per cent of the basic words used by their teachers. In such a case, the words are not meaningful cues.

The teachers in the workshop, when they turned their attention to the matter of cues, found that there were many ways in which they could make the cues in their classroom activities more salient, more concrete, more meaningful, and more consonant with the known cultural background of the children they were teaching. Each of the following descriptions of techniques focuses on the cue aspect of the learning situation.

Using the opaque projector to project a large image of drawings, pages of a book, or small objects for observation and discussion has the tendency to make the cues more salient by increasing their relative size. It is possible to project an image almost the entire height of the classroom wall. Such large size also focuses attention.

To help children learn the names of the months, it is sometimes helpful to have them identify the name of the current month with some familiar object or person. For instance, for January, the teacher can have the children identify the first sound of the name of the month with a child in the class named Jacqueline. When the meaning or sound of a new word is related to the children in the class, the cue becomes more meaningful.

Cues Should Appeal to Various Senses

Carefully designed techniques for structuring the children as a group are frequently helpful in making cues meaningful. Even such a device as, on appropriate occasions, teaching primary children to respond to a "Ready, Stop, Listen!" stimulus, establishes an atmosphere in which the children can attend to the visual and auditory cues which are to be presented. Salience of cue depends upon the attention of the learner as well as upon the visibility or audibility of the cue.

In an attempt to demonstrate to children that wool keeps us warm, the teacher's own sweater was wrapped around a jar filled with boiling water. The other sealed jar of boiling water was not wrapped. The cues in this experience were concrete and salient and provided for learning through three sensory pathways: visual, auditory, and tactile.

Making a booklet called "Our Names" can go far to encourage reading. Each child brings a snapshot from home, or the teacher takes snapshots of the children. Each child's name is printed on a single page and his snapshot affixed to the page. The booklet is read and re-read. Children enjoy finding their own names, reading names of others, and recognizing the faces of their friends. When the cue concerns the child himself, it is more meaningful.

Words Defined by Direct Experience

Defining new words or concepts by drawings on the blackboard or by direct experience with or manipulation of objects is quite effective: for *valley*, a picture of a mountain and valley; for *gangplank*, a picture of a ship with a gangplank leading to it; for *pearl*, let children observe and handle an imitation or cultured pearl; for *cargo*, place candy or other objects in a net, even a hair net, let children contrive a hoist, and let them practice raising it and lowering it into a box, representing the hold of a ship. The more senses appealed to by the illustration, the more meaningful the cues become.

Very young children learn new sounds and the letters that stand for them more easily with additional cues. Giving a limited number of initial word sounds a name which appeals to the children's imagination or experience can speed learning. *M* is the delicious sound; *S* is the snake sound; *Sh* is the quiet sound; *Ch* is the train sound; *Wh* is the blowing sound. Giving the sound a name adds a concrete cue.

Reinforcement Means Reward for Response

Just as cues are essential in initial learning, *Reinforcement* is important in ensuring that the learning "sticks." Reinforcement refers to reward. The principle of reinforcement is central to many theories of learning. Acts which are rewarded are repeated. Some of the guidelines which the workshop participants adopted as important in securing reinforcement in learning situations are as follows:

1. In the absence of reward as reinforcement, no learning takes place. A child who never feels success cannot learn.

2. Reinforcement is necessary both for the learning and the maintenance of a habit.

3. Mere repetition does not strengthen a habit. Repeating an action through drill, in the absence of reinforcement, may destroy learning.

4. In the learning of a new culture, extinction of old responses must take place if the old responses are to be replaced by new.

5. A response which is not reinforced becomes extinct. A response which is not practiced is forgotten.

6. If learning is to take place, the response must occur before it can be reinforced. The most frequent danger in group instruction is the lack of opportunity for many of the children to participate.

7. Reinforcement is most necessary at the beginning stage of learning. Success is essential at the beginning as a basis for motivating further learning.

Many of the rewards or reinforcements are given so casually, so naturally, and so unconsciously by the teacher that he often does not consider them as rewards. A reward need not be something which can be handed to a child. In many instances, what the teacher can give of himself is more a reward to the child than is some tangible object. As one teacher put it, "We have unusual relationship—they're real proud." He felt that the feeling that he and his class shared was something so unique, and so deep, and so personal that they would do anything for him. In this kind of reinforcement would be included the smile, the nod, "That's right," "Good," "He got it right," also, especially with little children, the physical support of the teacher, such as the hand on the shoulder during a recitation. Teacher approval is a powerful influence, and the children are very responsive to it. The teacher's personal displays of interest in the child such as remembering his name and remembering the record of the day before or test performance on the previous day are all rewards. Approval by peers is a powerful social reward. The feeling of adequacy is reinforcement by oneself, and enjoyment of the learning for the sake of learning is an intrinsic reward.

Techniques Which Offer Reinforcement to Learning

Learning the names of other children in the kindergarten can be one of the first learning tasks of new children. To help children learn others' names, the teacher can have them play "Jack, Be Nimble . . ." using each child's name instead of "Jack." Children sit in a circle on the floor with a block and a ball in the middle. "What is your name?" "My name is Linda." "Linda, be nimble," and so on. All the children have practice in saying the child's name. To be so singled out is for each child both good participation and at the same time good reinforcement for his self-esteem.

Rewards in the concrete sense should be made as apparent to other children as possible. For instance, as a reward for completing work before others, children may have "bucket work." The "buckets" are plastic wastepaper baskets. The work in each bucket consists of lessons or activities of any appropriate kind inserted in brightly colored cellophane envelopes. When a child has some "bucket work" everyone knows it; thus his self-esteem is reinforced by the knowledge that both his peers and the adults present are aware of his reward.

After planting a seed in a milk carton, children watch for the seed to grow into a plant. For a first experience, something like grass or radish seeds works well, as they grow fast. Such activities, when they are carried out to successful completion, are a source of genuine reinforcement of the self—a feeling of command over environment arises from the child's seeing that he has "made" the seed grow.

A simple process such as encouraging children who finish assigned tasks early to help others acts as a kind of reinforcement. Still more strongly reinforcing is allowing a child who has, for example, learned how to solve a puzzle to show another child how to solve it. Helping another child produces social and peer reinforcement. Teacher approval of the helpfulness does the rest.

Socially Approved Behavior Increased by Reinforcement

Choosing a "Citizen of the Week" through a class vote—having each row select a candidate and then having the entire class select the winner on the basis of democratically arrived at qualifications—can provide great social reinforcement to a number of children in a term. Posting the picture of the winner and the runners-up each week offers another kind of reinforcement. This reinforces the kinds of behavior embodied in the qualifications set up for voting.

For very young children, writing in a regular place on the blackboard statements of performance of approved behavior can be highly reinforcing. "Roosevelt said, 'Excuse me' to Ernest." "Dolores helped Sylvia." "Catherine shared her candy with us." Such statements, allowed to remain in public view for a day or so and pointed out to visitors and others, can go far in reinforcing socially approved behavior.

Active Participation Key to Learning

The thought or act which results from the stimulus or cue is the response. In the classroom, response is frequently referred to as *Participation*. In large groups, it is difficult to know whether a given child is participating in the learning situation unless he makes some *overt* response—answers a question, nods his head, acts in accordance with instructions. A major aim of the teacher is to arrange the learning situation so that each learner in the classroom will somehow make the correct response as soon as possible after the stimulus has been given. Before a child can learn a new way of thinking or speaking, he must *try* the new way. No amount of repetition by the teacher gives the child the practice he needs. One cannot, for instance, learn to play tennis simply by watching others play. The child must try the response himself, and, if he succeeds, the response must be rewarded. He must know when he is right.

Ideally, every child should actively participate at every stage of every lesson. This ideal is, of course, usually not totally attainable, but every effort should be made to see that as many children as possible participate in as many ways as possible in *every* learning situation. Children learn to read by reading, not, usually, by listening to others read. The following are some techniques suggested by workshop participants for leading as many children as possible to participate in each learning experience.

Involving Each Child Essential to Success

In the study of boats and trips, one teacher took the entire class of fourth graders on an imaginary trip. Each child experienced each step of a real trip. Each had an imaginary "shot" with a hypodermic. Each had a passport complete with height, weight, thumbprint, and official stamp. Each child participated in the "actual" experience of a real trip.

When learning sound recognition and discrimination, the children can respond with bodily movements of some sort when they hear the critical sound or when they hear one unlike the critical sound. They can indicate that they hear, for instance, a word beginning with an "s-sound" by clapping, tapping, holding hands up, or some other means. Their participation thus becomes overt.

For the primary grade "show and tell" period the teacher can bring an object and not show it to the children. The teacher can describe the object and let each child "guess," or wrap the object in a cloth and let each child lift and feel it and then guess what it is.

Children can be led to make their own copies of charts or other materials to which they need to refer in their work. For instance, when learning the concept of "place" in arithmetic, each child can make his own copy of a place chart from a large one placed in front of the classroom. In this way, each child in the classroom participates directly in a careful examination of the chart.

The list of techniques and activities presented here is intended to be suggestive rather than complete. Each of the three concepts—cues, reinforcement, and participation—deals with an important part of every successful learning situation. Awareness of and attention to these essentials can improve learning by children of all cultural levels, but such awareness and attention is most essential in the instruction of culturally deprived children. The provision of cues which are salient and concrete, the ensuring of direct participation in the learning situation by every child, and the reinforcement of correct or desired responses will go far toward improving the instruction of those children whose success in school activities is crucial both to them and to our society.

༄·ཀྵ

An Experimental Curriculum for Culturally Deprived Kindergarten Children

༄·ཀྵ

JAMES L. OLSON AND RICHARD G. LARSON

There is a pressing need for urban educators to develop sensible curricula for culturally deprived children. Traditional curricular concepts do not seem to meet this need. Content is inappropriate and reflects the lack of an adequate theoretical curricular structure. If efforts to meet the demands of educating deprived children in depressed area schools are to proceed with logic and efficiency, then controlled attempts to meet these problems must be explicitly described and carefully evaluated.

This article describes the curriculum structure and implementation of a pilot project undertaken in Racine, Wisconsin, which represents one approach to the education of culturally deprived kindergarten children. An experimental group of 20 kindergarten children was identified. This group participated in the curricular activities described in this paper while a like group from a similar school setting was identified for purposes of evaluation.[1]

From *Educational Leadership*, May, 1965. Reprinted with permission of the Association for Supervision and Curriculum Development and the authors. Copyright © 1965 by the Association for Supervision and Curriculum Development. James L. Olson is Associate Professor of Exceptional Education at the University of Wisconsin-Milwaukee; Richard G. Larson is Assistant Curriculum Coordinator of the Unified School District No. 1, Racine, Wisconsin.

[1] A general description of this project, supported by the Johnson Foundation and Western Foundation of Racine, was reported in the *NEA Journal*, May 1962. The procedures used in identifying deprived children were described in the November 1963 issue of *Exceptional Children*.

Theoretical Framework

The writers agreed that both subject selection and curriculum development needed to be based on some logically consistent rationale so that hypotheses could be constructed and tested. Cultural deprivation was defined as having its most notable effects on school children along four dimensions:

1. *Language development.* Underdeveloped expressive and receptive language skills will be evident among deprived kindergarten children, and will negatively affect their school achievement. Speech patterns will conflict with the dominant language norms of middle-class teachers, thus heightening the improbability of a successful start in school.

2. *Self concept.* An inadequate self-image may characterize children raised in a substandard environment. Self-doubt or insecurity may result in low school achievement and a lessened feeling of personal worth.

3. *Social skills.* The deprived child will have had minimal training in the conventional manners and social amenities accepted by his middle-class teachers. He will be unskilled in relating socially to his peers or to authority figures, and will lack ability to function effectively in a school group.

4. *Cultural differences.* Most deprived children will come from lower socioeconomic strata. Many will be members of minority group subcultures. Therefore, their behavior and beliefs may differ from those of the dominant groups in the schools, and will be less readily understood and accepted.

Instruments were selected or designed to assess these four areas. Those children measuring lowest on composite test results were selected and arbitrarily defined as a sample of "culturally deprived" children (Larson and Olson, 1963).

The four dimensions also served as the framework for curriculum development. The investigators and the project teacher identified skills and understandings within each area which were assumed to be vital to school success. Thus, language development yielded receptive and expressive language skills; these were in turn subdivided, providing reasonably specific curricular objectives which could be translated into teaching plans with relative ease. This analysis is presented in Table 1.

The reader may wonder whether concentrating curricular efforts upon those factors which were assumed to differentiate culturally deprived children is a naive attempt to accomplish the impossible—that is, to superimpose middle class values and patterns of living upon chil-

TABLE 1.

A FRAMEWORK FOR CURRICULUM DEVELOPMENT: KINDERGARTEN[2]

Developmental Areas Differentiating Culturally Deprived	Persisting School Situations	Classroom Activities
Language Development	Receptive Language 　Auditory Skills 　　Listening to get meaning from auditory symbols 　　. . . for learning 　　. . . for fun in conversation 　Visual Skills 　　Interpreting interpersonal meaning from facial and bodily expressions 　　Recognizing relationships between symbolic and concrete concepts and objects 　　Gaining familiarity with traditional cultural symbols 　　　Flag 　　　Santa Claus 　　　Mottoes 　　　Slogans, etc. Expressive Language 　Verbal Expressive 　　Development of understandable articulatory habits 　　Using words in sequence 　　Adapting speech to different social situations 　Motor Expressive 　　Drawing 　　Writing 　　Rhythms	This column was completed by the classroom teacher as daily lesson plans.
Social Skills	Relating to peers Relating to authority figures Developing manners Functioning in a group 　Sharing 　Taking turns 　Making choices Adapting to required social roles	
Self Concept	Developing: 　Realization of individual uniquenesses 　Independence from family 　Realistic awareness of physique 　Positive identification with academic success 　Adjustment to success and failure situations 　Self-awareness as a group member 　Feelings of self-worth	

[2] The list under the heading "Persisting School Situations" is by no means complete. The possibilities for expansion are obvious.

Developmental Areas Differentiating Culturally Deprived	Persisting School Situations	Classroom Activities
Cultural Differences	Developing an awareness of differences in cultural patterns Eating habits Dress Recreation Home activities Personal relationships Expanding geographical limits Expanding psychological limits	

dren whose behavioral norms are solidly imbued with the values of a lower class culture. One may justifiably question whether middle class standards form a solid enough base upon which to structure a plan for satisfying the social psychological and intellectual needs of any man. The writers agree.

The purpose of this curricular structure was to aim instruction at those skills which deprived children lack, but which seem to be universal requisites to school success.[3] This may explain the purpose of the column headed "Persisting School Situations."[4] The criterion for entry in this column was the supposed potential for maximizing success in later school experiences.

A further criterion for analyzing the four differentiating areas was a consideration of those things which the writers assumed were expected of all students by their middle-class teachers. There was an attempt, therefore, to select those persisting school situations which required skills and attitudes which teachers might assume are taught to pre-school children in the average middle-class home, but which probably are not taught to culturally deprived children. Thus, the curriculum framework included such entries as the sequential use of words, role adaptation, and belief in one's own success potential.

The preceding description of a curriculum framework for culturally deprived kindergarten children is general; however, at least two qualifications must be observed. First, this framework applied only to one-half of the kindergarten day. Mornings were spent using the rec-

---

[3] The deep influence of lower-class culture on language development (Bernstein, '61), on mentality (Anastasi, '58), on mental health (Sexton, '61, Harrington, '63) and on school achievement (Sexton '61, Kirk, '58) combine to form a grim portrait of deprivation. Bernstein observes that the environmental influences on language may be the most crucial, since school success so greatly depends on that single factor.

[4] This phase is an adaptation of Stratemeyer's curriculum-building concept of "Persisting Life Situations."

ommended curriculum guidelines of the Racine school system. Second, it should be stressed that the theoretical framework was useful only to the extent that it was utilized by the teacher as a guide for the selection of classroom activities. The teacher and the investigators attempted in several ways to maintain a reasonable amount of unity between the theoretical curriculum structure and its practical implementation. All three were involved from the beginning in discussions on curriculum development. All met several times during the school year to review aspects of curriculum and instruction. Finally, the teacher kept a daily log throughout the year in which she recorded activities which seemed appropriate to the academic needs of the experimental subjects.

Activities

A number of classroom activities emerged as particularly promising practices with deprived children. The heavy use of a simple box camera by the teacher paid dividends. After taking candid shots of individuals, of classroom activity, or of the children on their many trips, the photographs were posted on a bulletin board. The photographs immediately stimulated high interest and discussion; many of the children had not seen photos of themselves previously. The teacher frequently changed the snapshots on the board and placed the old pictures in a large class book.

Puppets were used to present dramatizations of well-known stories and to project conversation into imagined characters. Since shyness and inhibited expression typified the speech of some of the children when placed before the class, this medium provided a means of projecting expression and speech without personal exposure.

The class made a monthly "newsletter." Children drew pictures on ditto masters, and the related stories they dictated to the teacher were typed on these sheets. The results were sent home to parents, and single copies were given to other rooms in school. Descriptions of trips, personalities and special classroom events were favorite subjects. The following example of a newsletter entry reflects the typical expressive style of the children, as well as the nature of the information which seemed important to them:

I liked the trip to the building. It had lots of windows, and we could see the water. The building was in Milwaukee. The heater felt funny in the bathroom. It was to dry your hands. There were pictures. They were all different. We have some pictures in our house. There is a picture of my mamma, and my daddy, and me. A lady was putting things in a box. We saw round things in a box. We saw cap waves on Lake Michigan. They were white and went high and low. Some hit the rocks and flashed. There were a lot of cars. Some were parked, some were going. There was a city bus, too. We went on the elevators. We went up and down. We sat down in it, and we were laughing. The building had a lot of windows and steps. They had a kitchen.

In order to give the reader a flavor of other kinds of activities developed by the classroom teacher, the following excerpts have been selected from her daily log.

October 23—We had quite a good time in the afternoon while Julie frosted her cake. Jeffrey Bogan got hold of the mixer and Julie put the frosting on. The small problem of finding an electrical outlet led to a talk on why we needed one in the first place. How did the use of the electrical mixer make the work easier? Julie didn't know what a birthday spanking was and started to cry when it was mentioned.

December 6—We went to Milwaukee via the Northshore. All went beautifully, and people were helpful and friendly. Individuals in stores and on the street and in the train were impressed with the manners and attitudes exhibited by the children. The store windows overwhelmed the children. Several said how pretty their mothers would look in some of the dresses we saw.

March 4—Used the earphones. They picked the songs and stories they wanted to hear. They knew a lot of the songs and I was able to better hear [sic] what they could do along with the phonograph. Omar responded exceptionally well with a loud clear voice.

April 23—The trip to the Buick dealers. We saw the new cars and watched mechanics at work. The mechanic gave each of them a book and we later looked at the books together.

These samples from the log reflect the teacher's attempts to provide situations which might stimulate growth in the four areas previously described—language development, social skills, self-concept, and cultural differences. The reader will also note references to the most frequent activity—field trips. Trips were assumed to be valuable in eliciting linguistic responses from children; language output could not be expected without provision for input. The planning and evaluation experiences relating to field trips provided key classroom opportunities for the growth of language facility.

Trips also provided chances for social skills to develop in a variety of contexts. Children learned to eat in restaurants and to use transportation facilities. They became adept at altering their behavior to meet the requirements of expected social roles in public places.

Further, trips provided a vehicle for self-concept development. The children were exposed to success in handling social situations, and felt positive responses from others. It was assumed that cultural differences were reduced as the geographic and psychological limits of the children expanded.

One of the most successful field trips took place when a group of university seniors majoring in education accompanied the children on a field trip to Chicago. The only instructions given to the university students were that they should choose a child, stay with him for the day, talk to him, and be good listeners. This experience provided excellent practice in learning to converse with adults. Here was an infrequent opportunity in the lives of most of the children —a chance to receive long and undivided attention from interested persons.

In all, over fifty trips were taken during the eight months the experimental kindergarten was in operation.[5] Total expenses for field trips amounted to $598.00.

Materials

Table 2 [below] presents a listing of the kinds of materials and equipment utilized in this experimental kindergarten program. No attempt has been made to list all of the devices and aids used in the classroom—only those which might be different from the typical kindergarten furnishings have been listed.

TABLE 2.

MATERIALS AND EQUIPMENT USED IN THE EXPERIMENTAL KINDERGARTEN

Language Development	Self Concept	Social Skills	Cultural Differences
Books	Negro family dolls	Safety signs	Records
Records	White family dolls	Family dolls	Garden and
—Listening games	Puppets	Costumes for role-	farming tools
—Folk songs	Full-length mirror	playing	Toys—cars,
—Rhymes	Camera	Lunch tables	trucks, trains,
Record players	Tape recorder	Rhythm instruments	tractors
Tape recorders (2)	Private storage	Dolls representing	Sand table
Listening center	cubicles	various	Cooking utensils
Earphones and dis-		occupations	Farm animals
tributor for small			Rocking chairs
group work)			Colored cubes
Montessori sensory			Model workers
education devices			
Puppets and puppet			
stage			
Number manipulation			
devices			

[5] The project class began October 15, 1962, and ended in mid-June, 1963. The first few weeks of that school year were used in selecting experimental and contrast subjects.

Discussion

Parental Involvement. The experimenters decided at the beginning of this study that parental involvement would be one variable which could be controlled by simply assuming a typical school policy. That is, if the parents wanted contact with the schools, the schools were ready to provide this contact. If they wanted special help from any services provided by the school, it was provided. In turn, the school initiated routine home contracts which fell within the framework ordinarily assumed by schools in the Racine system. This allowed for a home visit by the teacher, a mid-year parent-teacher conference, and parent contacts for meeting unanticipated problems relating to health, school adjustment or academic attainment. However, the project teacher and the investigators made a considerable effort to avoid contacts which extended beyond the frequency of those utilized in other local kindergarten classes.

The Concept of Expanding Horizons. As was previously described, field trips were probably the most important curricular vehicle in this pilot program.[6] Before the beginning of the school year, it was decided that, whenever possible, the children would be out of the classroom from one to two days a week. This goal was fairly well achieved; an average of 1.6 trips were taken weekly.

This initial commitment to trips as a catalyst for stimulating academic and psychological development also freed the thinking of project personnel from ordinary channels, and provided a crutch for maintaining a well-paced and stimulating program.

One assumption made by the authors in beginning this study was that the typical kindergarten nap was unnecessary. The school day was lengthened from the half-day kindergarten class to a full five hour school day. In spite of this increase, the teacher was requested to introduce a nap only if the children seemed to require it. It was decided that naps would be avoided unless the children's behavior gave clear evidence of the need for rest. The experimental classroom teacher reports that throughout most of the school year no nap was required by these beginning kindergarten children despite the fact that they were attending school full days.

The Teacher. Miss Eleanor R.[7] was selected as the experimental

---

[6] It is interesting to note that William Raschaert indicates that many of our assumptions about the value of field trips seem to be untested. He found only one paper of significance since 1938 in a recent review of studies on field trips. (Personal conversation, Detroit, 1962).

[7] Miss R. is currently a staff member of the Laboratory School at the University of Chicago.

classroom teacher. Since her background, philosophy and attitudes undoubtedly had a great effect upon the curriculum as it was presented to the children it is necessary to describe her. She had obtained her degree in primary and nursery school education, and was working on a master's degree in mental retardation. Miss R. had nine years' teaching experience.

Her attitudes toward the experimental kindergarten were open and accepting. Her teaching style was informal, with use of a wide range of vocal tones and facial expressions. Often, her face communicated nuances of emotion without the assistance of a spoken word. She laughed and scowled often. She spoke firmly one moment, gently and softly the next.

The preplanning and post-evaluation of field trips were marked with Miss R.'s commitment to variety. She activated multi-sensory stimulation through the use of many projects and techniques within a short time span. Discussion, singing, rhythms, cut-paper projects, taped talks, creative drama, and role playing were standard. Free play periods were not restricted to a set time allotment.

In summary, this article describes a curriculum specifically designed to meet the assumed educational needs of culturally deprived kindergarten children. A theoretical framework based upon the psychological differences between deprived and typical elementary school children was described. Discussion also considered activities, materials and the teacher.

References

Anne Anastasi. "Heredity, Environment, and the Question 'How?' " *Psychological Review* 65, No. 4, 1958.

Basil Bernstein. "Social Class and Linguistic Development: A Theory of Social Learning." *Education, Economy and Society.* A. H. Halsey, J. Floud and C. A. Anderson, editors (Glencoe: The Free Press, 1961).

Michael Harrington. *The Other America* (New York: Macmillan, 1962).

Samuel A. Kirk. *Early Education of the Mentally Retarded* (Urbana: University of Illinois Press, 1958).

Richard Larson and James L. Olson. "A Method of Identifying Culturally Deprived Kindergarten Children." *Exceptional Child,* November 1963.

William Raschaert. Personal conversation. Detroit, 1962.

Patricia Sexton. *Education and Income* (New York: The Viking Press, 1961).

Florence B. Stratemeyer *et al. Developing a Curriculum for Modern Living.* (New York: Bureau of Publications, Teachers College, Columbia University, 1957).

Ways to Improve Oral Communication of Culturally Different Youth

RUTH I. GOLDEN

Mark Twain once said in a sarcastic moment, "Nothing so needs reforming as other people's habits." Yet, I believe he would approve of our interest in the problem of how to reform the speech habits of culturally different students, for our purpose is to break down language barriers and to help each individual acquire a language proficiency that will help him to achieve his greatest potential. As Thomas Pollock has said, "Civilization depends upon communication. Language is the basic instrument through which human 'beings share their thinking. If a youth is to develop as an individual, contribute to society, and participate in its benefits, he must have command of the social processes of language."[1]

The schools and all the institutions in a democratic society exist for the purpose of promoting the growth of the individual. For his growth in oral communication, most public high schools offer elective classes for improving the speech arts. These attract mainly those who already possess some speech proficiency. Most schools also have speech correction classes which are staffed with specialists to take care of those with severe defects. If we define a speech defect as any deviation from nor-

From *Improving English Skills of Culturally Different Youth* (Washington, D.C.: United States Government Printing Office, 1964), pp. 100-109. Reprinted by permission of the editor. Ruth I. Golden is with the Detroit Public Schools, Detroit, Michigan.

[1] Thomas Clark Pollock, et. al.. "The English Language in American Education," A Report of the Modern Language Association Commission on Trends in Education, 1945, *Issues, Problems, and Approaches in the Teaching of English*, George Winchester Stone, Jr., ed. New York: Holt, Rinehart and Winston, Inc., 1961, p. 137.

mal speech that calls attention to itself or to the speaker in a negative way, the specialists could not possibly accommodate in their speech correction classes all the students who need help.

This problem of reforming, or changing, language habits, then, concerns all English teachers and particularly those in urban centers where we find a great many students of foreign extraction or of various ethnic backgrounds for whom English is either a second language or like one. For the student whose native speech, even though it is American English, contains a great many structural, articulatory, and intonational differences, learning to speak a language that is acceptable on the high school level is surely like learning a second language, which is not an easy task.

Virgil Anderson, who wrote *Improving the Child's Speech,* estimated as far back as 1953 that there were approximately 2,500,000 speech-defective children of school age in the United States—over 40,000 in a city the size of Los Angeles, for example, and around 350 in a small city of 20,000.[2] The number today far exceeds that of 1953 because of continued immigration and migration, along with growth in language awareness. During the past 10 years, Detroit's population alone has increased by more than 200,000 because of the influx of southern and foreign migrants who have brought with them their own speech habits. It is, therefore, increasingly important for the classroom teacher to be cognizant of the individual speech needs of his students and to have some means of coping with them.

I emphasize the speech aspects of language, for the oral symbols are basic and the child's written expression is likely to reflect his speech. Two examples of this from my own class papers are: "All people should be treated like *beans,*" spelled b-e-a-n-s (these students seldom use the sound of *ing*) and, "Use the right *can* of language," spelled *c-a-n* (*kind* was pronounced *can* following their usual substitution of the low front vowel *ae* for the dipthong *ai*). If we can improve spoken language, written language should also improve.

In adult life we spend at least 90 percent more of our time expressing ourselves orally than we do in writing; therefore, it is deplorable that so little emphasis is placed on improving oral communication in the English classroom.[3] Of course, the aim is to develop in the learner to the best of his ability the four basic aspects of any communications arts program—listening (or understanding), speaking, reading, and writing.

---

[2] Virgil A. Anderson, *Improving the Child's Speech.* New York: Oxford University Press, 1953, p. 7.
[3] Lecture by Preston H. Scott, head of the Speech Department, Wayne State University, Detroit, Michigan, 1940.

These are interrelated and all have to do with developing language expression. Although for many pupils they can best be taught concurrently in integrated language arts units, for children with special problems special practice drills are needed.

My own teaching experience has been devoted to meeting the needs of large numbers of pupils, particularly migrants or children or grandchildren of migrants who are mainly at a low socioeconomic level. Although the pupils speak American English, they speak and continually hear one distinctive variety of it at home or in the neighborhood, where they may continue to speak it for rapport. However, if they are to become employable or to succeed in business, they must learn to shift into the more dominant patterns of the area in which they may later live and work. For these pupils many of the techniques of second-language learning are applicable.

I cannot recommend too highly the book by Mary Finocchiaro entitled *Teaching English as a Second Language in Elementary and Secondary Schools*.[4] This book is full of practical ideas that would enrich teaching in any situation. For good oral drill games particularly suited for the junior high school level, I might suggest *Good English Through Practice*[5] by Marjorie Barrows.

Before we discuss method, let us review some of the factors we know about this very complex phenomenon called language. Because we express our individual personalities and communicate our wants and desires through language, and because we are judged partly by what we say, language is a very personal possession and we become highly sensitive about it. As English teachers, we must be aware of this sensitivity. It may help if we remember that, when we point one finger at someone else, we are pointing three fingers at ourselves.

We know that language is a living, changing set of symbols and the better we know the code, the more effectively we can communicate in it. Part of our job as English teachers is to preserve the basic code and to maintain respect for it. However, unlike the Morse code, there is no one exact set of symbols. Instead, there are many acceptable variations of what may be considered the standard code, and there are different levels of language which may fit various situations. To be most effective, one must be socially mobile in his use of language so that the listener's attention is on *what* one is saying, not on *how* he is saying it. A visit to the United States Senate convinces us of the many acceptable

---

[4] Mary Finocchiaro, *Teaching English as a Second Language in Elementary and Secondary Schools*. New York: Harper and Row, 1958.
[5] Marjorie Wescott Barrows, *Good English Through Practice*. New York: Henry Holt and Co., 1956.

varieties of American English typical of the particular areas from which the senators come. These variations are mainly in the pronunciation and enunciation of vowels.

To some people of one area, the variations used by those of another area may be very amusing. I'm reminded of the Yiddish dialect stories, the lovable Hyman Kaplan, the minstrel shows that depend on Negro dialect, and the comparisons of the Boston dialect of President Kennedy and Senator Lodge made by Frank B. Gilbreth in his "Dictionary of Bostonese." Whether we have positive or negative reactions to slight variations depends upon the personality of the individual, his educational and cultural level, and his freedom from structural deviations. So long as the speaker is effective in various situations, and so long as there are positive reactions from his listeners, we would not wish to change his language. Should a Bostonian come to live in the Midwest for any length of time, or vice versa, he might adjust his speech unconciously through imitation, or consciously to avoid being conspicuous. More than anything else, as human beings, we want to be accepted, to be approved, and to be recognized, each as an individual.

That variations will decrease and one common standard American language will, in time, prevail seems likely because of our humorists, our television commentators, and the fact that we are a Nation on the move. In one recent year, approximately one of every five Americans pulled up stakes and changed residence. Three and one-tenth percent of these moved to another state. It is already possibly to move from the Pennsylvania-Ohio line all the way across to the Pacific Coast without being aware of dialect differences. This is one of the largest dialect areas, or speech communities, in the world and represents the General American dialect that will probably become more or less standard for the Nation. This is the dialect that is used in teaching English to foreigners here and in teaching abroad through the United States Information Service, which has 389 cultural centers in 80 countries of the world.[6] There is, then, little chance of disagreement on what dialect we should teach.

We know, too, that speech is an overlaid process. Each organ that contributes to the speech mechanism has another primary purpose. Speech is a learned activity; it is not biological or racial. Only about 15 percent of those said to have defective speech have any physical basis for it, and only about 10 percent more have speech defects which could be classed as complicated or involved. In fact, about 75 percent of all speech defects, according to Anderson, are the result of bad habits

---

[6] Lincoln Barnett, "The English Language," *Life*, March 2, 1962, p. 75.

based on poor listening, carelessness, laziness, indifference, or imitating poor models.[7] Within this 75 percent are most members of the ethnic groups in the process of acculturation. They provide a challenge to the English teacher. Anderson does not include the challenge of grammatical or structural errors with which the English teacher has always been concerned.

Our Nation has progressed to an unequalled extent because of our principle that each individual is entitled to rise to his highest potential. In our public schools we hold that no child shall be handicapped by artificial restraints in his struggle to rise. It, therefore, becomes the task of every teacher to participate in helping each student to equip himself with the language habits used in conducting the affairs of our country and in making himself acceptable socially.

The teacher, however, can only point the way; it is the child who must change. His language is definitely related not only to his success in school, but also to his possibilities for subsequent employment. Much of the urge to change depends upon the child's concept of himself and of his place in the democratic society. What he does, what he learns or avoids learning is related either to building up or defending his self-concept.

How do we go about setting the climate so that the child will want to make the effort to change? For one thing, we must broaden his self-concept by giving him pride in his own culture and by making him aware of the heroes and leaders of his own ethnic group who have mastered his same problems. An assembly speaker, a book, or a picture on the bulletin board may provide the initial motivation.

We must let him retain pride in the language he already has, even guide him into taking classes in Spanish, German, or whatever foreign language he understands so that he can increase his proficiency in it. In the case of those who have retained through historical, regional, and social class influences a brand of English that contains many unacceptable structural deviations, the learning of a foreign language helps to focus attention on language as a tool and skill and to develop facility in usage. But we should encourage pupils to assume the responsibility of speaking English proficiently. We may say to them, "This brand of English you are using is a language in itself, which may have its uses for you. It is like an old suit of clothes that we don't throw away because we may still want to wear it on some occasions. But we would not think of wearing the old suit for a job interview or a dance, if we have something better to wear. Here in class you can acquire the language

---

[7] Anderson, op. cit., p. 13.

used by most Americans in the business world. This language will then be yours to use when you want and need it."

This is the approach I use with my students, many of whom use such structural deviations as "he have," "they is," "he taken," and "that's mines," adding the *s* sound, but saying, "ten cent," omitting the *s*. They may substitute *f* for *th* as in *bofe*, *I* for *e* as in *pInny*, the low front vowel *ae* for *aI* to confuse *rat* with *right*, and use a great many non-standard expressions. We must offer them alternate usages and so strengthen them that the English language of the business world will be for them a second language into which they can move for upward social mobility.

Let us review the speech process in order to arrive at a technique to improve these students' speech. As talking animals, we learn to communicate verbally through various stages of development from crying to babbling to lallation (the first ear-voice reflex), on to the stage of echolalia where we echo, or imitate, the sound patterns we hear about us. As Donald Lloyd says, "We learn to speak at our mother's knee and at other low joints."

It is in this latter stage, the echolalic, that the special sound pattern of the child's native language becomes established. As he goes on into articulate utterance, his speech become more refined and fixed so that by the time he is about 6 years old, the habits that will form his adult speech pattern are already set. To reeducate and build new habits, we must take him back to the stage of lallation, sharpen his ear-voice reflex, and carry him on through echolalia, giving him good standard forms to imitate. The language laboratories for teaching foreign languages have been successful in our schools because they have been established on this premise. It is time we English teachers had them, or at least time we began to make greater use of their techniques for the teaching of English to these pupils.

A year of independent study as a Ford Fellow led me to this conclusion. Part of the study included a questionnaire given to 11th- and 12th-grade students in six Detroit high schools. The study showed that the selected list of 102 nonstandard usages, which the students were free to check or not to check, were both heard and used at least four times more frequently by students in schools representating regional speech patterns than by students in schools representative of Detroit area patterns. The results of this study were published by Wayne State University Press for the National Council of Teachers of English. The book is entitled *Improving Patterns of Language Usage*.[8] It is divided

---

[8] Ruth I. Golden, *Improving Patterns of Language Usage*. Detroit: Wayne State University Press, 1960.

into three parts: "The Problem," "Possible Ways To Meet It," and "Suggested Remedial Lessons and Exercises."

The time needed to develop and test English lessons on tape geared to meet this problem was provided by the U.S. Office of Education in a 2-year grant. During these 2 years I have been relieved of school duties in order to direct, to test by analysis of covariance, and to evaluate a research project under Title VII of the National Defense Education Act.

The set of 14 taped lessons we developed are of the listening-repeating type, but they incorporate some writing. They serve as a type of teaching machine to explain the structure of the language as well as to change particular usages by giving the student the opportunity to imitate and to practice using better forms. Skinner's theories are involved in that the tapes give immediate reward and reinforcement. The taped lessons are also built upon linguistic concepts, but retain some traditional terminology. To hold interest, because each tape runs just under 30 minutes, we use a variety of rich voices, both male and female, and a variety of teaching techniques and student activities.

Ideally, the tapes could be used in the foreign language laboratory, but we included them as an English classroom activity in a three-group plan with the groups rotating their activities of speaking, reading, and writing during the 3 middle days of the week, while still carrying on other language arts units.

We find that the tape recorder has so many valuable uses for teaching English that we think there ought to be one in every classroom ready for use at any moment. There is much wasted time if you have to requisition a recorder from an audiovisual room or get one out of a closet and set it up. Bolting the recorder to a table seemed to be our best solution.

We have our basic spelling words recorded on tape. If a teacher expects to give the same spelling lesson more than once, he might as well hold a microphone in front of him the first time he dictates it. Thereafter he is free to take the roll or to do other work as he wanders around the room while the spelling test is on and the students are getting training in listening. If the teacher's voice over the tape sounds natural to the students, they will then believe that their own voices, which sound so unreal over tape at first, really do represent the way they sound to others.

Hearing one's own faulty articulation and structural errors over tape can be one of the greatest motivating forces for pupil self-improvement that I can imagine. After there is pupil awareness and desire to improve, the next logical step is to give pupils good forms to imitate and to give them practice in hearing themselves saying the approved forms.

Along 2 walls in the corner of our classroom are 2 phonojack boards, making 12 earphone stations in all, partitioned with plywood. Under the rotating group plan, one group will be at the corner using earphones for listening and repeating lessons. Another group will be reading, since lack of reading background is at the heart of much of the language problem. The third group will be in individual contact with the teacher in a small circle while working on their writing or speaking difficulties.

For the reading group, we have tried various materials including the *Practical English Magazine,* the *SRA Reading Laboratory,* and a Scholastic Magazines' reading kit which provides a classroom library of two shelves of books on a thematic unit. The unit we chose at Central High School was *Mirrors,* which pointed up our semester's theme of taking a look at ourselves, and particularly a look at our language.[9] One of the two books for common learning, *Best Television Plays,* edited by Gore Vidal,[10] contains a wealth of third-person singular verbs in the stage directions. Our students especially need to strengthen such forms of agreement between the subject and verb as in, "John laughs as he crosses the room and opens the window."

This three-group plan is conducive to creating an atmosphere of trust, cooperation, and a feeling of interest in the individual, which is what these students need so badly. Somehow through the earphones, which the students enjoy using, they also get the feeling that they are being individually instructed, and we have purposely tried to make our tapes seem warm and personal. The small circle contact is invaluable. This work, however, is not for an inexperienced teacher; it takes a calm, well-organized, friendly but firm attitude to manage any three-group activity successfully.

The experiment involved four classes, two control groups and two experimental groups. There were two oral and two written tests and an attitude inventory, all given before and after the special series of lessons. All groups were taught in the same way with the same material, the only difference being that the experimental groups went to the booths to hear the taped lessons while the control groups went to the booths to read the same material from scripts without hearing it. All groups had use of the tape recorder for recording the oral tests and for other speech activities, but we found that the special taped lessons in addition were highly effective in improving speech.

---

[9] Since the preparation of this paper, other useful educational materials, as well as revisions of the above titles, have become available.

[10] Gore Vidal, *Best Television Plays.* New York: Ballantine Books, 1957.

The teaching ideas I'd like to share in the rest of this paper are part-ly those used in the experiment, but mainly the result of almost 20 years of teaching in 4 Detroit high schools where there are culturally different students.

Much of the success of an English language laboratory class depends upon the attitudes and the individuals aims set at the beginning of the semester. In the orientation period, we discuss the purposes and the need for education. We discuss all aspects of language, stressing in real-istic terms the need for effective language in all walks of life. To clinch the discussion, students write letters to the teacher in which they intro-duce themselves and state their aims for the semester. This setting of aims paves the way for breaking into speech drills later whenever the need arises. We plan introductory talks to be taped, and individual or group projects to be presented later to the class.

These projects provide most of the composition work for the semes-ter, although purposeful letter writing is engaged in as frequently as possible. A sheaf of letters, usually written to an individual or to an organization within the school, will actually be mailed so that good writing is made meaningful. Replies to the letters lead to some infor-mal conversations later. The presenting of the booklets or other indi-vidual projects gives practice in strengthening needed forms such as, "This picture" not "Dis pitcher" and in stressing agreement as in "This shows" and "It has."

To orient students to the use of the tape recorder for critical listen-ing, we first give names or one-sentence introductions into a traveling mike from a relaxed sitting position. Even in so simple an exercise, we can learn the importance of emphasizing the surname so that it can be repeated in an introduction. Then we may try a sentence or two in "class on parade" order and hear a playback before giving introductory talks about our hobbies and interests.

"Class on parade" is a device I use frequently for many types of brief oral presentations. A whole row of students will rise at one time and take positions at the side of the class. Each student then waits for his turn, makes his brief presentation, moves to the other side of the room, and waits for his group to finish so that all can take their seats as the next group comes up. Barring illness, there are no exceptions. Anyone who is not prepared says so when his turn comes, but the moral sup-port given when several rise at one time and the atmosphere of encour-agement and informality seem to eliminate procrastinators.

This procedure works well and saves time during speech activities such as: the Inquiring Reporter, in which one student reporter asks each student two or three questions from a long list which they have all had time to consider; famous sayings, in which as a part of a unit on biography each student presents an adage or quotation and tells in his own words what it means to him;[11] memory work, such as a few lines from "The Gettysburg Address" in a ninth-grade Lincoln unit; or the explanation of a rule of courtesy.

Other classroom speech activities include various extemporaneous talks, introductions, business interviews, and panel discussions. A taped business interview with questions designed purposely to bring out deviations, if used, comprised the second oral test of our experiment. For choral reading, with the ninth grade, I especially like Alfred Noyes' "The Highwayman" because my particular students need practice in improving the *aI* sound through the repetition of *highwayman* and *riding, riding.* The correction of this one sound may be a key to changing the entire speech pattern. As students change this frequently used sound, they are often reminded to change other less desirable usages.

We have made up a little nonsense story about "The Rat Named Kite" which introduces the idea of having the students write what we call "stupid stories" to bring in the repetition of sounds or usages they particularly need to practice. We emphasize final consonants and the past tense signal *ed* by listing substitutions for words like *walked* and *said* and by classifying these words according to whether they have a *d* or a *t* sound at the end.

Besides the taped group lessons for usage drill practice, we frequently spend a few minutes on general oral drill. If someone says, "fave cent," we may take a minute to count in unison from "one cent, two cents," up to "ten cents," stressing the *s* sound. When trouble occurs in agreement of third person singular noun and its matching verb, or if we hear "seen" instead of "saw," we may take time out to drill on the conjugation of the verbs, jazzing up the rhythm to make the activity fun as well as to reinforce it in the memory.

For extracurricular motivation, we participate in speech contests and put on plays and variety shows. In two schools we have organized a speech and personality improvement club called "The Teen Talkers and Tapers." One club sponsored a schoolwide Better Speech Campaign complete with Tag Day, daily homeroom lessons in speech improvement, and colorful hall posters and bulletin boards.

We now have some proof of success, but one never knows how truly successful such speech efforts are because so much of the learning may

---

[11] We have typed a large collection of these sayings on 5- by 8-inch cards, and find them excellent for extemporaneous speech training as well as for uplifting values.

be a delayed action process. If we hold to high standards, yet make speech activities pleasant and memorable, there will be positive results. We cannot change the student's speech habits for him, but we can help him to become aware of the need for change by becoming a more critical and discerning listener; we can give him good examples to imitate; and we can encourage his efforts at self-improvement.

An Experiment in Oral Language

ELLEN NEWMAN

The culturally disadvantaged youth often speaks a substandard English —a language which is a handicap in the classroom and in life. This normal language pattern learned at home is usually different from the one employed by teachers. Communication is further hindered by frequent short attention and listening spans so that much of the teacher's language must undergo a personal translation before what is expected in class can be understood.

In addition to the above, the culturally disadvantaged child often has difficulty expressing his thoughts in the standard English of the classroom. When faced with the assignment of a composition he is apt to state "I don't know nothing to write about!" More likely, however, the child suffers from not being able to express his thoughts. He has been told that his substandard language is wrong, and consequently is afraid to use that language in the classroom. At the same time he is not fluent in the more standard languages.

The language of the disadvantaged child is also unacceptable in the larger society. Prospective employers find a substandard language difficult to understand and indicative of a lack of intelligence. If the disadvantaged child is to have a fair chance in our mobile society, he must develop a new language pattern—a standard language. This does not mean that he must forget or repress his substandard language, but he must learn to distinguish between the two and to use each in its place. Just as the substandard speaker is handicapped in the school and job world by his language, so he is often socially handicapped by a

Printed with permission of the author, who is a second-year teacher at Madison Junior High School in Oakland, California. The experiment described in this paper was a pilot program for the Ford Foundation, developed in January, 1965, at Madison. English supervisor was Jean Wilson; principal, Norman Shapiro.

standard usage in his home environment. Emphasis should be on effective communication. The substandard language is an effective way to communicate at home, but the child should be taught that there is another, more effective way to communicate in the larger society.

When the child's verbal expression is improved, his understanding will also improve and from improved understanding greater social mobility is possible. Language can become an access to society rather than a barrier from it. With these problems and goals in mind, then, this program of oral language has been developed.

What Is Oral Language?

The oral language approach is a method similar to that employed in the foreign language laboratory wherein emphasis is placed on speaking and listening—prerequisites for effective writing. It is believed that the normal way a language is learned is by hearing and imitating sounds. The next logical steps are reading and writing with grammar presented by teaching the student to recognize that something sounds "wrong" rather than by studying the rules involved.

Drills helping to increase the child's vocabulary and expression are employed. He is not taught that his speech is wrong, but is made aware of the many possible ways to use language, and learns which language usage is most effective for the particular situation. The child's own speech patterns are not disregarded, but are compared to standard language. The child is given a chance to make language work for him.

The Value of the Approach

A quiet classroom where emphasis is placed on grammar rules, drills, and sentence diagraming offers few situations for the disadvantaged youth to express himself and to improve his language usage. Often he cannot generalize from the drills and practices to his own experience, and much of the content consequently lacks meaning for him. He is resentful of the teacher who says his language is wrong and he is frustrated because he knows no other way to express himself.

The oral language approach gives the student a chance to use his language. He is listening and speaking. Difficulties in writing are avoided by letting the student tell his story. He is given a chance to organize and express his thoughts and to listen to the thoughts of his friends. At the early stages of this program, the teacher does not stop him and say, "What you said was wrong." Instead, she listens and encourages him, thus proving that it becomes worthwhile for him to talk. Then as the child becomes less bothered by his substandard usage of English, he is better able to accept the standard practices. The child thus develops a second language with which he is able to achieve success in the classroom and society.

Experiment

In an effort to test this oral language approach, an experimental program was developed in an all-Negro junior high school in Oakland, California. The purpose of the program was to develop techniques for teaching standard English to students who speak a substandard language. The experiment was based on the assumptions that

1. Listening and speaking skills are essential for effective communication. By listening, the individual learns what others think and what they expect from him. By speaking, he expresses his ideas and desires and can respond to the thoughts of others.

2. Language changes with time and place and effective communication rests on the individual's ability to adapt to the situation. The child must be able to express himself in a variety of ways. Various language patterns are employed in varying social situations; when to use each must be taught.

3. Only after a child uses language effectively at the oral level can his speaking and writing benefit from the rules of grammar. To teach rules before a child can use his language freely serves to hinder and to repress the child's expression. Continued oral use leads to a greater range of word choice, greater fluency, and a pride and enjoyment in being able to make himself understood and in being able to understand others.

Procedure. This class in oral language met two days a week before school. Fifteen seventh graders representing a cross section of abilities were selected to participate in the experiment. Attendance was voluntary. There were no grades issued, no books distributed, and no homework assigned. The class met in a small conference room where seating was organized around the tables to encourage discussion. A tape recorder was available and there was ready access to the foreign language laboratory.

Some Methods and Techniques. For purposes of evaluation and comparison, all class work was taped. Our first sessions were devoted to interviews of each student. From these tapes it was discovered what some areas of language difficulty were and what individual problems needed attention. The students then listened to the tapes and were asked if they noticed anything "strange." The obvious grammatical mistakes were not noticed by the students. Thus at the beginning of the semester the students could not pick out the substandard usage in their own speech.

In an attempt to test the students' ease in speaking, their ability to express themselves spontaneously, and their logical thinking processes, later sessions were devoted to creative oral responses. The students were assigned parts in sociodramas, given a problem, and asked to work out the solution. They also were involved in short talks expressing a point of view or defending a stated position. These techniques were used throughout the semester.

Role playing was also used and with this technique a short intensive unit on social manners was introduced: how to answer the door, how to apply for a job, how to introduce friends at a party. This unit was used primarily to give the students an opportunity to use their language and to offer practice in social situations common to everyone. Again, practical real-life situations were employed. The students ordered groceries, answered advertisements, and delivered messages.

Later in the semester pictures were brought into the classroom and the students were asked to tell stories about them. At this point it was interesting to note the improvement in student presentations. They enjoyed the oral emphasis and were extremely creative in their responses. At this time short written assignments were introduced into the program.

Much of the work during the semester centered on the study of verbs and tenses, though these terms were not employed. The students were not given any rules. Instead, corrections were made when the child realized that something sounded strange. For example, a sentence was placed on the board and students were asked to replace the underlined word with one of their own choice. Thus: "Yesterday I *washed* my sweater." First the sentence was read with the substitution for the verb, then in later practices the word *yesterday* was replaced by *tomorrow*. The students realized that other changes were now necessary.

Through this technique the students soon learned verb tenses. They knew the sentence was no longer correct when it read "Tomorrow I *washed* my sweater." Also, this device helped students to increase their vocabularies and to become aware of new thought relationships. Similar techniques were used for other parts of speech.[1] The foreign language laboratory was employed throughout this program, enabling the teacher to give individual attention to students.

The students were frequently reminded of the purpose of the class. Also, their speech was never referred to as bad. Instead, additional

---

[1] Barrows, Marjorie, *Good English Through Practice*, New York: Holt and Company, 1956. Many of the games and drills suggested in this book were very valuable.

ways of saying something, of dressing up their language, were offered. For example, students were given practice in using substandard language in speaking and listening and in changing this substandard usage to normal usage. They were asked to listen to commercials, talks, language at home and in the classroom, and to see what differences were noticeable. Language and its uses became the topic of many classroom discussions so that by the middle of the semester the students were increasingly aware of the complexities of their language.

Success of the Program. Comparison of later work with early tapes shows marked improvement in thought organization, standard usage, and creative response. Students were able to correct their own mistakes and to become conscious of these in others. More importantly, students learned to distinguish between standard and substandard usage of English. They respected the corrections of others and were responsive to criticism from the group as well as from the teacher. Feelings of success were evident so that students began expressing a desire to enroll in the class again even though it was in addition to their regular class schedule.

Suggestions for Improvements

This oral approach must be greatly expanded. The class was not designed as a panacea for all the language problems of the disadvantaged. It was, rather, a starting point so that the program could be integrated with regular English programs or expanded to supplement or replace programs. It would be hoped that this natural approach of hearing and speaking the language, which has proven to be so successful, could be used in place of some of the more traditional procedures being used in the classroom. There is little value in memorizing the definition of a verb. The value is in being about to use the verb effectively.

Much of the success of this technique, however, will depend on the creativity and flexibility of the teacher. No one program is right for everyone. The success of oral language lies in the ability of the teacher to shape her basic ideas to the needs of her students. But only when the teacher is ready to listen to the child will the child be ready to speak.

Some Approaches to Teaching English as a Second Language

CHARLOTTE K. BROOKS

Linguists say that all languages and dialects are really of equal merit, and that "good" language is simply language which gets the desired effect with the least trouble for the user. Yet, there exist in our schools two kinds of children who have language or dialect problems and whose language, from this point of view, is not "good". I would like to discuss their problem at this time.

Of course, I am still interested in the eager, relatively untroubled youngsters who study the language arts with enthusiasm. I am always happy to see, hear, and read about the excellent teaching they are getting. I am glad to know that they share experiences readily—both orally and in writing—and that they learn to read with little difficulty. As a teacher I enjoy working with such youngsters and now I find great pleasure in visiting them and observing their growth in reading power, their skill in writing, their articulate and perceptive discussions, their joy in literature, and their creativity. But these youngsters are not my major concern at this moment.

Like many others, I have taught—and now watch with a troubled mind—the two other kinds of pupils: the culturally different and the culturally deprived. I am concerned because I think that in spite of a growing awareness of the long-neglected problems of these children, educators have not yet learned the best ways of dealing with them. And unless teachers of the language arts salvage the youngsters—and do so

From *Non-Standard Speech and the Teaching of English*, ed. William A. Stewart (Washington, D.C.: Center for Applied Linguistics, 1964) pp. 24-32. Reprinted by permission of the editor. Charlotte K. Brooks is with the District of Columbia Public Schools.

very early in their school lives—these potentially useful citizens will be lost forever to all education and will become our problems, our drop-outs, our hangers-on, our failures. I say "our", because if this happens, the loss will be ours as much as theirs, for in our rapidly changing, au-tomation-geared land we can no longer afford such losses.

Earlier, I said "two kinds of children" quite purposely, because I want to differentiate sharply between the culturally different and the culturally deprived. Many people, even those who have made careful studies of the needs of children who perform below par, tend to lump the two groups together. In my own city of Washington, D.C., where we have attempted to help normal children who are retarded in school, basic classes sometimes include not only these children but also the mentally subnormal and the emotionally maladjusted. A cursory read-ing of newspapers and magazines and attendance at professional meet-ings has elicited for me the not too surprising information that all over this land totally unlike kinds of culturally different and culturally de-prived children are thus grouped together. Too often there is little consideration given to the great difference among them or to the best approaches to teaching them.

Limitations of space and time will prevent my exploring more fully the variations among these children and all of the approaches that can be used in teaching them. Therefore, I shall concern myself with the users of non-standard English among the culturally different and cul-turally deprived, and with some approaches to teaching them standard English as though it were a second language. However, it must be men-tioned that among the culturally different should be included those perfectly intelligent (or even superior) children who are immigrants from foreign lands, and many of whom are non-English-speaking. Still others are pupils with physical or emotional problems, or pupils from other English speaking countries. In short, they include all who differ from the average child of middle or upper level American city or sub-urb. No teacher must make the brutal error of considering these different children as necessarily deprived. They have rich cultural heri-tages and can offer much to their fellow pupils and teachers if properly approached.

What, then, is the culturally deprived child? Of course, there can be some overlapping, because the culturally deprived child may also be culturally different. However, he is essentially the child who has been isolated from those rich experiences that should be his. This isolation may have been brought about by poverty, by meagerness of intellectual resources in his home and surroundings, by the incapacity, illiteracy, or indifference of his elders or of the entire community. He may have come to school without ever having had his mother sing him the traditional lullabies, and with no knowledge of nursery rhymes, fairy stories, or the folklore of his country. He may have taken few trips—perhaps his only one the cramped, uncomfortable trip from the lonely shack on the tenant farm to the teeming, filthy slum dwelling—and he probably knows nothing of poetry, music, painting, or even indoor plumbing. He may live in the slums; he may reside in the suburbs. He may fool the observer with his quiet and cleanliness or he may disgust with his dirty appearance and crude manners. He may disturb because of his loud, vulgar ways or frustrate because of his sullen silence; he may well be the child of a minority group, a product of inferior schools, staffed by inadequate, poorly prepared, or—to him, at least—culturally different (or indifferent) teachers. Such a child, though potentially of average or above average ability, often comes to school for the first time able to speak only some non-standard variety of English.

Since being relatively happy and successful in the middle and upper reaches of the English speaking world requires the ability to use standard English, and since the old ways of attempting to teach its use have not been notably successful, other ways must be tried. In order to prepare for experimentation in this area, I have visited schools in which English is being taught as a foreign language, have watched speech and language arts teachers at work on elementary and secondary levels, and have talked with and observed the work of teachers of the culturally different and the culturally deprived. At least one teacher of English in Washington is now working on the design for a research project in which she will teach standard English as a second language to culturally deprived as well as culturally different pupils. Others are interested.

This is my first assumption: that standard English should and can be taught successfully as though it were a second language to children who speak non-standard English as a result of cultural differences and/or cultural deprivation. Why do I assume that this should be and can be done? Many teachers of the language arts—themselves the products of the so-called middle classes—teach as though a modern linguistic science did not exist and as though standard English speech and usage were historically and geographically fixed and immutable, with certain well-known laws that always have been and always must be obeyed. Textbooks, those "best of all authorities" to many such teachers, have blandly stated these laws and the teachers have inexorably taught them. Middle class little girls and boys have easily learned and practiced the "correct" forms simply because this is the kind of usage that they have always heard and seen. The basal readers have always pictured their milk-cum-vitamin way of life. Later, these children have identified with the characters of stories in school and in the stories their parents and teachers have encouraged them to borrow from the libraries. Their parents and teachers have talked in identical socially acceptable ways, lived in the same kinds of worlds. With few problems in the language arts, these children have moved from elementary to secondary school, then usually to college and on to professional careers.

The other type of children? On entering school they learn very quickly how unlike the socially accepted pattern they are. Dress, manners, speech—so much of their behavior is strikingly different from the established norms. The stories—even the pictures in the books—are certainly not about their lives, and the language spoken by the teachers and prescribed by the grammar books is not like theirs. The situation may be worsened if the teacher attempts to remodel the child without adequate scientific knowledge about the reasons for and the nature of the differences between the child's behavior and the established norm. One linguist maintains that this kind of teacher is a quack and should be just as liable to prosecution as the medical fraud. The non-standard speaker, meeting this snobbery in school, is puzzled and discouraged. Some teachers can be heard to say, for example, "A person's speech reflects his personality traits", or "Careless, sloppy speech reveals a careless, sloppy person". And the non-standard speaking pupils have often believed this, and have shrunk from or resisted learning.

Let us now consider some examples of the kinds of pupils whom I am discussing. Carlos is culturally different. His parents, born in New York City, are the children of parents born in Puerto Rico. Because one grandparent lives in the home, Spanish is often spoken there, although his parents are able to speak English. They have little money, but Carlos and his family love music and dancing and often attend free concerts or go to art galleries. The grandfather has shared his store of tales and poetry with the boy, and sometimes takes him on long rides into the country, or to beaches and parks. Carlos has even visited Puerto Rico, where other relatives live. But the boy does not say much in school because he is shy, and is not sure that he always has the right English word. As a result, his teachers in primary school, harassed with overcrowded classes, few materials, and little training in dealing with the culturally different, lumped him with other Puerto Rican children in a slow class.

Fortunately, the program described in the October 18th *Christian Science Monitor* came to the rescue before it was too late. A trained volunteer now works with Carlos, often in this way. The boy picks up an interesting picture.

"I hab a tree, with leebs", says Carlos.

"Yes, you *have* a tree, with *leaves*", replies the teacher. "Say *have-leaves*".

"Have-leaves", replies Carlos, learning the /v/ sound in English. Because this boy already knows some English, he needs mainly to have someone take an interest in him to draw out what he knows, to involve him in the life around him, to help him share with others—orally and in writing—his valuable contributions, and to correct some speech difficulties.

Mary, on the other hand, is a culturally deprived child—a small brown girl, whose mother moved North with her non-working husband and six children. Mary's mother is too tired at the end of a long working day to do much more than a minimum of housework. She says little except to reprimand; the father, seldom present, says nothing unless he is cursing in a drunken fury. The rooms are small, noisy, and unclean. Loud parties are given constantly next door, cars and trucks clash by, sirens, dogs, radios, and television assault the ear, and Mary long ago learned to "turn herself off". Mary seldom opens her mouth in her first grade classroom deep in the slums of a big city. *Conditioned inattention,* they call it, when Mary cannot "turn herself on" in school. Apathetic, vacant, she seems stupid. She is not, really—not yet, anyway.

A special language arts program, like those that are a part of the Great Cities Project, may save Mary. In Washington and in other cities with such programs trained teachers work with pupils like this girl. Such children can become interested in fascinating objects like bells with many different sounds, and can learn to listen, to talk, and to write about them. They are given new experiences—something new to talk and write about. Perhaps, unlike Carlos, Mary must be taught about fire stations, museums, concerts, art galleries, the zoo and the country. Like Carlos, though, she must be taught standard English as a second language. Mary may say, "Dis here a leaf". The teacher could then reply, "*This is* a leaf, Mary. Put your tongue between your teeth and say 'th'." The teacher should surely *not* say, "You have a lazy tongue". That kind of value judgement would defeat her purpose, and would simply vanquish, in the time-honored way, the already nearly defeated child.

Mary, enjoying this special attention, and not told she is wrong at every word, will try. And she will learn to say *this, teeth, that,* and other standard English sounds and words. I know, for I have seen this done.

My second assumption is based upon the first: If standard English is taught as a second language it is not necessary to insist that the child reject entirely the other or "first" language.

With Carlos, this poses no problems. Most people realize that non-English or minimally-English speaking persons must retain the first language for use in the home and sometimes in the community. They even accept with equanimity those errors in English usage that come obviously from primary use of the other language: "leebs" for "leaves"; "I no want to go", and such interesting dialects as Pennsylvania Dutch and 'Cajun'. How many teachers, though, are able to accept Mary's non-standard "dis" and "dat"? For Mary *will* use incorrect English. She will be affected by her community and her peers more than she will be affected by her teachers. She will say:

"You done it".
"Dis is mines".
"I ain't got none".

This language will get the desired effect in Mary's community with the least difficulty for its user, while,

"You did it."
"This is mine".
"I haven't got any" or "I don't have any",

from Mary might cause an embarrassing sensation in the home and among her friends.

Perhaps Mary can use both kinds of language, each at its appropriate time, if her teacher will show her the way. Must the teacher reject the non-standard English as wrong—and with it reject Mary's family, friends, and her values? Many teachers feel that they must change the language of children like these. They have tried, but how successful have they been?

Certain questions are well worth asking at this point. For example, what right has a person to impose his cultural pattern upon another? How does a teacher know what this *is* the right way? What does the teacher know about the history of English? Does he or she know the linguistic facts about *shall* and *will*, and the double negative (perfectly right, by the way, in Spanish), the possessive, or forms like *ain't I?* Who made the rules, and who changes them? Who decides upon standard American English? Is is different from standard British English? Does it differ regionally within the United States?

After a year spent teaching English in Birmingham, England, I revised many of my own attitudes about pronunciation (Birmin*gham,* Alabama; Birmin*g'm,* England), as spelling, usage, pronunciation, and meaning. I learned to spell *labor* as *labour,* to say *contróversy* and *A to Zed,* to put a comma after the salutation of a business letter and to use Esquire and *Yours faithfully*. I learned to say "The team are ready", and to know that *napkins* are diapers after my husband brought some home for use at my first grand English high tea! I met men and women from Wales, many of whom speak their own Celtic tongue among their countrymen. At my school there were six who spoke English well—though almost always with a musical lilt—but kept Welsh as a "first" language. They had no trouble shifting from one to the other at will, or from formal to informal (and sometimes non-standard) British English. Most of us move from formal to informal American English quite as readily. Will not our pupils, if their own first language is not rejected, be just as able to shift into standard English when such a shift is required by circumstances?

Before briefly summarizing some of the suggested approaches in a final statement, may I reiterate my reasons for feeling that these rather tentatively suggested and not yet completely tried suggestions are needed?

Constant admonition has not, we know, taught correct usage to those who habitually use non-standard English. Red pencils have seldom changed the way of resistant pupils. Why, then, should teachers not exploit the tremendous psychological uplift implicit in the idea of acceptance by saying in effect to Carlos and Mary, "I accept you and your language; use it when you need it for communication with your family and friends. But, if you really want to be a free and successful participant in other areas of American life, why not learn the kind of language accepted and used there".

The teacher must, of course, fit this little speech to the age and mental ability of the pupil, but with it he or she may be able to destroy the barrier to communication built up by the usual, unknowingly insensitive rejection. Perhaps by the same device he can build a foundation for the kind of teaching he must do. This initial acceptance can lead to some of the approaches I shall mention.

Incidentally, if language laboratories are used in this program as they are for foreign languages, we in the language arts should be in an excellent position to request some of the NDEA funds now going into those other languages. Furthermore, if linguistic science is truly a science—and I believe it is—we have a second reason for requesting participation in the NDEA grants.

What, then, should we do?

1. We should not reject outright the first language of any child, but should accept the view that we leave his language alone, and teach him a second language as though it were a foreign tongue.

2. We should point out as early as possible in the child's school career that there are certain advantages in learning and using standard English. Specific examples should be pointed out.

3. Culturally deprived children might be started earlier in school—perhaps in a pre-kindergarten or nursery school—so that they can be given some of the rich experiences that are not now being provided by the home or the community.

4. The same media used for teaching foreign languages should be used for teaching standard English as a second language: interesting objects and pictures, tape recorders, records, television programs, language laboratories, films and new textbooks based upon the findings of linguistic science.

5. Teachers and pupils must learn the history of language, and must understand the nature of standard English.

6. Books, especially basal readers and grammar books, must be revised to include more material directed toward the culturally different and the culturally deprived.

In terms of this approach, concern with matters like ending sentences with prepositions becomes sadly antiquated and trivial. Does this mean that the more traditional teacher will no longer be needed? She needn't worry; there will be plenty for her to do. Pupils will still have to be taught to read well and critically, to speak clearly, to write correctly and accurately, and to avoid those mechanical errors in the use of English which interfere with communication. But these errors are found everywhere, not just among the different and deprived. Indeed, Dr. Edwin Sauer says in *English in the Secondary School*, ". . . the really serious language faults of our time are more likely to be heard in high places than in low. The gardener who says to his employer, 'I ain't hardly got no room for them tulip bulbs' will be understood . . . But what can a reader do with a statement like this from a top industrial executive? 'Gentlemen: In re your communication as to the expediency of our continued controls of merchandisable materials, may we state that, pursuant to many requests . . .' "

If Miss Fidditch, our traditional teacher, can help eliminate jargon, gobbledygook, tautology, euphemisms, and clichés in addition to what has been suggested already, she will have a more than full-time job.

Culturally different and culturally deprived pupils like Carlos and Mary may well be happier and more successful "sayin' what comes natur'lly" where this is perfectly acceptable, but learning to use standard English in the appropriate situations. And if the "natur'l" talk is not rejected completely, and the standard English taught from the beginning with the very best approaches used in teaching a foreign language, Miss Fidditch and teachers of the language arts may be happier and more successful too.

At least, it's worth trying.

꙱ • ꙰

Give Him a Book That Hits Him
Where He Lives

꙱ • ꙰

Culturally, he is bounded on the north by comic books, on the south by the pool parlor, on the east by the racing form, on the west by neighborhood small talk. Born into a home at cultural ebb tide, often raised midst turmoil and trauma, living in an intellectual ghetto, he sits in my classroom—annoyed to the point of hostility. I have asked him to read a book—any book—for a first report of the term.

The "he" I mean is no figment of my imagination. He is Barry Saltz, a 16-year-old future butcher of America (one of many such in my classroom); a present reluctant reader (one of many such in my classroom). Despite his 20/20 vision, it dismays him not an iota that he has never read a book cover to cover in all his 16 years, that he has never spent a rainy afternoon browsing in the library.

Scan the printed page? Not he!

I search my brain for a *book* that may appeal. "How about *Questions Boys Ask*,"[1] I recommend ever so naively, as I brandish a copy I own.

"Naaah. . . ."

I try sports, hobbies, deep-sea fishing—everything from prehistoric man of 5 million years ago to the stars millions of light years away. But I get a look that warns me—"Mister, you're wasting your time."

I am beginning to lose heart when one day it happens! I find the

From *Improving English Skills of Culturally Different Youth* (Washington, D.C.: United States Government Printing Office, 1964), pp. 91-99. Reprinted by permission of the editor. The author is chairman of academic subjects, New York City High Schools.

[1] David W. Armstrong. *Questions Boys Ask*. New York: E. P. Dutton & Co., 1955.

link I need to help move Barry Saltz from the desert island of igno-
rance about books he has for so long inhabited to the mainland of
written words and ideas. It is a tiny link—no bigger than the cluster of
warts on Barry's index finger.

Those warts really worry Barry, butcher-to-be, because as he put it,
"They're gonna drive away my customers." So I ask him one day,
"Why don't you get rid of them?" and learn, to my surprise, that he
has an *idée fixé* about warts. They come from touching frogs, and
maybe will vanish one day by magic, if you're lucky.

Sensing how deep his supersitition about warts really is, I recommend a book, *Superstitious? Here's Why!*[2] urge him to read the section
on warts, and agree to accept this as a report.

The result? *Mirabile dictu!* Barry Saltz practically memorizes that
paragraph on warts and reads the book through cover to cover in one
4-hour sitting. Moreover, having finally gone to a library, he has now
become aware of some very readable books about health and strength—
a major interest. Before the semester is over, Barry Saltz can tell you all
about *The Wonders Inside You*[3] by Cosgrove, *Magic Bullets*[4] by Sutherland, and *Boy's Book of Body Building*[5] by Pashko. True, he still refers to de Kruif's *Hunger Fighters* as "Hunger Pains"! Who cares!
Barry Saltz is on his way!

Does it matter? Does it really matter that the Saltz nose now goes between the covers of a book? Is this a "summum bonum" commensurate
with the effort expended? Yes, indeed! For, of all youth's divine rights
during that precious period we call "The school years," I place very
high the enjoyment of books. Learning how to earn a living is one
thing; but in an age of steadily increasing leisure, learning how to live—
joyously—is, to me, prime. And learning how to do it, among other
ways, through books—is quintessential.

Perhaps no one has said it better than Paul Bueter, a 17-year-old senior who, after viewing *A Night to Remember*[6] on TV, was one of doz-
ens who had remembered it vividly enough to ask for the Walter Lord
original. Queried on why he wanted the book, having just seen the TV
version, he gave what seems to me the classic answer to those who see
TV as the substitute for reading—"Sure, it was good," he says of the
TV performance, "but I don't know . . . I didn't really get the feeling

[2] Julie Forsyth Batchelor and Claudia De Lys. *Superstitious? Here's Why*. New
York: Harcourt, Brace & World, 1954.
[3] Margaret Cosgrove. *The Wonders Inside You*. New York: Dodd, Mead & Co., 1955.
[4] Louis Sutherland. *Magic Bullets*. Boston: Little, Brown & Co.. 1956.
[5] Stanley Pashko. *Boy's Book of Body Building*. New York: Grosset & Dunlap.
[6] Walter Lord. *A Night to Remember*. New York: Holt, Rinehart & Winston, 1955.
Bantam Paperback, 1962.

of how it was on the *Titanic* on that black night. . . . How could you, with all those camera lights on the people?" In order for Paul to "really get the feeling" of that black night to remember, he needed more than brilliant camera lights. He needed the glow of his own imagination.

Yes, I'm glad I got Barry Saltz to read for other reasons. Just as we learn to write by writing, we learn to read by reading. It's not always that "Johnny doesn't read because he can't." It's often that "Johnny can't read because he doesn't."[7]

Yes, I am glad I got Barry Saltz to read because I know that the meat upon which our Caesars feed is anti-intellectualism, "know nothing-ism." In the growing struggles between freedom and authoritarianism, it is better for us all that the Barry Saltzes be thinking, questioning, probing citizens—not vacuums or vegetables. Though there are many paths towards this end, I respect reading as one of them. I'm glad I got Barry Saltz to read.

As chairman of an academic subjects department in a New York City vocational school (from 1956 to 1961), I have had the chance to study hundreds upon hundreds of Barry Saltzes in their raw, untutored state. Coming from homes where the bedtime story at twilight had never been heard and where the television set had replaced the reading lamp, they sat in our classrooms with all the symptoms of cultural blight. Their median IQ score was 85, their reading scores were poor, and their practice of the language arts was unique. One boy who was asked at an assembly to read from Proverbs in the *Bible* prefaced his oral reading with the announcement that he would read some "proud verbs" in the *Bible*. Youngsters asked to write on the "Star-Spangled Banner" began with "Oh, say can you sing by the doors early light?" A lad, reporting on a TV show he liked insisted that the hero was "Quiet Earp." Once in a discussion, I used the term *bachelor of arts* and asked for a definition—"He's a guy who got away by staying single."

Family ties, as the ordinary middle-class youngster enjoys them, were *terra incognita* to many of my boys. Fully 20 percent lived at home with but one parent, the second having vanished, run off, or died. I had boys who had never been served a warm breakfast by mother since they could remember. I had boys who had never had a heart-to-talk with father. Yet let mother or father be called to school, on some matter disciplinary, and we were often invited to "Hit him! Whack him! I mean treat him like he was your own!"[8]

---

[7] Estelle H. Witzling, "Johnny Can't Read Because He Doesn't" *High Points*, 38: 52-59, January 1956.

[8] Charles G. Spiegler, "A Teacher's Report on a 'Tough School,'" *The New York Times Magazine*, Nov. 24, 1957.

Spawned in such homes, the Barry Saltzes never go much beyond talking of "Who's gonna win the fight next week?" watching crime shows on TV, going to the movies with their dates, ogling the girlie magazines. Of the 900 boys at my city vocational school, no more than 20 ever found it worthwhile to take in a Broadway play or a concert at Carnegie Hall even though both are little more than an hour from any boy's home. "That's for eggheads," Billy Brenner, 16, tells me when I offer him a ticket. "It's too far, anyhow. You come home too late." Yet two nights a week, religiously, instead of sitting down with his homework, he marches to the bowling alley where, until midnight, he enjoys a few short beers and the thrill of crashing a 16-pound bowling ball against the varnished pins.

Small wonder, then, that when we talk to them of *Silas Marner* they hear us not. Their ears are tuned to the change-of-period bell. We may appeal to them with a lovely print of an English landscape. They see it not; their eyes are on the clock. Desperate, we bring out the great, beloved classics which are on the world's permanent best-seller lists. With pomp and ceremony, with a laying-down of red carpets, with a lighting of candelabra, we introduce children to these classics. But we leave them unmoved. So, in quiet resignation, we affix to them the label "retarded readers"; and that great cultural divide between the middle-class teacher (reared on Shakespeare and Browning and Eliot) and the sons and daughters of "blue-collar" America (so often raised on comics, the movies, and television) becomes deeper and wider.

We've got to heal that breach, and we can! But this can be done only with understanding—the understanding that the Barry Saltzes are, as the late Elizabeth Rose of New York University put it "allergic to print"; that much of what we, his teachers, choose for him to read is not only *not* a cure for this allergy but also an *extension* of it; that only the book which "packs a wallop for him" may hope to effect a cure. The remedy? Begin with a book that hits him where he lives![9]

I learned this back in 1954 when, as a new departmental chairman, I walked into the middle of a cold war between most of the 900 students in the school and most of the English teachers. The issue at first was books, *required* books for classroom study. The battleground was the bookroom piled high with *Silas Marner* and *Giants in the Earth* (grand books for college-bound youth, but sleeping pills for vocation-bound youngsters). There was a curtain dividing pupil and teacher, which, though made only of paper and print, was no less formidable than today's Iron Curtain. You walked into classes where teachers were

[9] Elizabeth Rose, "Literature in the Junior High School," *English Journal*, 44: 141-147.

devoting a full term to *Silas Marner,* and you saw children with heads on desks and eyes shut. You walked into the library and rarely saw a youngster except with a prescribed booklist based on the predilections of his teacher. The long and short of it was that children were not reading, and teachers had thrown in the sponge with the excuse, "They can't!"

I believed they could, if we would but give a boy a title, a book jacket, a theme that rang true; if we could but talk to him colorfully about the world of books! Don't limit him to the confines of prescribed booklists or restrictive formulas for making book reports. Let the world and its infinite wonders be the subjects he may choose from, I begged. Let him begin with what he likes, appeal to his interests—and he will read.

When we inaugurated a 3-day book fair, displaying 2,000 books dressed in jolly jackets and written on hundreds of lively subjects I was sure youngsters liked, there was a shaking of heads among some members of the faculty. "I'll bet you won't sell a hundred books," one asserted smugly. "All these kids want is comics and girlie books. They won't buy anything decent!"

But they did. For 3 days, while English classes were cancelled, children browsed, read at random, bought or not as fancy struck them. And when the fair was over, we knew that these were the 3 days that had shaken our smug little world. The Johnnies who would buy "only comics and girlie books" had dug into their after-school-odd-job savings to take home 1,123 good books. Granted, Bill Stern's *My Favorite Sports Stories* and *The Real Story of Lucille Ball* were best sellers, but not far behind were the *Burl Ives Song Book, The Red Pony,*[10] and books of science fiction. And higher than anyone dared predict were *The Cruel Sea*[11] and *Mutiny on the Bounty.*[12]

Though no teachers were panting down the students' necks to "read this!" they did guide student choice. Some, like the big, broad-shouldered lad who was about to buy *The Scarlet Letter*[13] because he thought it was a football story, needed guidance. Some, like the nature lover who was about to buy *A Tree Grows in Brooklyn*[14] because he thought it was on target for a report he was making on trees, needed guidance. Others passed by the proffered help, however, and bought many books with vocabulary loads somewhat beyond their level. It didn't matter. "Interest," George Norvell, former New York State Su-

---

[10] John Steinbeck. *The Red Pony.* New York: Viking Press, Inc., 1959.

[11] Nicholas Monsarrat. *The Cruel Sea.* New York: Alfred A. Knopf, Inc., 1951.

[12] Charles Nordoff and James Norman Hall. *Mutiny on the Bounty.* Boston: Little, Brown & Co., 1932.

[13] Nathaniel Hawthorne. *The Scarlet Letter.*

[14] Betty Smith. *A Tree Grows in Brooklyn.* New York: Harper & Row, 1947.

pervisor of English, has said, "leaps over all reading barriers, including vocabulary."[15]

Johnny wasn't sleeping through "Lit" class by now. We relegated *Silas Marner* to a basement storeroom and gave the youngsters livelier fare. Booker T. Washington in his struggles for an education became a far more genuine superman to them the comic book man with wings. It was *Kon-Tiki*[16] on the perilous Pacific that replaced Eliot's nineteenth-century England. You could now walk into a class studying *Kon-Tiki* and see Jimmy Kolofney at the blackboard writing a letter of congratulations to Thor Heyerdahl. While he is expressing his admiration for the Skipper and "that crazy, wonderful think you done," seven boys are rehearsing in two separate corners of the room: three of them in one corner play the crewmen of the *Kon-tiki;* the other four make up a TV panel that will ask the intrepid voyagers all about the dangers, the thrills, the uncertainties of their venture.

Before long all eyes are focused on Jimmy's letter on the blackboard, to correct it—because "You can't send junk to a big shot like that." Later the class turns to the TV panel, which raises some incisive questions on the madness, the glory, and the thrill of adventure dear to any boy's heart. It also raises a question or two that better-bred boys might not ask: "Didja ever 'chicken out'?" "Hey, didja miss girls?" The end-of-the-period bell rings in the nick of time.

By the end of the year, the majority of our 900 students were reading at least a book a month. Many were doing far better. Library circulation had gone from 600 to 1,500.

Neither "climax" nor "denouement" cluttered up book reports now. As make-believe salesmen, kid critics, Hollywood producers, television panelists, they reported in terms they knew. "I like," "I love," "I hate," "I get mad," "It's great," "exciting, "heartwarming"—these terms indicated how books hit them. "I love that book because it suits my taste," wrote Johnny Gallardo about *Lives of a Bengal Lancer.*

Whatever the individual taste, we have given each of those 900 students a sporting chance to satisfy it. Now that the fair was over and the appetite whetted, I began to observe, ever so occasionally, especially after lunch, a paperback under the arm of a lad or two where earlier in the day there had been a lunch bag. Boys were beginning to walk off their hero sandwiches with short strolls to the neighborhood paperback gallery, sometimes bringing back a sample or two. Soon we discovered the Teen Age Book Club[17] whose titles caught the fancy of

---

[15] George W. Norvell. *The Reading Interests of Young People.* Boston: D. C. Heath & Co., 1950.

[16] Thor Heyerdahl. *Kon-Tiki.* Chicago: Rand McNally & Co., 1950.

[17] Teen Age Book Club, sponsored by *Scholastic* magazine.

many. We were beginning to establish a rapport between children and books, helping many of our boys buy them cheaply, start their own libraries, and see for themselves how "even the smallest library is a veritable Treasure Island that takes no *Hispaniola* to reach—its buried riches no pirate's chart to locate."

This is not to boast that success was absolute and universal. We still had lots of lads like Lenny Kalter who equated the carrying of books with the role of the sissy. It wasn't until Miss Isenberg (public librarian assigned to visit our classes regularly to bestir the reluctant dragons) had introduced young Master Kalter to Henry Gregor Felsen's *Hot Rod*[18] that Lenny could identify with a character in a book—in this instance Bud Crayne, *Hot Rod's* hero, and lover of speed. Lenny borrowed the book, devoured it, then became so avid a reader on the subject that *Street Rod*[19] (also by Felsen), *Mexican Road Race*,[20] *Thunder Road*[21] and *The Red Car*[22] were finished within 2 weeks. Then he began searching the stacks all over the city for "anything by Mr. Felsen." When he heard that we were planning to invite an author to visit our assembly and set the keynote for our next Book Fair, he volunteered to write the first formal letter of invitation he had ever written in his life—you guessed it—to Gregor Felsen.

Last, but hardly least, let me suggest how television far from proving a menace to reading, as is so often alleged, proved a boon. My major premise here is that culturally deprived youngsters limit their horizons to the four walls of the home, the four corners of the neighborhood, and, as with many of my boys, the six pockets of the pool table. Television is their new window to the world. Through it they find the fullest, richest array of new interests man has ever known. Where or when, for example, in all recorded history could so many Americans in the year 1962 with a flip of the dial take an hour-long journey through the White House, with its gracious First Lady as hostess and guide?

My minor premise is that interest is the key to reading. My conclusion follows naturally. Television, by creating interest, can become the road to wider reading.

I saw it strikingly one morning in April of 1956. I was sitting in my office composing my weekly bulletin when the door burst open and two of my boys came dashing in.

"Got somp'n by Ogden Nash?" came the breathless query.

Slowly I raised my head.

---

[18] Gregor Felsen. *Hot Rod*. New York: E. P. Dutton & Co.

[19] Gregor Felsen. *Street Rod*. New York: Random House. 1953.

[20] Patrick O'Connor. *Mexican Road Race*. New York: Ives Washburn, 1957.

[21] William Campbell Gault. *Thunder Road*. New York: E. P. Dutton & Co., 1952.

[22] Don Stanford. *The Red Car*. New York: Funk & Wagnalls Co., 1954.

"Who?"

"Ogden Nash—you know," they exclaimed, "the guy wid dose crazy rhymes."

My pen dropped; my ears perked up. Surprised, indeed delighted, that my boys were interested in reading one of America's most literate creators of verse, I asked: "You boys doing a book report on Mr. Nash?"

"Nope!" they parried, "no book reports—we just wanna read sump'n by him. We went to the library, but the other guys beat us to it. *You* got sump'n?"

Happily I had. And happily, Tommy Gorman, a 15-year-old butcher-to-be, and Peter de Stafano, a 16-year-old baker-to-be, walked off with every copy I owned of *I'm a Stranger Here Myself*.[23] When you realize that before this day the closest Tom and Peter had come to voluntarily exposing themselves to rhythms and rhymes was the "popular song sheet," you realize what a move forward they had made.

This did not erupt full grown from the head of Zeus. It happened at a time when their English teacher found the going rough as he started a unit on poetry. So he looked for help. Since television was not a dirty word in our school, he looked to see how that week's TV programing could help. And lo, that Sunday Ed Sullivan could! For Sullivan had invited Noel Coward to read from the works of Ogden Nash to the background music of Saint Saens, as played by Andre Kostelanetz. So the homework assignment for that Sunday said, "Watch Sullivan"—not just the song, not just the dance—but *all* of it! With the results we have seen.

Teach a little "dialmanship" and TV can become an Aladdin's lamp far more wondrous than the Arabian original. Our librarian, too, recognized that and arranged a bulletin board entitled *IF YOU WATCH: WHY NOT READ*. If you watch the weather spots, why not read *Weathercraft*[24] by Spilhaus, for example? If you watch Leonard Bernstein, why not read *Leonard Bernstein*[25] by David Ewen?

If, in fact, we really want to introduce the culturally deprived youngster to books he can read on subjects he wants to read about, we are living in an age of huge abundance. For, in truth, this is the Golden Age of Writing for Youth, with many magnificent series available to them; with real writers (Quentin Reynolds, Dorothy Canfield Fisher, John Gunther, to name but a few) writing for them.

I cannot begin to tell you of the many, many hundreds of "juveniles" I have read myself with admiration, and been privileged to review

---

[23] Ogden Nash. *I'm a Stranger Here Myself*. New York: Little, Brown, 1941.

[24] Athelstan Spilhaus. *Weathercraft*. New York: Viking Press, 1951.

[25] David Ewen. *Leonard Bernstein*. Philadelphia: Chilton Books, 1960.

and annotate, with a very high respect for what they can mean to children, and, with genuine appreciation for what they have meant even to ancient old ME.[26]

The job of preparing the proper materials for the customer we are talking about is, however, far from complete. So formidable, indeed, is this task, with both the textbook and the trade book, I would take a leaf from the book of the Ford Foundation man who recently recommended a *Vice President-in-Charge-of-Heresy* for every school system—by proposing a *Vice President-in-Charge-of-Searching for-and-Finding-Materials-Written-So-That-the-Children-We-Are-Concerned-With-Will-Read-Them-With-Interest.* As my first piece of advice to said VPI, I would urge: "Listen to the children you are serving." Here are their answers:

1. The subject has to be worth it to us. We like books about animals, aviation, careers, hobbies, sports, the sea, westerns. We love lots of adventure, plenty of excitement, slews of interesting facts about science and things.

2. Don't treat us like babies. We may not be such "hot" readers, but that doesn't mean if you give us an easy book about ducks on a farm we'll cackle over it gleefully. We had that stuff in the third grade, remember?

3. Give us lots of good pictures, good drawings, and big print. As one of the fellows said, "I can't read when the print on the pages is so small. After a while I lose my eyesight."

4. You have to know how to write. Maybe the fellow who likes to read a lot will stand for some boring parts, but not us. If you want us to read don't beat around the bush but come to the point. Give us a story that pushes us to go on to the next page and the next page—and we'll stay with it.[27]

Let us search out the books which, as Robert Lawson has put it, will give these kids ". . . the chuckles . . . the gooseflesh . . . the glimpses of glory" they love. The books are here, now, asking to be discovered and enjoyed.

Books and reading are a staple in such a program not only for the well-endowed, but also for all the children of *all* the people. Only in the faith that there are no "second-class" citizens in our schools, a faith conceived, nurtured, and cherished in pride for nearly two centuries, can we hope to rise to the urgent tasks ahead. I am supremely confident that we shall.

---

[26] The reviews of the books under this category appear in the section called "Books You May Like," in Marion Monroe, Gwen Horsman, and William S. Gray. *Basic Reading Skills*, Chicago: Scott, Foresman & Co.

[27] Charles G. Spiegler, "Reading Materials for Retarded Readers," *Materials for Reading*, Supplementary Educational Monographs, No. 6. Chicago: University of Chicago Press, 1957.

An Experience Approach in a Senior High School Reading Lab

MARY K. ABBOTT

A specific class usually has a personality. After a few weeks, it is possible to characterize a given group in the same way as people are labeled: quiet, slow to get started, curious, friendly, dull, or perhaps even plain unbearable. A class in reading should share this attribute, and if the class is composed of students who come from backgrounds described as "disadvantaged," the class personality might be expected to parallel the characteristics which experts say the disadvantaged possess.

Instead of the loud, physically active, somewhat aggressive class I had come to expect as a remedial reading group, one semester's selection brought me 22 students whose individual personalities had defeat imprinted on them and whose collective class personality could be summed up as utterly apathetic. Although they had been chosen for our special program because there were signs indicating intelligence and ability, the only emotion indicated in class was the desire to sit through the hour and get out. There was, however, no hostility—just nonviolent resistance. It was difficult to get them to talk enough to find out if they had trouble articulating words. A written assignment was out of the question; the books might be open, but the time would be spent staring at the page, which might as well have been upside down. When I attempted to explain anything—to the class, a small group, or an individual—I found that I was the sole participant. The usual motivational pitch about the necessity for learning to read well for school and jobs was received with bored patience.

Printed with permission of the author, who has been a secondary teacher in the San Francisco Unified School District and a member of the School-Community Improvement Program staff of that district.

And yet, no student was upset or hostile. It was simply as if the classroom and I did not exist for them. Many students who come to Reading Lab are won over after they find that there are reading materials they can handle; they attempt to work with such materials in a fairly enthusiastic manner. This group would have none of the enticing books, paperbacks, individual work kits, or filmstrips with which the Lab was stocked. Ordinarily, I divided the reading class into groups because the span of reading achievement usually ran from second- to eighth-grade level. This survival device often enabled me to work on specific kinds of difficulties, and it also reduced the level of competition for the students. With this group, it just didn't seem to matter. They were unreachable and therefore, unteachable.

All of these students, of course, were having problems in most of their other classes. They exhibited all of the symptoms which students with reading disabilities have, plus those specific handicaps which mark students as being disadvantaged. Not only were they unable to figure words out, but they were also unaware of the meanings of words that are thought of as common vocabulary. Their hall conversation told me that they had used a kind of dialect-English, a part neighborhood patois and part school slang, which almost made English a strange language for them to listen to, to speak, or to read and write.

It was obvious to me that this gap would have to be bridged, but that the students were not about to take the first step. That left me. I was familiar with the technique of using experience charts, and in fact, had often done this with a few students who were just beginning to learn to read. I thought that trying this approach would not hurt; I'll admit that in the back of my mind I thought nothing could be worse than the present state of teaching in a vacuum.

Ordinarily, in descriptions of successful approaches, the students all fall over themselves being entranced with the new method, the teacher emerges victorious, and everyone lives happily and educated ever after. I came in with my new approach, all right. I brought in six objects: a flashlight battery, a wooden block, a sponge, a 45-rpm phonograph record, a pencil, and an orange. I said that we were all going to look at these things and try very hard to remember one point about each item. They looked at the items and the collective class unconsciously said, "What's she giving it?" They did try to discover what the objects were, though. When we had all looked, I said that I would write their ideas on the board for them and asked them to finish the sentence, "The battery (holding it up) is——." Blank—utterly blank—faces greeted this pronouncement. It took several more repetitions and much turning of the battery before someone finally ventured the word "round?" The complete sentence was written on the board. We did consider the orange and the record as round also, and we finished with listening to the "r" sound in "record, orange, battery, and round" and listing one or two other objects that had this characteristic as well as words that had this sound. They had perhaps learned a word or two, and I had learned that six things were too many for the attention of the group.

The next day I reviewed the vocabulary and found that "record" led the list of words remembered, recognized, and spelled. The question for the day then became, "What is your favorite record?" Several titles spilled forth, most of them unintelligible to me. "O.K., so I don't speak the language; now tell me so I can write it down." And they did tell me—not enthusiastically—but with care, so that I would write properly. And, of course, they knew how the titles should look. I asked which one was the best, and about four students attempted to explain the relative merits of "Itty-bitty purple polka-dotted yellow bikini" as opposed to "I loved you, I lost you, and I'm glad." (The titles are reasonable facsimiles.) We did decide on a favorite and after determining that everyone would be able to listen to it before the next class, I asked them to decide what the song was trying to tell them and how it made each of them feel. The blackboard the next day had on it: "We listened to a song yesterday." About six other sentences about the song, answering the general questions provided, were pried loose from various students. After considerable work at choosing the clearest words and sentences, these were arranged on the board in reasonable order and from these sentences, we chose words we should know.

For example, "like" was used. This word gave me the opportunity to show them the long "i" sound at work with the silent "e". In the sentence I had written on the board, the word "listened" was hard and unfamiliar to some students. The use of context helped us discover that the only thing we all did to a song yesterday was to listen. The beginning "l" sound and the fact of silent letters were both pointed out. The difference between listening and hearing was explored. Finally, the class was asked to copy "our" paragraph in their notebooks and told that we would review the words tomorrow.

This pattern of common experience, the writing of an experience chart, vocabulary and word-attack work, and individual writing practice was carried out for about three weeks. The experiences included the fortunes of our football team, the appearance of the classroom (a metal shop), the current mode of dress, the viewing of a film, and a current school crisis over grades. In all cases, it was necessary to give the students something to look for or to decide about the event or thing. Class participation in formulating the charts did increase; one or two students brought objects or told of an experience like participating in a sports event. In some cases, the subject matter of the charts led to further discussion and exploration. For example, discussion of a current civil rights demonstration led *one* student to find out who Martin Luther King was. At no time was there an enthusiastic rush to acquire more information on a topic of vital interest to all. In fact, there was little enthusiasm expended on anything chosen, whether it was picked by them or by me. The area that came closest to generating feeling was a kind of personality exploration that centered on what people like about other people. But even in this case, none of the books I imported hurriedly was more than picked up and put down. A few students did allow themselves to be volunteered to write the story on the board.

During the course of the three weeks, though, the students had acquired very respectable looking notebooks in which all of the stories were written and in which their vocabulary work was kept. I constantly told them how much work this was and how well it was done. Each page had to have some kind of a mark on it or it had no value to the student. Most of the students had been faithful about keeping this notebook up, and a few of them were even somewhat proud of having a whole notebook full of work.

The time had come when I felt I had to begin working with some individuals on their specific problems. I wanted to continue to use the chart approach with the students having the most severe disabilities, while allowing the more advanced students to do work that would challenge them. I made the break by talking about reading as a way of finding out what someone else has said and by reminding them of how well they had done with their previous work. We would continue to do our stories, but not as often.

The class did respond, and the barrier of complete apathy was broken. At times, of course, they needed booster shots of encouragement and a return to our experience approach. We did attempt more challenging group paragraphs, though. For example, the class had some definite ideas about executives that were caught stealing their company's funds, and the story that emerged from this discussion was thoughtful and clear.

The students were never overwhelmingly enthusiastic about the class; they never ran to obtain books so that they could sink into the enjoyment of reading something they wanted to; most of them did improve their reading skills, and some of them benefited from a changed attitude toward their own work. A few of them occasionally volunteered that they had something about which they would like to write a story with me. These individual stories were done with the help of a typewriter I had available and did create pride in their authors.

The experience approach made them important people in the classroom; their ideas were used, and their words and sentences became the text. I believe this did lead them to view reading as a natural activity and one that did not belong only to the world of teachers. With the experience approach, everyone does have a chance for success and a certain amount of cooperation is built in to the formulation of the story.

I would have liked to have been able to provide more variety in the experiences; perhaps have taken the class someplace of interest that we could have talked and written about; perhaps have worked on further. The transition from the total experience approach to a partial use of it is difficult to make, and the timing is hard to judge.

In this particular situation, the experience approach was used to combat apathy. The students did become involved in learning, and the air of defeat which they carried was lessened. Perhaps the greatest value of this approach is that it opens the way for the culturally disadvantaged to accept help and to feel that he is helping himself.

‽•‽

Choosing Books for the Disadvantaged:
Reading Can Provide Fruitful Experiences

‽•‽

MARCELLA G. KRUEGER

Should educationally deprived children be offered only the most basic of materials because of their supposedly low potential? It has generally been conceded (3, p. 15)[1] that social class has an effect on school aptitude of children because of differences in the amount and kind of mental stimulation they receive. A child's life chances are strongly influenced by his social stratification (15, p. 17f.). However, these children need not be permanently educationally deprived if schools and teachers use the presently available knowledge and the results of many empirical studies to guide them into all that is best in the culture that they have embraced by living in America's large urban centers. This includes an introduction to a variety of the best kinds of books which have been written for children.

The complexity of the problem should not be minimized. It has been estimated that by 1970 more than half of all children enrolled in large city schools will be disadvantaged (12, p. 1; 10, p. 367). The disadvantaged child early discovers that there is little relationship between school life and the life he knows. Nevertheless, authorities agree that "the central need, the precondition to the success of every other remedial or preventive measure, is better education" (14, p. 1 and 7, pp. 69ff.). It has been suggested (7, p. 89) that the problem is not whether to imbue the deprived with middle class values or to strengthen the posi-

From *Chicago School Journal*, March, 1965. Mrs. Krueger is an assistant professor of education at Chicago Teachers College North.

[1] Numbers refer to the bibliography listing.

tive aspects of their own unique cultural forms, but rather to provide skills and knowledges so that they can select their own future direction. In general the curriculum should be planned realistically, yet with high expectations, and should include experiences which change the self image of the child. Economic survival should be ensured through increasing command of standard English. The curriculum should be "rooted in use value for the children" (4, p. 303).

Appealing Materials Promote Reading

Because success in reading and language arts constitutes the key to academic progress, they are stressed by most programs. These disciplines have to be particularly planned for these children in order to avoid failure experiences which further prejudice them toward schools and education. For these children print is often "a devious and impoverished medium" (12 p. x) in comparison with television and movies. Special transitional techniques are needed to bring such children into the academic mainstream. Frank Riessman and others (12, p. 33; 11, p. 335; 7, p. 92; 13, p. 225; 8, p. 226; 6, p. 120) who have studied the problem agree that the teacher needs to exert special effort to give children language experiences related to the realities of their lives and to their interests. The personal effort to locate materials which will be likely to appeal to the pupil not only strengthens his interest in reading, but his ego benefits from the personal attention.

Harry Hayes, an experienced Chicago teacher of the deprived, says that the use of a variety of materials in a room library "acquaints children with more books, creates more interest in reading, and probably improves general reading ability more than any other classroom activity" (8, p. 226). The books chosen for a room library will, naturally, be mostly curriculum-related and have the criteria suggested by Arbuthnot (1, p. 424 f.) represented in their choice. Strong child appeal, good themes and plots, memorable characters, problems common to all people, and democracy in action should be the guiding basis for selection.

In addition to curriculum-related books, those chosen specifically to present and illuminate the pervading problems of disadvantaged children in Chicago can be of great help in overcoming the impediments to urban acculturation which seem to militate against school success for educationally deprived children. There are a number of categories into which such books fall. Those in the list at the end of this article offer material for dealing with language difficulties, for improving the self-image of the child, for changing attitudes and values, and for helping the child adapt to urban living. To illustrate the sort of assistance books can offer, some indication follows of how some of these books can be of assistance in the last two of these categories: changing attitudes and values, and adaptation to urban living.

Anti-School Attitudes Can Be Changed

What are some of the values and attitudes toward school which these children bring to the classroom? In what ways are they in conflict with the essentially middle class, urban values of the school? Are there children's books which could be used to help bring these attitudes into harmony?

Dr. Daniel Novak, Chicago Parental School psychologist, (10, p. 370) finds in his experience that there is often a severe lack of mutual understanding between the children and school personnel. The one-third of elementary children who come from the lower-lower class usually find school very uncongenial. Some researchers believe (5, p. 178; 12, p. 2) that the lower class child probably enters school with a nebulous and essentially neutral attitude, but in the school situation highly charged negative attitudes toward learning evolve. Literature and the arts as they have been presented in the schools are considered as irrelevant to the actual problems of living in slum conditions. The home rarely negatively predisposes toward the school situation, although there is little positive motivation or correct interpretation of the school experience. There is a lack of books and formal language. The depressed child is "present" oriented, physical strength and skills are valued, and he is used to the direct expression of aggression in the home and on the street.

Books Make Learning Seem Worthwhile

Reading is not valued highly. The parents do not read, and "neither they nor the child's social group urges the child to practice reading or school exercises or sets him an example for attainment in this field" (3, p. 14). Studying homework seriously is a disgrace, and good marks are concealed. There is a relative lack of achievement motivation (13, pp. 124f.).

Fears are quite different for this type of child. He fears being "taken in by the teacher, of being a softie to her" (13, p. 125). He fears *not* to be a street fighter. He fears his subgroup should he have excessive school success. There are, however, literary experiences which might help to alter these views.

Early in the school year, Columbus Day arrives. "Columbus" from *For Days and Days* by Annette Wynne (2, p. 51) might be used to suggest the value of learning, of bucking odds, and of persisting in the face of discouragement.

There are some materials which could be presented to revise negative attitudes toward reading in addition to the daily enthusiastic presentation of all reading materials by the teacher. In Beim's *Thin Ice* (18), Lee, a reluctant second-grade reader, finds a use for reading and probably thereby saves his brother's life. This could be related to city danger signs and to winter-time skating on lagoons and on the lake. It could be read independently by primary children.

Folk tales often present situations which can crystallize values teachers are trying to inculcate. In "School for Crocodiles" (55, pp. 110-116), when a boy loses a book, a jackal finds it and proudly starts a school. There is good humor, enjoyed especially by the underprivileged children, in the attempt to teach nonsense syllables. In Glen Rounds', *Ol' Paul, the Mighty Logger* (45), there are many tales that would enthrall these children. Paul is certainly the masculine prototype many of these children need. Paul's experiences in providing food for his large crew (pp. 14ff.) will have identifying elements. There is Johnny Inkslinger (177-183) to promote mass production for "figgering." He figgered just for the fun of it! "Paul Goes Hunting" could relate to experiences of the Kentucky in-migrant whites. Then there is the story of Backward Bill, which has an amusing compensation switch angle because he could be so easily replaced. Is there material here for discussing automation and its effects on the uneducated?

Teacher Should Read Aloud

In another group of folk stories by Courlander (25) there is an African Gold Coast story called "Why Wisdom Is Found Everywhere" (pp. 30-31). It explains the Ashanti saying, "One head can't exchange ideas with itself" and concludes, "Should you find a foolish man, he is one who didn't come when the others did to take a share of the wisdom." This ought to make an interesting discussion. The source of the stories should be especially interesting to the Negro children.

At this point it should be stated that oral presentation by the teacher and much story telling is a preferred method with all of these kinds of children because of their lack of formal language readiness. It is recommended, too, that formal reading instruction be delayed in the primary grades. Reading levels of class materials should be lower than grade levels. Therefore little that is suggested here is lower grade material unless it is to be introduced by the teacher.

An example of upper grade material in this area of values is Skippen's *I Know a City* (50, p. 120) in which there is a description of the establishment of schools in New York City quoting John Dewey as stating that the "primary business of the school is to train children to cooperative and mutually helpful living." For upper grade readers there is the beautiful story by Elizabeth Speare, *The Witch of Blackbird Pond* (51), in which there is much made of the value of reading and of the teaching of reading. This is a book about colonial days, but it is very relevant to the present.

There are two suggestions for vicarious outlets for aggression. Zolotow's *The Quarreling Book* (63), which is relatively easy reading, might help children to understand unreasonable parents, teachers, and classmates. Doing the "Pirate Don Durk of Dowdee" as choral speaking with its aggressive rhythm and swish and expressive "tough" words would furnish a wonderful release for emotions as well as an excellent literary experience. Middle grade readers would enjoy this.

Books about Urban Living

Although attitudes and values are important in and of themselves, they are related to knowledge. Newcomers fear the city because of its strangeness. If they are hostile to teachers and to other agents of urban society, it is at least partly because they do not understand the helping role those agents are attempting to play. Therefore, recent in-migrants can profit greatly from reading experiences which introduce them to views of the city and its ways and which will reduce their fears and hostilities. Although all of the material available for elementary school children in this area is not of equal value, the following suggestions indicate the range of such material available.

Most of the newcomers to Chicago have come from rural areas and their cultures are not compatible with modern, urban life. They need help to adjust. Teaching materials should be urban oriented not suburban. The content should concern housing, occupations, and transportation, and should be interracial and interethnic (7, p. 93). Present experiences and future opportunities should be presented.

Education Should Be Practical, Useful

In some cases urban acclimatization is difficult. There is much intracity mobility and much "back home" feeling especially among the Puerto Ricans and the Appalachian whites. This lack of a real break with the "old country" impedes acculturation. For instance, Puerto Ricans are citizens but are looked upon as foreigners because of their language difference. It takes only a short plane ride to go back to welcoming relatives and friends.

Urban education for the average deprived person must be practical and useful. "Education provides the means for more and different kinds of employment, provides a more secure future. Jobs that interest him, like firemen, policeman, postal clerk, all require detailed civil service examinations, and education is sorely needed to obtain those coveted positions" (12, p. 13).

There is a relatively large number of books that could be used in this connection. In almost any classroom a unit could be developed in this area. Perhaps it would be good to hearken back to rural memories first. In *Danny's Pig* (56), Danny adopts a lamb when the three piglets were all claimed by his sisters. The lamb, raised with the piglets, refused the company of her sheep relatives and preferred her pig friends. This is primary reading, and perhaps the analogy of moving to new friends in the city could be made even with small children. "Gypsy Children" (29), a poem by Rachel Field, expounds on the rural life and on nature's wonders.

Several books contrast city and country life. Schlein's *City Boy, Country Boy* (47) is for beginning readers, has colorful illustrations, and says, "the nicest thing about the city is all the wonderful people." Each boy likes the other's environment, but "I live where I live. I love where I live." "City Streets and Country Roads" by Eleanor Farjeon (2, p. 154) would furnish nostalgia for the South, Puerto Rico, and for the mountains. How many of the children would agree with

> "Oh take me away
> To the country again."

A discussion about this should help in establishing rapport with the children. For older children, *The Witch of Blackbird Pond* (51) contrasts a warm climate with a cold New England one. Strangeness in a new place and different customs can be identifying aspects. Kit Tyler learned to love the new place and to appreciate a different scale of values. Will these children do likewise?

Books Stress City's Diversity

Then there are the practical books which are valuable for pointing out the many possible city vocations, and the variety of people who live in a city. Tensen's *Come to the City* (54) has photographs to illustrate the city's activities. At the back of the book are riddles with page numbers for answers. This is for the youngest readers. Hader's *Big City* (30), readable by experienced beginners, is rather thorough in depicting occupations, transportation, foreign neighborhoods, public servants, museums, etc. A rather contrived book, Hall's *The World in a City Block* (32) will appeal to middle grades, and does present many nationalities, each with choice objects from their country of origin. Discussing it could lead to appreciation for many people and to a study of the various migrants who have been part of Chicago's past.

Slum Clearance a Part of Life

Books on special aspects of city life should inspire field trips which are essential for these children who need objectivity and physical activity to help them learn. The following are usually most appropriate for the upper primary and intermediate grades. Sanders, *Behind the Scenes in a Super Market* (46) is a real contribution because it goes beyond the electric eye doors and obvious aspects to the relatively unknown management occupations and activities. Meat cutting on a large scale, the care and cleanliness of vegetables, and the frozen food handling are examples to discuss with the children. Puerto Ricans, especially, find frozen foods strange and unpalatable. Romano's *This Is a Department Store* (44) could be the background for a trip to Marshall Field's and a ride on the subway. Again, various employees are mentioned.

The Schneiders' book, *Let's Look Under the City* (48), points out the ways in which a city's utilities are planned and operated. This could lead to a discussion of Chicago's unique waste disposal system, and, perhaps, to a trip to a sewage treatment plant, to a trip to a telephone exchange, or to a cruise on the Chicago River. *Tear Down and Build Up* (23), although difficult to read, could be used by the teacher to relate to urban renewal and to slum clearance, which is part of the everyday life of most of these children. Neighborhood field trips could be taken to note the various workers who are employed on these projects.

In a separate category are the city's policemen. They are in the ambivalent position of holding a coveted occupation and, on the other hand, being often the target of subgroup hostility. It would be necessary for the teacher to indicate an awareness of these attitudes. No saccharine presentation of the benevolent policeman would be accepted. Phyllis McGinley's *All Around the Town* (2, p. 26) has a policeman poem which might serve as a springboard to combat negative ideas among the youngest. For older children contemplating vocational choices, Colby's *Police* (23) gives a good overview of police duties including protecting the polls and the use of air patrols. This could be related to our helicopter traffic reports. Shippen (50, pp. 71-81) gives the history of New York's "finest" with fascinating anecdotes and source materials.

Shippen also gives other fascinating details concerning city problems. Children should be most interested to compare colonial food prices (meat at ten cents a pound, butter at sixteen cents a pound) with present day prices and prices in the South, in Puerto Rico, etc. Housing and schools are presented with illuminating details. This is indeed a valuable source book, readable in upper grades. Pedro of Puerto Rico starts the story of big city transportation by Urell (57). Mrs. Small's class studies transportation in New York City. This could easily be related to Chicago. It is a middle grade book.

Winter and Snow Naturally Interesting

There are several books concerning winter in the city. This is an especially vital topic because most of the inmigrants have come from warm climates. Often they are unprepared for cold as far as both clothing and shelter are concerned. In *The Snowy Day* (37) a Negro boy enjoys the new experience. His home is pictured with an iron bed and a pedestal bath tub. It is easy reading as is the Hader's *Snow in the City* (31). The city is obviously New York City with Macy's Thanksgiving Day parade, Music Hall, Rockefeller Center, etc. Our children have probably seen these on television. There is a good part on snow clearance and about the effects of heavy snow on transportation. It is beautifully illustrated. "Snow in the City" from *Branches Green* by Rachel Field (2, p. 366) gives snow poetic beauty.

> "And not a million people,
> Not one of them at all,
> Can do a thing about the snow
> But let it fall!"

Most of the city life books concern Manhattan. A juvenile "gang" is part of *Russett and the Two Reds* (59). There are values concerning group action, friendship, and pet care. *It's Like This, Cat* (43) has discerning father-son relationships, and top-notch humor for the middle and upper grades. Frieda Friedman has several books for middle grade readers on family life in New York. *Ellen and the Gang* (28) has a plot revolving around some juvenile delinquents and including a girl friend from Puerto Rico. The denouement is a bit pat, but there is much that is relevant to modern city life. Other books by Friedman are the following:

> *Carol from the Country.* Illustrated by Mary Barton
> *Dot for Short.* Illustrated by Carolyn Haywood
> *The Janitor's Girl.* Illustrated by Mary Stevens
> *A Sundae with Judy.* Illustrated by Carolyn Haywood

In Wood's *Fun in American Folk Rhymes* (60) there is "East Side-

West Side" and a "Chicago-New York" rhyme which could introduce children to city game rhymes. Did they have game rhymes in their previous environments?

Children's Literature Can Advance Learning

The preceding discussion of books related to two categories—changing values and attitudes, and adapting to urban living—is meant to be suggestive for teachers and for children as is the bibliography of books which follows. It is hoped that the suggestions made here about the use of children's literature will help the teacher of disadvantaged children to be supportive and accepting as well as imaginative and creative. The goal of reading such books as have been described here is not simply to entertain the children by indulging their interests—although that is, in the situation, a worthy aim—but to help them to build upon what they have and to develop the kinds of understanding and competence which will enable them to adapt to the school, succeed in learning, and become useful, productive members of urban society. This kind of education can be accomplished, at least partly, by exposing the children to the best appropriate and relevant materials available.

Professional References

1. Arbuthnot, May Hill. *Children and Books.* Chicago: Scott Foresman and Company, 1964.
2. Arbuthnot, May Hill, Compiler. *Time for Poetry.* Chicago: Scott Foresman and Company, 1951.
3. Charters, W. W., Jr. "Social Class and Intelligence Tests" in Charters, W. W., Jr. and Gage, N. L. *Reading in the Social Psychology of Education.* Boston: Allyn and Bacon, Inc., 1963. Pp. 12-21.
4. Crosby, Muriel. "A Portrait of Blight" in *Educational Leadership.* Vol. 20, No. 5 (February, 1963). Pp. 300-304.
5. Deutsch, Martin. "The Disadvantaged Child and the Learning Process" in *Education in Depressed Areas.* Passow, A. Harry, Editor. New York: Teachers College, Columbia University, 1963. Pp. 163-179.
6. Eller, William. "Reading Interest: A Function of the Law of Effect," *The Reading Teacher.* Vol. 13, No. 2 (December, 1959). Pp. 115-120.
7. Goldberg, Miriam L. "Factors Affecting Educational Attainment in Depressed Areas" in *Education in Depressed Areas,* A. Harry Passow, Editor. New York: Teachers College, Columbia University, 1963. Pp. 68-99.
8. Hayes, Harry. "Some Ways to Teach Culturally Deprived Children." *Chicago Schools Journal.* February, 1964. Pp. 221-228.
9. McClelland, David O. "Measuring Motivation in Phantasy: the Achievement Motive" in Dulany, Don E., Jr. et al, *Contributions to Modern Psychology.* New York: Oxford University Press, 1963. Pp. 237-251.

10. Novak, Daniel. "Counseling Culturally Disadvantaged Requires Special Understanding," *Chicago Schools Journal,* May, 1964. Pp. 366-372.
11. Passow, A. Harry. "Education in Depressed Areas" in *Education in Depressed Areas,* A. Harry Passow, Editor. New York: Teachers College, Columbia University, 1963. Pp. 332-351.
12. Riessman, Frank. *The Culturally Deprived Child.* New York: Harper and Row, 1962.
13. Smith, Louis M. and Hudgins, Bryce B. *Educational Psychology.* New York: Alfred A. Knopf, 1964.
14. *Teachers College Topics.* New York: Teachers College, Columbia University. Vol. 12, No. 3 (Spring, 1964).
15. Watson, Goodwin. *What Psychology Can We Trust?* New York: Teachers College, Columbia University, 1961.
16. Yandell, Maurine Dunn and Zintz, Miles V. "Some Difficulties Which Indian Children Encounter with Idioms in Reading" in *The Reading Teacher.* Vol. 14, No. 4 (March, 1961). Pp. 256-259.

Children's Materials

17. Beim, Lorraine and Jerrold. *Two is a Team.* Pictures by Ernest Crichlow. New York: Harcourt, Brace, and Company, 1945.
18. Beim, Jerrold. *Thin Ice.* Pictures by Louis Darling. New York: William Morrow and Company, 1956.
19. Bontemps, Arna. *We Have Tomorrow.* Illustrated with photographs by Marion Palfi. Boston: Houghton Mifflin Company, 1945.
20. Chase, Richard (Compiler, Editor). *Grandfather Tales.* Illustrated by Berkeley Adams, Jr. Boston: Houghton Mifflin Company, 1948.
21. Clark, Ann Nolan. *The Desert People.* Illustrated by Allan Houser. New York: The Viking Press, 1962.
22. Clark, Ann Nolan. *The Little Basket Maker.* Illustrated by Harrison Bagay. Los Angeles: Melmont Publishers, Inc., 1957.
23. Colby, C. B. *Police; the Work, Equipment and Training of Our Finest.* New York: Coward-McCann, Inc., 1954.
24. Colby, Jean Poindexter. *Tear Down to Build Up.* Illustrated by Joshua Tolford. New York: Hastings House, 1960.
25. Courlander, Harold. *The Hat-Shaking Dance, and Other Tales from the Gold Coast,* with Albert Kafi Prempeh. Illustrated by Enrico Arno. New York: Harcourt, Brace, and Company, 1957.
26. Evans, Eva Knox. *All About Us.* Illustrated by Vana Earle. New York: Capitol Publishing Company, 1947.
27. Evans, Eva Knox. *People Are Important.* Illustrated by Vana Earle. New York: Capitol Publishing Company, 1951.
28. Field, Rachel. "Gypsy Children" in *Gaily We Parade,* John E. Brewton, Compiler. Illustrations by Robert Lawson. New York: The Macmillan Company, 1949. Pp. 149.
29. Friedman, Frieda. *Ellen and the Gang.* Illustrated by Jacqueline Romes. New York: William Morrow and Company, 1963.

30. Hader, Berta and Elmer. *Big City*. New York: The Macmillan Company, 1947.

31. Hader, Berta and Elmer. *Snow in the City*. New York: The Macmillan Company, 1963.

32. Hall, Natalie. *The World in a City Block*. New York: Viking Press, 1960.

33. Holl, Adelaide. *Lisette*. Illustrated by Roger Duvoisin. New York: Lothrop, Lee and Shepard Company, 1962.

34. Hughes, Langston. *Famous Negro Music Makers*. New York: Dodd, Mead, and Co., 1955.

35. Jackson, Jesse. *Call Me Charley*. Illustrations by Doris Spiegel. New York: Harper and Brothers, 1945.

36. Justus, May. *New Boy in School*. Illustrated by Joan Balfour Payne. New York: Hastings House, 1963.

37. Keats, Ezra Jack. *The Snowy Day*. New York: The Viking Press, 1962.

38. Keats, Ezra Jack and Cherr, Pat. *My Dog Is Lost!* New York: Thomas Y. Crowell, 1960.

39. Lenski, Lois. *Blue Ridge Billy*. New York: J. B. Lippincott Company, 1946.

40. McCord, David. *Far and Few*. Drawings by Henry B. Kane. Boston: Little, Brown and Company, 1952.

41. Meigs, Mildred Plew. "The Pirate Don Durk of Dowdee" in *Gaily We Parade*. John E. Brewton, Compiler. Illustrations by Robert Lawson. New York: The Macmillan Company. Pp. 73 f.

42. Morgan, Carol McAfee. *A New Home for Pablo*. Illustrated by Harvey Weiss. New York: Abelard-Schuman, 1955.

43. Neville, Emily. *It's Like This Cat*. Pictures by Emil Weiss. New York: Harper and Row, 1963.

44. Romano, Louis G. and Georgiady, Nicholas P. *This Is a Department Store*. Illustrated by Jim Collins. Chicago: Follett Publishing Company, 1962.

45. Rounds, Glen. *Ol' Paul, the Mighty Logger,* New York: Holiday House, 1949.

46. Sanders, Ruby Wilson. *Behind the Scenes in a Super Market*. Illustrated by Baldwin Hawes. Los Angeles: Melmont Publishers, Inc., 1957.

47. Schlein, Miriam. *City Boy, Country Boy*. Illustrated by Katherine Evans. Chicago: Children's Press, 1955.

48. Schneider, Herman and Nina. *Let's Look Under the City*. Illustrated by Bill Ballantine. New York: William R. Scott, 1954.

49. Shapiro, Irwin. *John Henry and the Double-Jointed Steam Drill*. Illustrated by James Daugherty. New York: Julian Messner, Inc., 1945.

50. Shippen, Katherine B. *I Know a City; the Story of New York's Growth*. Illustrated by Robin King. New York: The Viking Press, 1955.

51. Speare, Elizabeth George. *The Witch of Blackbird Pond*. Boston: Houghton Mifflin Company, 1958.

52. Sterling, Dorothy. *Mary Jane*. Illustrated by Ernest Crichlow. New York: Doubleday and Company, 1959.

53. Sterns, Emma Gelders. *Mary McLeod Bethune*. Illustrated by Raymond Lufkin. New York: Alfred A. Knopf, 1957.
54. Tensen, Ruth M. *Come to the City*. Chicago: The Reilly and Lee Company, 1951.
55. Trumbull, Lucia. *Fairy Tales of India*. New York: Criterion Books, 1959.
56. Udry, Janice May. *Danny's Pig*. Illustrated by Mariana. New York: Lothrop, Lee, and Shepard Company, 1964.
57. Urell, Catherine; Jennings, Anne; Weinberg, F. R. *Big City Transportation*. New York: Follett Publishing Company, 1954.
58. Weiss, Harvey. *Horse in No Hurry*. Illustrated by the author. New York: G. P. Putnam's Sons, 1961.
59. Will and Nicholas. *Russett and the Two Reds*. New York: Harcourt, Brace, and World, Inc., 1962.
60. Wood, Ray. *Fun in American Folk Rhymes*. Drawings by Ed. Hargis. Philadelphia: J. B. Lippincott Company, 1952.
61. Yashima, Mitsu and Taro. *Momo's Kitten*. New York: The Viking Press, 1962.
62. Yates, Elizabeth. *Amos Fortune, Free Man*. Illustrated by Nora S. Unwin. New York: Aladdin Books, 1950.
63. Zolotow, Charlotte. *The Quarreling Book*. Pictures by Arnold Label. New York: Harper and Row, 1963.

〜•〜

Compensatory Education Programs for Secondary School Students

〜•〜

MARY K. ABBOTT

Seven senior high schools in San Francisco are involved in the compensatory program; the student population in these high schools ranges from the most poverty-stricken youngster to the most affluent and from the functional illiterate to the genius. The smallest senior high schools have 1,700 to 1,800 students, and the largest have around 3,000 students.

Given this set of circumstances, what can be done to "compensate"— to make up for—those social and economic factors which bring students to the senior high school unable to take advantage of its offerings? The compensatory program has had as its core the necessity for instruction in the language arts, especially reading. Students from culturally different, socially disadvantaged backgrounds have difficulty with all of the language arts; they find it impossible to operate in any of their classes without competence in reading, writing, speaking, and listening. Instruction in reading has been an important beginning and has led to the realization that much more than a set of remedial reading classes is needed for a program to be truly compensatory.

Each of the senior high schools has a program geared to the needs of that particular school. These needs have been agreed upon by the administrators and program personnel and, while there is a high degree of similarity in purpose from one school to another, each program fits the situation in each school. . . .

Printed with permission of the author. Mary K. Abbott presently serves as a resource teacher at the senior high level in the San Francisco Unified School District's Office of Compensatory Education, which directs the programs described herein. A further note concerning the author appears with her article "An Experience Approach in a Senior High School Reading Lab."

The class size in the compensatory program is set at a maximum of 18. Often the compensatory class will be smaller than the maximum, especially when the students have been selected because of very severe learning and reading disabilities. Emphasis in these classes is directed toward making the student aware of his strengths and his weaknesses and his potential; the skills taught in the classes are aimed at giving the student a chance to compete and to become as good a student as he is capable of becoming.

Information about the Compensatory Staff. One of the major problems of the students in the compensatory program is that failure in school has become a way of life. In order that the cycle of apathy and failure be broken, instruction in the compensatory classes must be of exceptionally high caliber. The compensatory teacher must be an extraordinarily good teacher to be able to reach the culturally disadvantaged student and convince him of the value of what he has to offer. The teacher must be able to perform in the face of hostility, apathy, and suspicion; he must be able to overcome the gaps in the student's education and to use the very considerable street sophistication which the student *does* have. In short, the compensatory teacher is an outstanding teacher and a compassionate, yet firm, human being.

The compensatory teacher must be comfortable with students who come from backgrounds much different from his. He values each student as an important person and respects the dignity of each of his students. The compensatory teacher must be "firm, kind, and somewhat ingenious." He needs a sense of humor and adaptability and ease in operating a classroom which departs from stereotyped procedures. He has superior skill in teaching the basic subjects and a fine subject matter background himself. These qualities are needed by all teachers, but no assignment places more of a premium upon them than placement in the compensatory program.

The most important qualification for working in the compensatory program is interest in students from culturally disadvantaged backgrounds and the desire to work with them. One administrator says,

The compensatory teacher must, above all, be interested in this type of student and be willing to give him a feeling of confidence that he can succeed, the attention he needs, and the support that he frequently needs.

The background experiences which lead to this interest and to possession of the necessary teaching skills are many and varied. Most often, it is an interest in the teaching of reading which leads a person to become involved with the compensatory program. Many of the compensatory teachers were chosen because of their special competence in reading instruction. Others became involved because of previous work in special education programs, elementary schools, or classes for the foreign-born.

Role of the Resource Teacher. Much of what is being done in the compensatory program is new and different. Even the teaching of reading at the senior high school level is a relatively recent development. In addition, even the experienced compensatory teacher requires help in the form of special materials, evaluation of equipment, and preparation of bibliographies and bulletins. Constant in-service assistance is necessary as the compensatory teachers attempt to cope with new and different problems throughout the year. In order to provide such assistance, the position of resource teacher was created and filled with a teacher who had been active in the program since 1961.

The main duty of the resource teacher is to provide help for the teachers working in the schools. This means that the resource teacher must be available for conferences with compensatory staff members. In such conferences, the topics covered range from the general area of programming and goals of the program to specific diagnosis of one student and suitable techniques for overcoming his difficulties. Much of the time of the resource teacher is spent working with the compensatory staff, the head of various academic departments, and the administrators in the schools to ensure the smooth operation of the program. Approximately 75% of the resource teacher's time is spent in this type of service in the schools.

The resource teacher has also met with publishers to explain the kinds of materials needed in the compensatory program—high interest, low reading-level materials built around the background of the students—and to evaluate the materials which are being published currently. It has also been the function of the resource teacher to find new texts, units, bulletins, and other various materials for specific teachers to use. Some of this material is for the students to use, such as the day-old copies of the newspaper provided free of charge or special subject-matter dictionaries to use in social studies classes. Much of the material is for the information of the teachers in the program; for example, manuals showing how reading skills are taught in the elementary schools have been furnished to all compensatory teachers, and a variety of informal reading inventories have been formulated for their use.

One other important aspect of this position is that of working with teacher-training institutions. There are very few trained reading teachers in the senior high schools; the teacher-training institutions must bear the responsibility for providing their graduates with instruction in this specific field as well as in the more general area of teaching techniques suitable for working with culturally disadvantaged students. The resource teacher has worked with members of the English and Education Departments at various teacher-training institutions to acquaint students and faculty with the needs in this field and to give assistance in planning programs to fill these needs.

The resource teacher has also given demonstration lessons for many faculty members in the various schools, arranged field trips and other events for students in the compensatory program, and normally acted as coordinator for this program and general consultant in reading for the senior high schools.

Characteristics of the Students. Compensatory students are individuals. Each of them has a specific story to tell, an individual path which led him to his state of frustration with learning. It is possible, however, to make some general statements about the background, skills, and attitudes of the students who are in the compensatory program.

These students have experienced genuine deprivation; they have been caught up in the cycle that leads from poverty to frustration to apathy and back to poverty. They come from backgrounds in which parental and community involvement has been insufficient. While getting an education is considered important, knowledge of the specifics which lead to this education is not available.

Many of the students in the compensatory program are bright youngsters, able to work efficiently and effectively once they are shown how to do so. In this program, the schools are not dealing with retarded students but rather with students who have not been able to use the abilities which they have.

The major skill which they lack is that of reading competently. Tied in with this skill are the other language arts, writing, speaking, and listening, which also pose problems for these students. Many of the students cannot hear accurately because their environment trains them not to listen. Many of them have major speech difficulties either because they have a background in a foreign language (although they may not speak it well enough to say that they are truly bilingual) or because their speech environment has consisted of dialect patterns and structure. Such students cannot communicate adequately in a normal academic situation; neither can they be communicated to through the medium of written or oral language.

Students who have experienced this constant communications handicap have a very unrealistic self-image. They see themselves as persons of little or no value, unable to accomplish anything asked of them. One teacher commented that these students have given up completely and feel that they will fail before they even start.

Many times this attitude will lead to an apathy which it is extremely difficult to shake. The student will refuse to believe that he has ability which will enable him to succeed. On the other hand, many of the students want to improve but have no idea how they should accomplish this improvement. Their work habits are poor and try as they might, nothing seems to come of their efforts.

Some compensatory students have a poor understanding of the adult employment situation which they will enter. They are unable to perceive the long range value of academic skills in the vocational fields they might like to enter.

For those students for whom the compensatory program offers instruction in English as a second language, the major difficulty is inability to handle English fluently and unfamiliarity with American culture. The backgrounds of these students do not enable them to understand either the concepts or the language they are expected to use.

Techniques Used in Compensatory Classes. The problems to be overcome are formidable and deep-rooted, yet the very capable compensatory teachers in the senior high schools are achieving success with these students. What are some of the techniques by which they are accomplishing these results? It should be noted that there is no panacea, no magic pill that makes either student or teacher succeed. The secret, if there is one, lies in the fact that exceptionally good teaching takes place in compensatory classes and that the classes are small enough for this fine teaching to bring results.

The techniques used in the compensatory classes stem from the attitude of the teacher toward the class. One teacher comments:

My techniques begin with the realization that irritation, criticism, and speed are obstacles.

Other teachers have this to say:

Nothing succeeds like success; each group begins with material a bit too easy for them and then moves into material of greater difficulty.

Individual assistance is of the utmost importance.

This theme runs through all comments about the compensatory classes. Teachers believe in and use group and individual work—sometimes tailoring specific assignments and use of different textbooks to meet the exact needs of given students. Classwork is not discarded but used only when a general discussion by the entire class is profitable. Through this procedure the student understands what his weaknesses are and realizes that he is doing work which will overcome them. He knows he is being regarded as an individual with both strengths and weaknesses and that his teacher will help him and values his work. Students who have not succeeded in school before do accomplish great gains when they work in this encouraging atmosphere.

Very often, compensatory teachers gear their lesson plans to the interests of the students. One teacher searched out many articles, at various reading levels, on the problems of automation because this was a topic that the students were very concerned about. This class considered the nature of automation, the effects it was having on industry, and the possible changes automation would make on the job market they would be entering. They read, asked questions, and read some more. They wrote and talked and asked more questions. They stood in line to use the vocational materials this teacher had available for them. And finally they decided that what a person really needed was a high school diploma and maybe some additional training in order to be able to get a good job.

Many compensatory teachers build part of their work around vocational units; the students learn about the realities of getting a job and holding it, and at the same time, they develop the language arts skills they need. They will accept instruction in how to fill out job application forms and use it immediately by completing sample forms which have been supplied to the compensatory teachers. Often the students participate in mock job interviews and realize the quality of information and the type of attitude they must have for a successful interview. The criticism of speech patterns and mannerisms which other students in the class present are much more effective and far-reaching than anything the teacher might say. The students gain practice in needed skills and much helpful information and guidance from such vocationally oriented units.

Compensatory teachers are constantly searching for materials of high interest value but low reading level. Senior high school students will not accept books which are obviously intended for elementary school students. They will, however, react very favorably when an adventure story of genuine worth—written at the fifth grade level—is "sold" to them as a book they would enjoy reading. Many teachers use nonfiction material to accomplish this involvement in reading; books dealing with science, automobiles, and personality problems seem to be especially valuable.

Since the development of skills presents the major challenge to the student and the teacher, many teachers have worked out a framework in which to teach these skills. The work is organized for each student with responsibilities he can meet. His work is checked and graded with the emphasis on having him see what he has done successfully. His errors are noted, and he is asked to explain how he arrived at the answer or how he would say that particular sentence. He is then given a chance to correct his mistake and to hand in a "good" paper. Students keep records of their progress, and the comment of one youngster that he didn't ever think he could do that much work in one report period shows the way in which such a technique changes the student's concept of himself. When a student can look at his own record and see that he got a "C" for the last three days instead of the "F's" to which he had become accustomed, his ideas about his own abilities change, and he will attempt work with the confidence that often spells success.

The compensatory teacher will use all the tools of the reading teacher's trade—whether or not the particular class he is teaching happens to be a reading class. He will get students to participate and then show them how to read what he has written from what they have said. He will use text material in which the students are interested to teach them the various means of figuring out words they do not know. He may work very long and hard on getting them to hear differences in sounds. He may have them repeat sentences, phrases, and words as teachers do when giving instruction in a foreign language. He will show them that there is a relationship between letters and sounds and how best to use this relationship to say words. He may work with prefixes, suffixes, and root words. A compensatory student may know very well what "take" means but be completely baffled by "overtake." The student must learn that words have meanings dependent upon the ways in which they are used—that "run" may have many different meanings and he must figure out which one applies in a given case. All these fundamentals the compensatory teacher must work into his teaching while keeping the class interested and encouraged.

The students and the teachers use many devices to accomplish these goals. Filmstrips with built-in word attack patterns are quite popular and allow the teacher to build the instruction as he chooses. One teacher of Social Studies uses vocabulary flash cards with a high degree of success. Students write the term to be defined on one side of a 3 × 5 card and then are encouraged to formulate a definition from their own experiences or from various reference sources. These cards become their own dictionary and review file. Each student may have different terms to learn; as soon as a concept is mastered, the card is put in the inactive file. One class, after using this system for two semesters, formulated this sentence in their Civics 2 class:

One of my *stimulating* and *unrestrained assets* was brought on the *installment plan* from a *shoddy dealer* who appeared *literate* and *optimistic* in his *alleged* statement that it was particularly *complex* and *intangible,* but very important to the *technology* in a *stabilized* modern *society.*

And, what's more, they knew exactly what it meant!

Much oral work has been done in the compensatory classes. Teachers use the tape recorder to overcome pronunciation difficulties which the students have. Because the classes are supplied with listening center attachments, the students are able to listen and use the recorder in privacy. Many teachers, especially those teaching the bilingual classes, use oral drill and conversational work to teach the patterns of spoken and written English. Choral reading helps students to get a feeling for fluency in the reading of English.

An oral assignment in front of the class can be agony for a compensatory student, so teachers introduce such work very gradually. The student speaks a sentence from his desk; then he participates in an explanation of a single paragraph. He may move from this to a group or panel discussion with a very definite assignment. In all cases, he is shown how to prepare his contribution, and the class is made aware of their role as audience.

Teachers work from the student's speaking to the skill of writing. After a student has told the teacher about the job he has just acquired or the game he played in yesterday, the teacher may say, "That was great. Write it down for me, will you?" From this may come the beginnings of ease with written communication.

Much work is done with the writing of individual sentences. The "chalk-talk" is a popular vehicle for the teaching of this skill. The students and the teacher put sentences together, and then everyone writes and corrects the written product.

Because the compensatory student has difficulty with many of his subjects, the teacher tries to provide immediate practice of the skill on subject matter material. If a student has been working on learning how to skim to find specific information, he practices, this skill in his science or history text to help him with his actual assignment. There is an attempt made to bring students to see how these skills can be used in their other subjects; this is difficult to do because of the range of subjects and the fragmentation of the student's day.

One constant problem is that of motivating the student to continue with his work. There is no such thing as instant success, and often, the pull toward achievement is long and hard for both the student and the teacher. Teachers are overcoming this obstacle by using "success stories" of persons from similar backgrounds. A visit from a college student who is achieving his goals at City College is worth three months of talking, especially when the student came from that school and had some of the same problems those in the class do. One area in which this procedure has been highly beneficial has been in a Latin American Relations class taught to Spanish surname students. Although this class is not formally part of the compensatory program, its aims are the same. Through talking with a number of Spanish surname adults (lawyer, FEPC representative, college students, podiatrist, clergyman), these capable students have realized the possibilities open to them and have increased their pride in their culture and heritage.

Motivation is also concerned with creating the desire to do something specific—in this case, to be able to read and write, to speak and listen with competence. Teachers often read to the students in order to motivate them to want to read. Listening to a book that is genuinely well-written, that says something that the students know to be of value (or that the teacher can make valuable for the student), and that holds his interest leads to the next and most important step: "Can I have that book to read myself?"

The "Lively Art" of Language

GAIL DONOVAN

English literature was my field of concentration in college. Yet not until I taught in Roxbury did I realize how profoundly language is at one with our lives. What we are depends very much on our possession of and responsiveness to the language. I learned this with my students.

For my student teaching experience at Harvard I was assigned to a class known as Operation Second Chance. This is a program designed by the Boston Public Schools for potential dropouts in the seventh and eighth grades, as part of the current compensatory endeavor. The program calls for homogeneous grouping of boys according to reading ability for the purpose of intensive remedial work, and language arts are to comprise their entire curriculum for a period of two years. The format is certainly a departure from traditional procedure; yet one wonders whether the total project does not still reflect our general unreadiness to adjust educational programs in ways radical enough to meet the real needs and nature of such children. The emphasis on language arts represents a recognition that a basic need for these children is to achieve some degree of literacy. But the glazed eyes and mute silence that met my arrival as "the new English teacher" testified to their tedium and frustration in trying to learn.

It did not take many days for my eyes and spirit to become almost one with theirs. There was an awesomeness to the venture from our first lesson, when some students wanted to know the meaning of

From *Harvard Graduate School of Education Association Bulletin*, Vol. X, Summer, 1965, No. 2. Reprinted by permission of the publisher and the author, one of five Harvard students assigned for practice teaching in Boston's Roxbury section. She took part in a small experimental project concerned with problems in urban teacher training, undertaken by HGSE with the cooperation of the Boston public schools.

"dream" in a sentence we were unjumbling. A day later one child shaved a strip of hair down the center of his scalp because he "don't want to do English!" Very little prepared me to accept the responsibilities of teaching such children or of knowing where or how to begin. These children were not only severely behind their peers, but their frustration with the kind of language required of them was so acute that they were hostile. My first semester of teaching preparation had centered about the more sophisticated possibilities in the teaching of Shakespeare, modern poets, and linguistic grammar.

For more than one week I was a mercurial combination of blundering insensitivity and painful hyper-sensitivity. What I thought was alertness to our different frames of reference led me to select the same terribly dull essay topics that are the bane of the worst "English" classes. Not wanting to demand much on their first written assignment, I asked them to write about their February vacation. Burnis' tearful "I didn't do anything, Miss Donovan!" forced me to consider just what it was that we were trying to do in this class and, for that matter, every other language class.

I came to feel that what the Second Chance program has not recognized is something that we tend to forget even in the most established classrooms: that the whole being is involved in verbal abilities and disabilities. The accomplishment of some degree of literacy in these children will be generated not by the repetitive study of vocabulary, synonyms, antonyms, and multiple meaning words. Rather it can be cultivated through the encounter with experiences felt vicariously through literature, encounters with imaginative experiences that will nourish and, quite possibly, release the child's creative potential and responsiveness.

It is easy to make such a diagnosis from a distance. I made the one above when I was only observing. Faced with a live classroom in which the children have overwhelming verbal disabilities, I know from my own blunders how very vulnerable we are to forgetting that language is only acquired "within the context of its lively use."

It was their reaction to the literature that I mimeographed and read to them that awakened me. They were utterly delighted with "The Lady or the Tiger," and went off to lunch engaged in heated arguments and hypotheses. I was leaving by a basement door when Gladstone tore out of the cafeteria to say "Miss Donovan, we can't decide. *We're* all boys. You're a girl. Which door do *you* think the princess sent the man to?" Several were so dissatisfied with Stockton's ending that they presented me with their own conclusions the next day. One or two had very curious twists wherein the courtier did not follow the princess' gesture but went to the opposite door only to find the lady—or the tiger.

I read many stories to them: Langston Hughes' "Thank You Ma'am," Saki's "Interlopers," O'Henry's "Retrieved Reformation" are but a few. Their reactions were always exuberant and very often surprising. Murray Hyerts "The New Kid" and Philip Apente's "The Wise and the Weak" are two stories of teen-age gangs that I thought would particularly appeal to them. Yet whenever we rated our stories these were always at the bottom of the scale. The story invariably rendered first place was Quentin Reynolds' "A Secret for Two," a tender story that I had almost felt afraid to read to them. They were disturbed by this story of a simple, blind milkman and there is much in their reaction that moved me and that I wish could be communicated to those engaged in textbook planning. Pierre represents heroism and nobility in a context common to their experience; his tale is beautifully related. And they regarded the story with a kind of reverence. I have studied aesthetics and literary theory but it was their reaction that demonstrated for me the dynamic impact art has upon us, not only by informing us about aspects of human life, but by stirring and enlarging our deeper natures.

Oral reading was the most difficult, and most disquieting, of their activities. Some would readily volunteer, others would consistently refuse. Anybody who made the slightest error was assailed with a barrage of taunts and jeers. Often I think I was more vulnerable than whichever child was the momentary object of it all, but I always remarked about their cruelty to each other. One day looked particularly dangerous. *En masse* they had discovered that a very quiet boy named Lance had never read aloud for the entire class. At that point Lance, who had rarely spoken since he witnessed his mother's shooting in the South last summer, looked like their trapped prey. When they demanded that I make him read, I responded that I most certainly would not like to read either if they jeered at me. They mulled this over and decided perhaps I was right. Still "he *should* know how to read!" One very large boy stood up and said: "Lance—we *won't* laugh. READ!" and Lance read. He needed prompting with every second word. But he read.

We talked a lot, too. There was much in the air that concerned them especially: Selma and Reverend Reeb's death, Martin Luther King's visit and the march, and dropping out of school, the pros and cons. All the talking and reading began to affect their creative writing. Their vacation compositions had contained mere lists of words or phrases, but now they joined sentences. In the beginning when I had individual conferences, they would not handle or look at what they had written. The very paper represented something contemptible to them and if I could get them to look at it for a minute, the look would be prefaced with "this is *bad*, Miss Donovan!" Praise for their written work was almost shocking to them. But somehow, as we talked and read, I think they gradually realized that writing was an extension—a very necessary one—of these other activities. When we studied folksongs they suddenly saw that it was very forceful for Odetta to repeat "no more, no more" in "No More Auction Block for Me" and that Pete Seeger was implying many different things when he sang "If I had a hammer . . . if I had a bell. . . ."

The last compositions that these boys wrote reflect some of the delight they discovered in using words. I gave them a topic sentence: "If I were banished, I would live in. . . ." I think this topic made amends for my first poor choice. Evidently it offered them the opportunity to explore their inner fantasies in a manner that illuminated but did not threaten. What they wrote is not "grammatically" correct. But several have the telling quality of some of the folk songs and spirituals we studied. Some would seem to reflect the compassion and awareness of reality that Reynolds' story stirred within them. All were written with verve and without apprehension.

I think it is David Holbrook, the British poet and educator, who says that the creative efforts of such children may be compared with the artist's impulse that forges a work of literature. For me, at least, his statement puts a particular perspective on their "banishment" compositions. I know from our months together that the writing of these compositions represents an expression of themselves not unlike very real artistic creations.

The "Banishment" Compositions

[The names of the children and the facsimiles of their actual compositions are omitted.]

If I was banished I would live in the wood because I don't have to were [worry] about light bill and gass bill and I could cauth [catch] my own food and sell some of it to use the money to buy new things and I dont have to were [worry] about hear the landlow mouth all day and I would live in a cabin and I could lay [all] day and dont have to were about houn [horns] on car buses and trouk and people yellow [yelling] and screaming and pecles [police] blowing wishsell and peopl konock on your door mostly evey minnit and I could cauch fish when I was hungry and I could shote a deer and sell it to the market man in the town.

If I were banished, I would live with my grandmother. I would get a job so that I could help pay for the food and bills. Then after I come from work I would help around the house then I would go out and play a little bit of basketball then I would eat supper look at a little television then go to bed and be ready for a new day of work. I would go to the factory were I work and start to sweep up the place. Right before I get read to go home I would take the cups of the tables and empty the trash.

If I was banished, I would live in the biggest home in the world. It would had a big room went woll to woll carpeting and in verd [every] room it woll had mahogany furniture. In the bard yard I had marble verde way. I woe the king of a king on Quincy Street that migt in my dreams.

If I were banished I would live in New York on 42d streets were you meet all kined of pepol then night come I would go in the show for all night. Then I come out it would be morning Then I would go over to the job centean for a job if I can get a job will go oven my frend when if he can not get me a job. Then go banished to a city after city looking for a job and end my life looking for a job in big city.

If I were banished, I would live, in a house that I will never forget it will be the best house on the street. The color of the house will be fril [fire] red I will have flowers in front of it. It will be [a] one apt. house and ther are one or two house on the street in the house ther will be a fril [fire] plast in it and ther will be pepple the banished too.

Then I will have a prity [party] that know one will sade anything to me but ther is on place like thath in the wood, so I will keep on drean of thing like this. This place will be in desert grandeur in Arizona. Ther is on cities ther. The city is sex miles away.

If I were banished I would live in Jamaica. Why? Because it is always warm and sometimes its so hot that if you were bare footed your feet would have been hurting. Jamaica is a glorish land to see, cocnut trees, small streams, beutiful water falls so cleam that you can drink from it. And that why I like to in Jamaica.

If I were banished I would live in Australia I would go to the Jungles and live with the navtive. I would learn how to uses a boomrang and help the navtive get their food. Some years later I might leave the navtives behind. Come back to civilization and get a Job

If I were banish I would go fare away I woin'd go to particular place I travel fron town to town fron city to city state to state to contry to contry to world to world. the renises for this is that well like you go to New York and you stay there for a whiled yo would want to go agin so that's why differnet places then wher I'an finsh here I av go to another plantet

Postscript on HGSE Students and the Urban Schools

Gail Donovan's "Operation Second Chance" classroom was one of five in the Patrick T. Campbell School that were shared this spring by

Harvard student teachers. Beyond their small joint project, M.A.T.'s were doing student teaching in other parts of Boston and in Dorchester, Medford, Cambridge and Somerville schools selected at their own request as representative of problems facing urban systems around the country.

Increased student interest in such schools has been marked. In applying for student teaching placements last fall, 62 out of 125 apprentices indicated interest in urban-only or in urban-or-suburban placement, and 35 of these asked for urban only. As recently as three years ago, a variety of HGSE affiliations with area schools considered particularly advanced were reflected in student teaching placements: virtually 100% were in prosperous middle-class suburbs.

Stephen J. Fischer, who initiated the Campbell School project this year as a small-scale experiment related to his interest in urban teacher training programs, sees this interest as the result of three converging influences: locally, the publicly-stated interest of the Boston Public Schools in drawing further upon outside resources in tackling their problems; the increased concern with problems of the city among members of the Faculty of Education; and the awakened concern of society as a whole in the problems of poverty and Negro rights.

This interest crops up in other places too. Of the several tutoring sections affiliated this year with the M.A.T.s' course in supervised teaching (C-16), two—those with Gerald Lesser and John Herzog and with Dean Sizer—by student request chose to concentrate exclusively on urban school problems. The Admissions Office finds that this year's entering students include applicants like Harvard seniors Richard A. Geist, who will direct a Head Start program in a Cambridge housing center this summer, and Chester E. Finn, Jr., director of a Harvard tutoring program employing 70 volunteers last year, and founder of another, college-oriented tutorial program for gifted Cambridge children from poor homes.

The HGSE Student Association cabinet, in response to local student inquiries, has established for next year a tutor advisory service to work with area colleges. Advanced students at the School will provide expert advice on how to attack certain teaching problems that arise in the tutors' work, as well as some training in such specialized fields as remedial reading, the "new" math, and career counseling. A certain number of students have spent summers in Freedom Schools in the South and, the last two years, in summer institutes for low-income city children. Many have been tutors.

Beyond interest, problems exist. Not a few students who request practice teaching in "the slums" are discouraged by the experience, and decide against later work in such schools. Others retain their commitment, but feel compelled after this student-teaching encounter to go to more stable, surburban school environments for their first full-time teaching experience.

James M. Wallace, Assistant Director of Student Teaching Programs, warns that the problems posed in these schools—especially that of "culture shock"—may be too much for many student teachers until they acquire more experience. He also believes it essential that student teaching situations be structured in a way that success in reaching his students is possible for, and may be verified by, the teacher. Stephen Fischer points to special problems created in discipline, always a problem for student teachers, when students from middle-class backgrounds prove reluctant to further "impose upon" children from lower-class settings whose lives appear already grim and blighted.

In career placement, the Peace Corps appears still to draw more of HGSE's new graduates than the great cities. But the number of urban placements is growing. It appears that the trend is there and, with the President's call for a National Teachers Corps, will likely grow stronger.

—Ed.

ᔕ•ᔐ

Stimulating Retarded Readers

ᔕ•ᔐ

ORIS BEANE

California State Legislature Act AB464 established special reading classes in Berkeley schools in the spring of 1963. I have had contact with the program as it deals with the retarded reader in the secondary school who stays in school a full day but whose difficulties in content subjects are due mainly to an inability to read properly. This does not discount the fact that many of these students are so-called behavior problems. However, according to medical and psychological tests, teacher judgments, and counselor evaluations (all necessary before any student is admitted to the 464 program) these students are able to learn, and, hopefully, will profit from instruction in a small group. Class size is limited to seven.

The Class

My ninth-grade class of educationally handicapped students started with seven students but ended with five. One boy and one girl were transferred to the Continuation School during the year. Of those remaining, none had ever liked reading. The exception was Sue, a Caucasian girl with an imaginative mind, who "didn't mind a certain kind of reading." To a great degree she lived in a dream world. Not surprisingly, she was the one who showed the most progress at the end of the year.

The other girls in the class were Negroes but not friends in or out of school. Lorna was quite critical of May but appeared friendly with Sue during the reading class period, sharing notes and a common interest in one of the Negro boys, who ignored them both. This boy was to me the most challenging member of the class. A bright, handsome, hostile

Printed with permission of the author, who teaches first grade at Bayview Elementary School in Richmond, California.

boy with a quick wit and an engaging but rare smile, he defied the help of all staff members until the middle of the second semester. Then for some reason, our combined efforts began to be meaningful to Jim and all of us working with him noticed general improvement. Pat and Eddie spent a minimum of days in school throughout the year. Their antisocial pattern was so fixed by the ninth grade that school remained only a building to them. I was never able to convince them that I could help them in an important area. Jose was the class tease and practical joker. Among these students, interest in the reading class ranged from a willingness to let me try to interest them to absolute refusal. Reading diagnostic tests like the *Weekly Reader* Tests revealed a span of third- to fifth-grade silent reading skill. These results were substantiated by a standardized test (Gates Reading for Significance) which was administered by the end of the first six weeks of the semester. The three girls in the class did not mind reading aloud. One, in fact, preferred to do her assignments aloud rather than write them—a desire which I thought I indulged in, but one which resulted in real learning and motivation for this girl. The boys refused to read aloud until later in the semester when they had overcome, in part, insecurities about vocabulary.

All of these students possessed the attitude that school was the place to strike back at society. Interpersonal relationships were poor. Each student believed that the teacher's time should be all his whenever he demanded it. Two of the boys were chronic teasers; one of the girls was a compulsive talker who never missed an opportunity to make a comment—usually a derogatory one about one of the boys.

Only two of these students had the kind of home background that we would consider adequate for good performance in school. The other homes were characterized by lack of space for studying, few or no books, parents who did little or no reading themselves and who were worried about basic needs for living. All parents however, despite their various problems, wanted their children to succeed in school because they were aware of the need for education. They were willing to do all they could but only one parent admitted to me that she needed to return to school herself in order to improve in reading. Pertinent to this, the Caucasian family of this class could afford to seek psychiatric help for their child and did so.

Explanation of Problems

My procedure with the group included individual interviews, interest inventories, group testing, individual informal oral reading tests (much later, a standardized one), notes on each class period, analysis of the notes, and assignments according to the reading difficulties I had observed. In thinking about a program and planning for this class these considerations presented themselves:

1. I felt that these students had to be convinced about the worth of the 464 program before our reading materials could be used to advantage.

2. I realized that they had not learned the necessary study habits that would enable them to be better students.

3. There was a desperate need to improve and, in two cases, teach reading skills, chiefly in the areas of vocabulary and comprehension.

4. I recognized that my toughest problem would be providing, in a forty-minute period, the kind of situations that would make these students want to read.

Despite consultations with parents and students there was considerable hostility in half the group to being programmed into the 464 class. The feeling was one of separateness from the rest of the ninth-grade class. There was also a lack of understanding about the meaning of reading. They felt that since they could recognize simple words, they knew how to read. Most devastating to their ego was what they thought their friends would say if they knew that they were in the 464 class. These articulate, noisy students made the others feel as if they should agree in public although individually they had admitted a need to improve in reading.

Only two of the students in this program seemed to have the most elementary knowledge of penmanship, of heading a paper, or of working in an organized manner. Following written directions was difficult for all. Expressing a thought in a written complete sentence was a tortuous process. One boy did not even speak with ease in a complete sentence.

These students had reached the ninth grade without being able to find the main idea or supporting details in a paragraph. Two students had no techniques for working out unfamiliar words of more than two syllables. One student lacked proficiency in recognizing Dolch's Basic Sight Vocabulary. Oral reading ranged from halting, word-by-word reading to eager but repetitous efforts with little recall or comprehension. All members of the class were restless, with short attention spans.

Text books, workbooks, or SRA labs only reactivated previous failures or unsatisfying experiences with reading. What printed material would appeal to these students? What could I present that would move them to open a book voluntarily? One of the first questions one of the boys asked was, "What kind of book do we have in this class?" Then he added before I could reply: "I bet it's one of those baby books like *Days of Adventure*. I'm *sick* of those books!" Immediately, there was concurrence by the whole group!

Efforts to Be Effective

I decided that attacks would have to be on all fronts and continuous so that effects would be cumulative. We began with discussions of why the State Legislature had passed the law authorizing these classes, and about the cost of caring for delinquents. We explored all ideas that were offered and related all to the question of staying in school.

"Let's find titles that have to do with trouble," I suggested at one point. "Get up and look at the books we have in our room."

A paperback book, *Trouble After School*, was one of several books on the shelf. Another was on the table. During this part of the period one of the girls picked up a copy of *Trouble* and suggested that this might be a story about Pat and that she would read it. Pat was immediately interested but unfortunately even this simply book was beyond his ability for independent reading. When Eddie picked up the other book, he opened to a page on which he saw the word "engine." That word he knew well, for his hobby was helping older boys fix their cars. Happily, this was a book he could read with but a minimum of frustration, and eventually Eddie finished this mimeographed edition of an original story by a San Francisco teacher working with similar students.

What of the other students, you may wonder. The fact that three students became involved was a spur for the others. Of course, I had planted the books and the students knew this, but that did not detract from their willingness to pick up and to start reading. It should be noted that I did not suggest reading a book—only a title! And one boy did just that, I must admit. One step at a time is necessary with these students, but this can be the needed stimulus to move ahead.

At all times I advocated frankness—about the school program, about ourselves and our performance during a given period and the reasons for it, about expressing our views. To encourage dealing with the reality, each student had two record sheets. On one I recorded his reading problems, plans for correcting his weaknesses, evidences of improvement. On the other, were listed the social problems we were trying to improve. I checked with each student those items we could honestly say he had worked on each day. Evaluation came at the end of each six weeks. At first, some of the boys were most indifferent, but when they discovered that this progress was in black and white before their eyes, the sheets assumed a different meaning.

I had an idea that practice in doing the many operations called for in school work was what my students needed. Therefore, we practiced following directions in many ways. We had group lessons designed around finding facts, recalling facts, finding the main idea of a paragraph, and so on. Each student then applied the new knowledge by himself on his own level of reading material. The sample lesson always dealt with the familiar or with the very dramatic. For oral reading, I chose articles from newspapers or from *Scope*.

Pictures and unfamiliar words in print were presented as challenges. During the worst outrages in the South in the 1964-1965 school year, we had many interesting discussions. Words we used in speaking were put on the board, headlines were cut out, parts of articles were prepared for reading. This method enabled everyone to read parts separately, to match headlines and pictures, and to find reasons for choices. Interestingly enough, two of the girls began looking for "big" words to show me that they could "figure them out."

Meaning was stressed to great advantage even in phonics exercises. I encouraged the students to be inquisitive about meanings. As a result, one of the girls asked the question I had been hoping for: "I know what segregation is, but what do they mean by '*dee*' *facto* segregation?" These students will never take Latin, but they now know one Latin phrase and its meaning.

After the initial period of learning about my students, I talked with them briefly about the program we would follow and the materials we would use. Our activities included films such as *Morning with Jimmy*, and subjects such as reptiles, swamp life, and the like. All were correlated with reading materials. For help in developing a structure within which to work, we followed a program of so many minutes on each part of the lesson. Whenever I found one particular part that held a student's interest, I always allowed him as much time as he desired on that day. With two exceptions each student found that by the end of the year he was producing twice as much work.

Description of Results

By the end of the year, all students showed gains. Sue had advanced more than two years in silent reading ability (from 5.1 to 7.8). Her oral reading developed an expressive quality which pleased her considerably. A lengthy, complex sentence continued to confuse her although she did make efforts to decipher the thought. Sue and Lorna were the two girls whose interest in "big" words was quickened during the year. Lorna also attempted to pattern her speech after mine and informed the group that she was doing so. On that day we had one of our most effective discussions on speech and speech patterns of people, considering Negroes in particular. This led to an increased use of the tape recorder and to improved oral reading by all of them. Lorna developed a critical quality to her reading. She continued to substitute words and to repeat words and phrases, but now began thinking about what was being read and the corrections needed. These same habits had previously prevented improvement in silent reading so that a gain of slightly over a year from 4.9 to 6.1 was brought about.

Oral reading practiced almost every day proved valuable in increasing student recognition of basic words and ability to phrase intelligently. Since some comprehension questions were always asked, the importance of thinking was emphasized.

Discipline from the kind of silent reading material used in *Reading for Meaning, Reading Skills, Better Reading, and Practice Readers* for the less able in the group, enabled the students to find facts quickly, to understand the meaning of the words used in the exercises, to draw inferences, and to find the main idea in paragraphs. Attention was always directed to using these skills in subjects as diverse as history and homemaking so that the girls and two of the boys showed improved grades in history by the end of the year. To be sure, I had been in contact with those teachers interested in trying the same techniques with their slow-learning students since these students need constant reinforcing from as many sources as possible.

Two of the boys showed no signs of progress until near the end of the year. At this time, one of the teasers suddenly realized that he was reading on a higher level in his English and history classes. It was at that point that he stopped protesting his being in the reading class. He now had less need to annoy his classmates and began completing his silent reading work so rapidly that he could do two lessons in the time that it used to take him to do half of one exercise.

It is likely that I spent too much time discussing subjects not related to reading skills. I feel, however, that these students must have breadth of knowledge since depth if not likely. Because of their reading handicaps they have missed much and seem to be auditory-oriented besides. Because they seem to learn better when the approach is concrete and visual, an opportunity for learning through such media as the Controlled Reader, films, and guided discussion is needed. Through our discussions I learned much about each student and I feel that each one has gained much in self-confidence which is so important. I did and still do wish for closer contact with the parents, however, even though I did have several contacts with four of the families.

In considering the program, I feel that the success attained was due in large part to the size of the class. The "unclasslike" atmosphere invited freer expression of the students and relief from some tensions at the end of the day. The assistance of my principal and his administrative assistant in supporting the English department in requests for good materials and aids must also be acknowledged. However, no matter what the underlying reasons behind the results of this (and any) program, we can only hope and trust that what we have tried to sow will bear fruit before it is too late for the realization of these students' goals.

Mathematics and the Culturally Disadvantaged

WILLIAM F. JOHNTZ

It has usually been believed that one had to wait until a child was older before introducing him to abstract mathematics. This idea is precisely wrong; it is not that one has to wait, but rather that one cannot afford to wait.

——Professor David A. Page, University of Illinois

Basic to the Madison Project is the belief that mathematics is not the art of following rote instructions, but is rather, the art of discovering patterns and finding ways to make use of these patterns.

It has been observed that young children, in grades three through six especially, have great ability to learn abstract mathematics. This is very nearly the best age in the child's entire life for exploring abstract science and mathematics—indeed, a fifth-grader is apparently better qualified than a ninth-grader; to postpone the introduction of abstract mathematics until the ninth grade, as the traditional program does, is to squander the best mathematics-learning years of the child's life.

Abstract mathematics—that is, especially algebra and coordinate geometry—is easier for children than many arithmetical topics are; it is more exciting and more fun; it can be very valuable in helping children to learn arithmetic and for developing arithmetical concepts.

——Dr. Robert B. Davis,
Director of Madison Project,
Webster College, Missouri (Formerly Professor of Mathematics, MIT)

The above quotations exemplify one of the most important discoveries ever made in regard to the teaching of mathematics. Their implications for culturally disadvantaged students are enormous. In the

---

An original paper, reprinted by permission of the author, a mathematics teacher at Berkeley High School, Berkeley, California.

pages that follow, I will explore some of these implications and describe a two-year experiment in the teaching of abstract algebra and coordinate geometry to culturally disadvantaged elementary students in Berkeley, California.

When I use the term "culturally disadvantaged," I refer primarily to Negroes from lower socioeconomic environments. I do this for a number of reasons.

First of all, more than 90% of the students involved in my project were Negroes from low-income families with limited educational backgrounds. Second, I believe the "culturally disadvantaged" component of any large urban area in the United States today would likewise be composed overwhelmingly of Negroes from low-income families. Finally, and to my mind most important, the Negro experience is unique; the nature of his deprivation is qualitatively different from that of other ethnic groups. His own group identity has been shattered; at an appalling early age he internalizes a self-image that does little to give him confidence and everything to convince him of his inferiority. Consequently, I believe that his needs are far greater and more pressing than those of other ethnic and/or minority groups.

The term "culturally disadvantaged" is a favorite one these days. It is used loosely and sometimes meaninglessly. When I use it, I assume there is a certain minimum educational expectation which the average American parent holds for his child. He wants his child to go to college and then to become successful in terms of money, status, or self-fulfillment. (I won't question this goal philosophically; in any event, in our technological, soon-to-be-automated society, at least a modicum of success is fast becoming prerequisite to survival.)

With this goal in mind, the average American parent provides his child with books, experiences, tools, and the motivation to succeed in school. He has at least some education himself, so he possesses the know-how to enrich the child's life. Even if he has little money, he knows how to use the public library and how to get to the public museum. He can read. When his child begins school, even in kindergarten, he is already several jumps ahead of the average Negro child whose parents are probably desperately poor, burdened with twice as many dependents, barely literate, afraid to use public institutions, and so defeated themselves that they could hardly be expected to motivate their child to do more than find a job—any job—and stay out of jail.

There are, I believe, seven important respects in which mathematics bears a special relevance to the problems of the culturally disadvantaged. They are:

1. Mathematics, due to its highly abstract nature, is less culturally

conditioned than other areas of learning. For instance, many Negro children entering the first grade have spent six years listening to "bad English" spoken in their homes and neighborhoods. They have not, however, been subjected to six years of "bad math." No math, perhaps, but not "bad math." The Negro students often works from a negative position in English while in mathematics he more likely starts from zero.

Much of the advice given to teachers of culturally disadvantaged students emphasizes that the material taught to them should be concrete and specific rather than abstract. On the contrary, I believe the reverse to be true. These students learn abstractions more readily than they learn the concrete. Perhaps the average educated American has projected his own difficulties with abstractions upon the hapless Negro; yet another subtle form of discrimination.

2. Mathematics instruction bears fewer derogatory connotations than other subjects. If a Negro studies history, he discovers that his ancestors were slaves. If he studies sociology, he learns that Negroes have the highest crime and illiteracy rate of any major group in the United States. Mathematics, being abstract, simply does not have these connotations. This observation is in no way intended to imply that the Negro should not have objective knowledge of his past and present condition.

3. Success in mathematics increases the Negro's job and college opportunities more than success in many other subject areas because of the enormous role played by technology in our society today.

4. Success in mathematics helps enormously to destroy the popular stereotype of Negro inferiority: that the Negro is successful only in the areas of muscles, music, and the ministry.

5. Because of the high status that mathematics holds in our culture, the Negro who succeeds in this field enjoys an improved self-image. An improved self-image, of course, increases motivation in other subject areas.

6. Mathematics provides an excellent method of evaluating the native intelligence of culturally disadvantaged students who often do very poorly on formal I.Q. tests. Concept-oriented mathematics taught from a discovery point of view offers the sensitive teacher an unparalleled opportunity to see through the child's lower-class conformity to the raw intelligence rarely revealed by standard tests.

7. The teacher of culturally disadvantaged children often has very low expectations for his students. This is due partly to the teacher's prejudice and partly to the low achievement of the students. The expectations of the teacher can be raised dramatically when he sees the

children learn abstract, conceptually-oriented mathematics. The effect is particularly vivid when the children are of elementary school age, since they frequently learn the material faster than the teacher. Having held these beliefs for some time, I decided to test them by teaching algebra and coordinate geometry to disadvantaged elementary school children in Berkeley, California.

Table 1 describes the classes that were involved in the experiment.

TABLE 1.

Grade	Racial composition	Grouping (ability) *	Length of instruction
Second	Integrated	Heterogeneous	120 classes (1/2 hour)
Third	95% Negro	Top quarter	115 classes (55 minutes)
Fourth A	100% Negro	Bottom quarter	20 classes (55 minutes)
Fourth B	95% Negro	Top quarter	90 classes (50 minutes)
Fourth C	80% Negro	Top quarter	140 classes (50 minutes)
Sixth	Integrated	Heterogeneous	170 classes (50 minutes)

* The students were grouped on the basis of their prior teacher's judgment of each child's creativity, imagination, and intellectual curiosity eather than I.Q., achievement, or "conformity" scores.

Observations

Method of Instruction. I have used the discovery method exclusively. I answer each question by asking another question which helps the student along the route to understanding. The emphasis is on concepts and structure, not technique. I usually am able to ask each student about two or three questions in the fifty-minute period. Sometimes the students work on a problem at their seats while I walk around the room and check each paper. The majority of the class time is spent in animated discussion of ideas.

I do not use a text. I feel that a text lessens the effectiveness of the discovery method. If a student has a text he tends to search out and memorize generalizations before he understands them. Ironically, his knowledge of the technique lessens his motivation to understand the concepts that underlie the technique. Another disadvantage of using a text is that it tends to structure the course. The content of the course should grow dynamically out of the discussion, not arbitrarily out of the text.

Motivation. The general level of motivation is very high. The students evidence a much greater interest in concepts than do the students in my second-year high school algebra class. During class discussions the students literally leap out of their seats when they have an insight or perceive a generalization. Often at the end of a fifty- to fifty-five minute period they will spend the whole of their recess asking questions and proposing new solutions.

Ability to Conceptualize. Their abilities seem as great or greater than my best high school classes. Several teachers of university level math who have visited the class compare them most favorably with their students. One logic teacher said the fourth graders' understanding seemed better than her university students. All of these university teachers (eight have visited the fourth-grade class) indicate that they see no intellectual limits to what these fourth graders can comprehend. One of the teachers is interested in teaching them a unit on limits.

Homework. I give homework to the fourth and sixth graders regularly; to the second and third graders rarely. With a little persuasion about 80% to 90% of the fourth and sixth graders will turn in their homework. This is one of the very few respects in which my high school students make a better performance. This is probably due, unfortunately, to the threat of grades at the secondary level.

Grades. I do not give letter grades to the students. We do a small amount of informal testing. The endless verbal questioning, however, gives me an excellent idea of what they know and understand.

Discipline. If the class' regular elementary teacher is experienced and competent, discipline problems are minimal even in the free and informal atmosphere of the discovery method of instruction. Their intense interest and success with the subject matter has given them internal control. Teachers whose experience is limited to the university and secondary level should realize, however, that elementary children are highly animated not only intellectually but also physically.

Transfer. Even more important for the culturally disadvantaged child than his mathematical success per se is the effect that this success has on his own self-image. The primary causal factor in the low achievement of culturally disadvantaged children is the low, negative image they have of themselves. For example, the most tragic aspect of the whole tragic history of the Negro in America is the fact that he has believed the myth of inferiority that has been perpetrated by the white man. If a child has an I.Q. of 150 at birth but believes himself to be stupid, he will perform as though he actually is stupid. The only way to break up the devastating fulfillment of the white man's prophecy of failure is to create a learning situation in which the Negro achieves up to the level of his innate talents. If he can have success in even one high status subject area, this can result in an elevation of his own self-image. The improved self-image then increases motivation and, consequently, achievement in other subjects areas.

The above phenomena have apparently occurred in the experimental program I have been working with. The regular teachers of these classes report that the success these children have had with algebra has not only "rubbed off" on their arithmetic but also on their reading, writing, speaking, and thinking. Greater conformity to acceptable standards of behavior in nonclassroom situations has been observed.

In one of the classes, there has been an average increase of ten points in I.Q. scores. One girl's score rose 38 points.

Grouping. During the two years of this experiment, I have come to some rather definite conclusions about the best method of grouping students. The fourth-grade class labelled "B" in Table 1 was grouped by drawing together four or five of the most creative and original students from each of four heterogeneously grouped classes for one hour each day to study algebra. During the hour they were with me, their intellectual performance was excellent, but they were totally unprepared psychologically to compete with other bright students. Their behavior fluctuated between aggression and withdrawal. They lacked a positive group identity. The intellectual excitement and values that I was able to build in that one hour period were swiftly undone by their peer groups in each of their heterogeneously grouped regular classes.

I came to realize that these students should be grouped together for the *whole* school day if they were to be able to fight off the educationally negative values that pervade the predominantly (90%) Negro school in an urban setting. So this year, in the same school, we grouped an entire class of students homogeneously, using the criteria described above.

They remain together all day, under the general charge of one teacher. I come in for one hour each day to teach them algebra. The results are startlingly different. The class has developed a group identity that places a high value on intellectual achievement and scholarship. They lend one another psychological support in fighting off the academically negative peer pressures.

Most of the compensatory education programs in the United States today pay only cursory attention to the culturally disadvantaged student who is genetically college-capable. It is still assumed that the ultimate goal of the Negro is to obtain a white-collar job in a bank. For a Negro whose I.Q. at birth is 150-plus to end up clerking in a bank represents, in my mind, an appalling failure. The gifted Negro must be identified early in his elementary school years, grouped with others of similar abilities, and then given an academic program of challenge and excellence that will prepare him to enter our major universities. Culturally disadvantaged people everywhere desperately need models of success to identify with and emulate.

None of the above discussion is intended to imply that an algebra program for elementary students should be limited to only the most intelligent. The fourth-grade class labelled "A" in Table 1 was the lowest of four fourth-grade classes in a school that is about 95% Negro. After three weeks of instruction, the students are able to add positive and negative numbers with an understanding of the role of the additive inverse in this process. They can also write true and false sets of simple inequalities. They show great interest in the work. Their regular teacher reports that their interest in other subject areas has increased and certain behavior problems have been minimized. As one might expect, some of the children in this low-ability class have been misplaced. One boy who had been described as close to mentally retarded has, I think, an I.Q. of over 120.

I do feel, however, that since the funds for compensatory education are limited, whatever money is available for an algebra program for culturally disadvantaged children on the elementary level should be spent on the most able students.

Recruitment of Teachers. I believe that in order to use the discovery method in teaching algebra and coordinate geometry to elementary school children, the teacher should have at least the equivalent of a secondary teaching major in mathematics. He must be sufficiently secure in his knowledge of mathematics that he is willing to let the intellectual ball roll wherever the students throw it. Even second-grade children ask rather profound mathematical questions.

My second and third graders are graphing the solution sets of linear equations in two unknowns; the fourth graders can solve simultaneous linear equations, simultaneous inequations in one unknown, and simultaneous inequations and equations in two unknowns. They are now working on solutions of quadratic equations. They were completely fascinated by trying to devise a geometric model of an ordered triple.

A mathematics instructor from the university who visited one of my fourth-grade classes indicated that he thought one would need to have a Ph. D. in math to keep up with these children after a couple of years of this kind of training.

In order to obtain people properly trained in math to do this work, I think it would be necessary to set up the program in such a way that (1) the algebra teacher teaches only mathematics; (2) the algebra teacher does not teach arithmetic skills (this should be done by the regular classroom teacher); (3) the regular teacher is present when the algebra teacher is teaching in order (a) to free the latter from responsibilities of red tape, discipline, and the like; (b) to provide an excellent means of in-service training for the regular teacher;(c) to allow the regular teacher to take notes for the algebra teacher (a set of notes is very helpful when one uses the discovery method without a text); and finally (d) to preclude the necessity, required in some school districts, that the special teacher be certified to teach elementary school.

If the conditions described above are provided, I believe that programs such as mine can attract people with graduate training in mathematics. Already a man with six years of graduate work in mathematics has expressed a desire to join this program on a full-time basis. Several other teaching assistants in mathematics from the University of California wish to teach in the program on a part-time basis of one or two periods per day. Part of their desire to work with elementary school students is based on a desire to help disadvantaged children. However, most of their desire, I believe, has grown out of their realization that elementary school children can do things, mathematically, that are not only interesting, but also intellectually very exciting. Several of these teachers are willing to give up their university teaching assistantships in order to involve themselves in this program. This is probably the greatest tribute of all to what these students are achieving.

I personally believe that a major portion of every compensatory education should be devoted not merely to bringing the culturally disadvantaged up to average, but to devising learning situations in which these students reach levels of achievement where they are models of excellence—not only to other culturally disadvantaged students but to our most advantaged students as well. Not only mathematics, but other abstract subjects such as philosophy, logic, linguistics, and the like, are well suited to this function. Negro slum children who graduate from the sixth grade probably will not speak what we consider to be excellent English, but I see no reason that they could not have an excellent French accent if their studies of French had started in the first grade.

Above all, I would like to see compensatory education programs stimulate an atmosphere of intellectual excitement and discovery for both student and *teacher*. To accomplish this we must set our goals higher than the purely remedial.

Our culturally disadvantaged urban schools contain thousands of children with fine minds. We must identify those minds and challenge and stimulate them in such a way that no amount of adversity in the culture can ever crush their intellectual spirit.

Summary

1. The number one problem of most urban school districts in the United States today is the very low achievement of the culturally disadvantaged students in these districts. Because the percentage of cultural-

ly disadvantaged children in our large urban centers is rapidly increasing, the urgency for a solution to this problem is becoming more crucial.

2. The most important cause of this low achievement is lack of motivation, which is in turn based upon the low self-image that culturally disadvantaged students have of themselves.

3. The most effective way to raise a student's self-image is to create a learning situation in which he can have success in a high status subject.

4. Abstract, conceptually oriented algebra and coordinate geometry, taught from a discovery point of view, are ideally suited to provide this successful learning experience for the disadvantaged student for the following reasons:

a. Mathematics is high status in our technological society.

b. Because mathematics is abstract, it has been less affected by the negative aspects of the culturally disadvantaged child's environment.

c. Abstract algebra can be learned in the early elementary grades before the student's low self-image has become indelibly imprinted on him.

5. The most neglected student in our entire educational system is the highly intelligent student who is culturally disadvantaged. These students should be identified as early as possible, grouped with students of similar abilities, and given an intensive compensatory education program built around a mathematics, English, foreign language curriculum. In brief, we should start getting them ready for college in the early elementary grades. These students must be kept together all day long to enable them to withstand the negative peer pressures.

6. If the culturally disadvantaged child is ever to close up the gap between himself and the more advantaged children, the schools that he attends must be the very best schools in the community. They must have smaller classes, better teachers and plants, more counseling and guidance, a longer school day and school year. Only in this way can the schools partially compensate for the negative aspects of the student's non-school environment.

꠹•꠹

Some Practical Ideas for Teaching Mathematics to Disadvantaged Children

꠹•꠹

NATALIE MINTZ AND HERBERT FREMONT

Suggestions to teachers about helping disadvantaged students to learn mathematics are in very short supply. Although the number of articles about these children is on the increase, specific and practical ideas are still sorely needed if teachers are going to open the horizons for these students of currently limited outlook. We have the feeling that much more is at stake than the mathematics experience of the disadvantaged. How many average students from middle-class homes have many of the same problems as their less fortunate peers? Is it possible that they too may be troubled children whose needs are not being met by the present school program? Certainly, teachers generally become involved in the personal problems of their students when these problems interfere with the planned instruction. Is it conceivable that many of our less outgoing students can achieve an acceptable level of work in mathematics and yet be troubled by some of the very concerns and frustrations that are so obvious among disadvantaged children? Can it be a matter of similar problems but different intensities? Of course, we cannot supply a definite answer. The feeling does persist, however, that, as we study the difficulties of the children we classify as "disadvantaged," we will begin to gain insights into the troubles of all students and develop the ability to help all children learn about mathematics.

In an attempt to build lessons based upon the notion that school is a place where important things are happening, we decided to use experi-

From *The Arithmetic Teacher*, April, 1965. Reprinted by permission of the publisher and authors. Mrs. Mintz is a teacher of science and mathematics at Junior High School 8 in South Jamaica. Professor Fremont is mathematics specialist in the education department, Queens College, and mathematics consultant to the North Shore Public Schools, Long Island, New York.

ence-type units in a seventh-grade class in a difficult school. The mathematics learnings involved in this unit, while of an incidental nature to the students, were very carefully planned for by the teacher. The use of a variety of teaching aids is generally a prerequisite in work with children who have a history of difficulty with mathematics experiences.

A useful teaching aid for the teacher who is attempting to give purpose to his instruction in mathematics is the catalog generally published by large department stores around holiday time.[1]

Teaching children who have great difficulty abstracting mathematical concepts can be a frustrating experience for both teacher and student. Doing percent problems can be an odious task for students who do not understand the mathematical concepts involved, and who see little purpose in doing such problems in the first place. For the perplexed teacher in such a situation we have a helpful suggestion. Make use of the department store catalogs when they become available, and plan a unit based upon holiday shopping and gift buying.

Such a unit is best planned to begin about Thanksgiving and continue until Christmas. The mathematical concepts to be taught are multiplication and division of decimal fractions; the meaning of percent; equivalent percents; converting percents to fractions, and the reverse; all kinds of problems involving percents, and general problem solving techniques.

As an introduction to the unit, each child received a catalog. The contents of the catalog together with the holiday season generated spontaneous student interest. The children were permitted to look freely through the catalog and to examine the contents. They were encouraged to talk about the array of gifts they saw. In this discussion of the various items careful attention was given to the spelling of each name in an attempt to enlarge student vocabulary. We did not limit ourselves to purely mathematical goals.

The class then considered the problem of using the catalog to buy gifts for friends and relations. On the last page of the catalog was an order blank listing each of the items in the catalog. The children understood that the gifts could be bought by completing this form. The form brought forth many questions:

"Do we charge it, or send a check?"
"What does it mean to charge it?"
"What does C.O.D. mean?"
"What is a money order? How do you make one out?"
"Why must we pay tax? How do you figure out how much?"

---

[1] In the case described the Gertz Department Store catalog was used at the suggestion of Gertrude Downing, Coordinator, BRIDGE project.

As the children considered these questions, they began to complete the order form which called for much information, such as item, quantity, description, size, color, price, tax, total cost. The activity generated much student interest. In addition, the students had a real need to learn how to carry out the mathematical computations involved so that they could purchase the items. Thus, before the process was taught, a situation was created that helped each student want to know how to do the necessary work. In addition to the development of the desire to learn, the unit provided meaningful experiences of many kinds: developing vocabulary, writing clearly, completing forms, understanding the importance of taxes, understanding methods of purchasing, learning item names, writing item descriptions, filling out order blanks, computing item taxes, and deciding about payment.

The area of taxation was especially fruitful in the development of concepts. Determining how to compute the tax, deciding how much money must be set aside for taxes, determining what becomes of tax money, differentiating between local and federal taxes (some items had two kinds of taxes on them) all served as a rich fund of valuable mathematical and nonmathematical experiences. This topic suggests other possibilities. Extended studies of income tax, property tax, or amusement tax are but a few of the possible areas for further study.

Thus, our children now had some definite purpose for their work. Percents to them were concepts to be learned so they could figure costs properly. The catalog is real. Many students actually bought gifts in the moderate price range, and others had fun doing some additional dreaming. Many of the students began to pick up the topics discussed and ask questions about taxes on cigarettes, leather goods, and toys. The girls were extremely interested in cosmetics. Others who had marketing responsibilities at home recalled the tax on paper goods. A few asked about the restaurant tax. There was a genuine interest in these topics because they had meaning for the students NOW, in their present, everyday world. This is a far cry from the "learn-it-because-you'll-need-it-as-an-adult" approach.

A narrative always tends to give the impression that progress through the unit described was smooth and uninterrupted. Of course, this is seldom the case. For some children the problems were not easy. One of the principal areas of difficulty was the multiplication of decimal fractions. But such problems arising in a meaningful context help the student. It is interesting how the decimal points found their way to correct position when we were dealing with money.

Learning the basic algorisms is a lot easier when there is a definite need to learn them. In isolation they are meaningless and become rote drill experiences. These children have been drilled . . . drilled . . . and redrilled, only to learn how impossible mathematics can be to master, and how useless it is to try to learn. Disadvantaged children especially have been "cooked and fried" in skill work from their first day in school. If they haven't learned fundamental skills by the time they reach junior high school, we must try to invent new experiences to help them learn. It is not simply a matter of providing more drill. One helpful technique is to make the mastery of mathematical skills a stepping-stone to something of immediate interest and use to the student.

Evaluation procedures for this unit involved the completion of numerous forms. To the children this activity was not considered a test. Rather, they saw it as a natural activity growing out of previous work. They thought it was fun.

The entire unit was climaxed by the actual purchase of an item from the catalog for the fish tank that was in the classroom. As the children completed this task, we began to get a sense of the enjoyment the children experienced as they became aware of their newfound skills. Yes, they seemed to have learned a good deal more than simply "finding the percent of a number."

Social Studies for Disadvantaged Students

STATEN W. WEBSTER

There is an appalling dearth of articles dealing with the problem of teaching the social studies to disadvantaged students. This fact is surprising in view of the social and cultural importance of this component of the school curriculum.

Before considering some possible ways in which the social studies can be taught more effectively to disadvantaged learners, attention must be given to certain key problems that are involved. The first set of problems to be considered here is inherent in the very nature of the social studies. The second group of problems pertains to the learned characteristics of disadvantaged learners themselves.

Problems Inherent in the Social Studies

A basic problem of the social studies is their highly verbal nature. With the possible exception of English, no other school subject required of all students relies so heavily upon reading as does this area. It is well documented that on the average, disadvantaged learners from lower-class, oppressed ethnic minority, bilingual groups read below the level observed in students from more favored settings. Thus, disadvantaged students enter the highly verbal race for success in the social studies with severe handicaps.

A second problem inherent in the social studies is that their content too often is removed from the realities of life in both time and space. Disadvantaged students find it hard and often impossible to become emotionally and intellectually involved in learning something which seems irrelevant to their daily lives. Also, many of the values, desired attitudes, and behaviors advocated in the social studies are not congruent to those the learner encounters in his own environment and sees

---

An article by the editor. A note concerning him appears with his article "When Schools and Parents in a Disadvantaged Community Clash."

in the wider society about him. This value-behavior discrepancy is most pointedly felt by disadvantaged groups in our society.

These factors combine to make the social studies an unappealing and difficult subject to disadvantaged students.

Problems Related to Disadvantaged Learners Themselves

Membership in an impoverished social class stratum or in an oppressed ethnic minority group is productive of strong feelings of alienation. Students who see themselves as outsiders find little reason to motivate themselves to learn about the sociocultural heritage of a society of which they, in reality, are not fully a part. The great heroes of the country's past and present are viewed as strangers and the significant events of our historical evolution are seen as other-worldly events.

Encapsulated lower-class and ethnic-minority-group communities are productive of limited world concepts on the parts of the inhabitants. This is to say that disadvantaged learners perceive the world and reality in a way largely restricted to their immediate environment. That which is close and near becomes that which is real. Too often, imagination and imagery, which are so essential for learning, are stifled by the harshness of reality. Disadvantaged parents lack the resources required to provide their children with the extensive travel, excursions, books, and learning aids which made for learning readiness and interest in their children.

When the future seems to hold little promise for improvement of one's status, a here-and-now orientation develops. Much of the social studies involves the there-and-then which is antithetical to the frame of reference of the disadvantaged learner. For such students, the fruits of learning too often must be seen as being practical and useful. The rewards of learning must also be immediate. These outcomes unfortunately are not readily obtainable or easily provided for in a field such as the social studies.

A final problem of the disadvantaged learner involves his difficulty in handling abstractions. Mastery and learning of abstractions require an adequate command of language, a storehouse of varied experience, and sufficient practice in the utilization of these intellectual processes. Disadvantaged students are, in general, severely deficient in these requisites.

Essential Characteristics of the Social Studies

Before dealing with some suggestions regarding social studies instruction for disadvantaged learners, three key considerations inherent in this segment of the school curriculum must be discussed.

Space and Time. Much of the content of the social studies is arranged in chronological order and students are usually forced to begin their study of these subjects at a point distant in time and in space. As stated earlier, disadvantaged students approach learning situations with limited world concepts and time orientations which stress the here and now. This discrepancy between the orientations of the disadvantaged learners and the basic scheme of organization of the social studies must be given serious consideration.

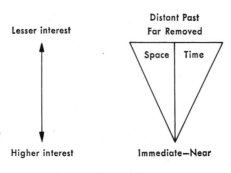

FIGURE A
TIME-SPACE ORIENTATION

Figure A illustrates that in dealing with the disadvantaged student, there is a better chance of arousing greater interest and higher levels of motivation if subjects, units, or problems in the social studies consider that which is here and now, before proceeding to content which is more removed from reality. Teachers and those developing curriculum must be cognizant of this fact and should consequently persist in instructional approaches which observe this point.

Intellectual Processes. The social studies are concerned with the production of ideational and attitudinal learning in students. Because of this, those basic intellectual processes most commonly used in seeking these modifications of student behavior involve the processes depicted in Figure B. Memorizing information and understanding its meaning are essential within the social studies. These basic processes provide the foundation for the higher intellectual activities of reflection, analyses of relationships among data, and critical thought. The processes of memorization and understanding are, perhaps easier to engender in students than those processes illustrated at the apex of the present schema.

All too frequently, social studies instruction is limited to the low-

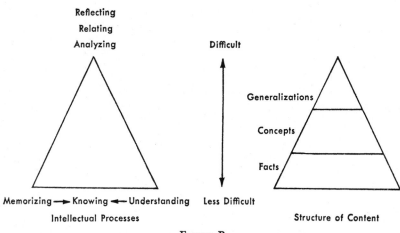

FIGURE B

level activities of memorizing and understanding isolated facts of the social studies. Teachers of disadvantaged students, frequently faced with additional problems of retarded reading and limited experience on the parts of their students, often resort to secondary processes for their class, and pay heed solely to those aims illustrated at the base of the triangle in Figure B.

It is the firm conviction of this author that disadvantaged learners are capable of engaging in higher intellectual processes. Consequently, teachers must include these processes as specific goals of their instructional efforts.

Structure of Content. The final consideration to be mentioned here involves the dimensions into which the content of the social studies is organized or structured for instruction and learning. The content of any social studies subject can be organized into three types of knowledge: Facts, Concepts, and Generalizations.

Facts are the foundation upon which learning in the social studies is based. They provide the basic matter required for the more integrative and sophisticated uses which can be made of knowledge. Too often, however, the mere mastery of these facts becomes the primary goal of instruction in numerous social studies classes.

Concepts are abstractions which can be used to construct classes of related phenomena. They allow man to integrate related knowledge, and they facilitate the communication of ideas. For example, the concept of government allows for the instantaneous pooling together of a number of facts regarding the institution of government and the various forms which it might take.

The fruitful development and utilization of concepts obviously necessitates the learning of a variety of facts. Concept mastery is more difficult to accomplish than the mere learning of facts, but is essential for the progression to the final dimension of content organization and utilization—the use of generalizations.

Generalizations are verbalized abstractions in the form of statements concerning relationships between or among concepts. Example:

A high level of industrialization in a country is usually associated with a high level of educational attainment.

The proper application of this generalization requires that the learner have prior understanding of the meanings and implications of the concepts of industrialization and education(al) attainment. If proven to be true during analysis, it provides the learner with a powerful tool for the integration of new and old knowledge.

The development of the ability to discover and to use generalizations is a difficult task, but one which is essential for meaningful social studies instruction. Nothing illustrates to students the power and utility of knowledge more clearly than do generalizations.

Too little of the social studies curriculum and instruction seeks to or does accomplish this level of content mastery with disadvantaged or advantaged learners.

Some Suggestions for Teaching Social Studies to Disadvantaged Learners

I firmly believe that the typical social studies programs being followed in public schools today fail to reach the majority of disadvantaged learners. These failures can be attributed to a lack of awareness or concern for the problems discussed above. In light of this situation, the following are offered as possibilities for the improvement of both the general social studies curriculum and of the instructional practices used therein.

Curriculum Modifications Needed. It is unrealistic to expect alienated, unmotivated, and often retarded readers to cover the content of a subject and to achieve the degree of masery of it as would more advantaged readers.

Despite possible opposition and criticism from certain groups, the social studies curriculum for disadvantaged learners must reflect parsimony and wise selections of learning experiences and content. Research on retention by Ebbinghaus[1] and others has clearly documented

---

[1] Ebbinghaus, H., *Memory, a Contribution to Experimental Psychology* (translated by H. A. Ruger and Clara Bussenius). New York: Teachers College, Columbia University, 1913, Chapter VI.

the fact that over one half the material mastered during a learning situation is forgotten after an interim of about six months. Because of this, only essential information which will supplement and augment material to be encountered later should be presented to the retarded learner in the social studies curriculum. Such material, after being carefully analyzed for content of concepts and generalizations, should be organized so that the more important issues continually reappear throughout the curriculum in degrees of increased complexity and sophistication. An example of such an evaluation for the concept of labor and its concomitant knowledge is shown below.

(Grades 1–3) *Work* (labor)	(Grades 4–6) *Labor*	(Grades 7–9) *Labor*	(Grades 10–12) *Labor*
Socially important; jobs and functions.	As specialization; as a resource essential for industrialization.	Division of labor; Labor as a determinant of social roles; Labor as a movement.	As a commodity; as a source of goods and services; as a basis for social differentiation and stratification.

In addition to the foregoing, it is equally essential that the social studies curriculum be organized to bridge the gap between the current status of the disadvantaged learner's interests, readiness, and perceptions and the content that is to be learned. A reversal is perhaps needed in the usual order of presentation of subject matter. For example, a consideration of some current civil or social strife (Viet Nam or the Los Angeles riots) might be used to introduce the study of the Civil War, Texas Rebellion, Boston Massacre, or slave rebellions. Parallels between the introduction and later class discussions might also be drawn to increase the student's understanding and realizations of the dynamics possible in the study of social studies.

Current textbooks and courses of study are not designed to accomplish the above, and because of this such efforts must be undertaken by teachers themselves.

As already stated, much of the social studies content is ego-alien to disadvantaged students. Such subject matter presented is viewed as uninteresting, unrelated to life, and even as threatening to those perceptions of reality held by the disadvantaged student.

Social studies are further alien to those members of ethnic groups whose past contributions to American life have been "white-washed" and obliterated from the pages of our textbooks. If appropriate books are not available, teachers must (a) prepare supplementary materials dealing with these omissions and (b) integrate them in a natural way into the content of the course. Units on cultural development and social issues appear to offer natural introductions for such materials. This can best be done in units dealing with cultural and social events during a certain historical period.

The lock-step pattern of requiring the same course for all students is a problem of the social studies curriculum. We continue to do things in a particular way because that is the way they have always been done. Dr. T. Bentley Edwards[2] has recently suggested a worthwhile idea for the revision of high school courses in United States history. Edwards feels, and I agree, that American history courses can be modified to appeal to a broader range of students. Envisioned is the provision for various sections of history, listed under the general rubric of United States History. Each section would then emphasize different aspects of this country's history. Sample course descriptions would include:

Sec. 1. U.S. History: Emphasis on the diplomatic affairs of the United States.

Sec. 2. U.S. History: Emphasis on the great social problems which have confronted the American people, for example, enlarging democracy, slavery, rights of workers, immigration, and the like.

Sec. 3. U.S. History: Emphasis on the scientific and technological development of the American people.

Sec. 4. U.S. History: Emphasis on the great intellectual and ethical ideas that have shaped American thought.

Sec. 5. U.S. History: Emphasis on the development of the arts (graphic, dramatic, literary, and others) in American history.

Such sections would be selected by the students on a voluntary basis. Advantages of this curriculum organization would include the utilization of special talents and preparations on the parts of the teachers and, hopefully, would arouse greater interest on the parts of the students.

Instructional Modifications Needed. The major responsibility in the battle of successfully educating the disadvantaged learner in the social studies falls upon the shoulders of the classroom teachers, who can be considered the infantrymen of education.

Ausubel[3] suggests three important considerations for these teachers. First, the readiness of these learners must be taken into consideration. This carries with it the in plication that, initially at least, much of the instruction should be diagnostic and should result in knowledge of the

---

[2] The author has been informed of this through a conversation with Dr. Edwards.
[3] Ausubel, D. P., "Teaching Strategy for Culturally Deprived Pupils: Cognitive and Motivational Considerations." *School Review*, LXXI, Winter, 1963.

real learning problems to be overcome. With this knowledge, teaching would be guided by the student's understanding, and repetitions of un-needed content would be avoided.

Second, that which is presented to students should be thoroughly learned before new material is introduced. Third, the content of the subject taught should be organized to promote efficient learning and retention. This last suggestion necessarily calls for the repetition of materials within a variety of contexts. Students must also be required to re-use in meaningful ways that which has already been learned.

Another major suggestion to the teacher is one which has often been stated. That is, initially at least, the presentation of content must proceed from the concrete to the abstract. For example, it is one thing to lecture, discuss, or conduct a recitation on the Federal Reserve System, and still another to set up a model example in one's class. Role playing is particularly effective with disadvantaged learners if well conceived because it is able to lead to greater emotional and intellectual involvement on the parts of the participants. Further, it provides opportunities for them to use oral language and critical thinking of the problems presented.

Discovery, a term frequently used today, seems to offer much as an instructional approach to the education of the disadvantaged. During the summer of 1965, this author had the pleasure of teaching a social studies class to a group of adolescents enrolled in the Special Scholarship Opportunities Program of the University of California, Berkeley. This program is designed to prepare and, hopefully, to increase the motivations of disadvantaged and ethnic-minority-group students for higher education. The social studies course was unlike the typical secondary school course in that it presented selected basic concepts from the fields of sociology, economics, and political science. Students complaints within this Opportunities Program about the difficult nature of reading assignments led to the application of the discovery method. Whenever possible, hypothetical situations involving groups or individuals and the concepts under consideration at the time were created. These situations were then analyzed and acted out prior to the time that the students were to read their text materials. For example, in stimulating the students to discover, learn, understand, and effectively use such concepts as social organization, roles, status, norms, sanctions (informal and formal), communication, and integration, a hypothetical small electronics factory was created in the class. Problems designed to elicit the discovery of concept objectives were also presented to the group and, finally, related text materials were assigned.

Because disadvantaged students are generally lacking in experiences required for efficient learning, teachers should aim at overcoming these weaknesses through the use of interesting instructional techniques. Audio-visual aids are useful for this purpose. Indeed, some English teachers report that the new films, records, and filmstrips available in their field have radically changed the levels of interest in and comprehension of such units as Shakespearean drama.

If such interesting graphic, audio-visual, and written materials are not available, teachers and those instructional divisions in central offices of school districts should create or devise them. Three student teachers of this author, for example, recently devised a twenty-page, objective, and well-integrated "textbook" on city, county, and state government. The duplicated text was supplemented by charts and drawings prepared by the teachers as well as by audio-visual aids obtained from a variety of sources. Prior to this effort on the part of these teachers, many of their students, who read two to three grade levels below that expected, had been forced to wade through those generally unstimulating books and pamphlets available from various agencies and governmental divisions.

From the foregoing then, it can be seen that a crisis faces the field of social studies instruction. The lawlessness on the parts of large segments of both our poorly educated disadvantaged white and Negro populations and the social apathy of our more favored social class strata are examples of the failure of our schools first, and other social institutions second, to develop the desired values and attitudes needed for the enhancement of a democratic way of life.

The above suggestions are minimal but serve their purposes, in light of this present situation, if they stimulate concern and thought, and result in creative innovations.

In a multi-ethnic and socioeconomically stratified democratic society there is perhaps no body of subject matter more important than the social studies. For a democratic society to persist and to grow toward a broader fulfillment of its goals for all persons, certain attitudes and values must be effectively taught, and then learned by each succeeding generation.

ฬ•ฬ

The Culturally Deprived Child
and Science

ฬ•ฬ

SAMUEL MALKIN

Educators have always had the problem of adapting the curriculum to the needs of children with special problems. Today teachers throughout the country, particularly in urban areas, are being confronted in ever-increasing numbers by the special problem of the culturally deprived or disadvantaged child. In New York City, it is estimated that 225,000 out of 573,000 elementary school children and 75,000 out of 186,000 junior high school pupils are in that category. Coupled with the disadvantaged or culturally deprived child is the non-English speaking child. About 11.5 percent of the entire elementary school population of New York City speak English haltingly or not at all.[1]

What are some characteristics of these children? In working with them, one quickly becomes aware of their general lack of achievement in the basic academic skills of reading, writing, and arithmetic; their general low self-image; and their lack of interest. Then one becomes aware of their limited experiences. What we tend to take for granted in youngsters—that they are familiar with gardens, pets, automobiles, trains, bicycles, elevators, and the country—is not necessarily true for these children. Indeed, many have never strayed from their own neighborhood or block, even though they may live in a city with many places to go and things to do.

Reprinted with permission from *Science and Children*, Vol. I, No. 7, April, 1964. Copyright by the National Science Teachers Association, Washington, D.C. 20036. The author is supervisor of Audio-visual Instruction, New York City Board of Education.

[1] *Higher Horizons Progress Report.* Board of Education of the City of New York. January 1963.

What are some of the conditions that cause cultural deprivation? Although poverty may not in itself be a cause, most culturally deprived children come from poor areas. Many come from broken homes or from families with deteriorated social standards; many come from areas where there is conflict between their own existing subculture and the standard American middle-class culture. Then, too, these areas may contain a constantly changing population with families moving in, staying awhile, and moving away again. The youngsters may have no roots, no feelings of loyalty, or no sense of responsibility to the community.

Teachers need orientation to work with these children since the children's expectations contrast sharply with the teaching and therapeutic processes which the teacher is normally trained to use. For example, these children desire authority and direction rather than training in self-direction; they desire action rather than introspection; they desire structure and organization rather than a permissive situation; they desire simple, more concrete, scientificallly demonstrable explanations rather than symbolic, circuitous interpretations; and they desire informal, sympathetic, nonpatronizing relationships rather than intensive ones.[2]

These desires and expectations of the disadvantaged child are positive elements upon which a functional and developmental curriculum can be built. Frank Riessman, in his book *The Culturally Deprived Child*,[3] strongly advocates such an approach. His observations identify other elements which have a direct bearing on the development of curriculum for these children. These are ability in abstract thinking, but at a slower rate than middle-class children; skill in nonverbal communication; greater achievement when tasks are motor-oriented; and greater motivation to tasks which have tangible and immediate goals.

An elementary science program for such children must be based on the positive elements of the characteristics, environment, and expectations of these children.

What Are the Features of Such a Program?

An elementary science program must be based on the pupils' environment.

Children are concerned with the world about them; the sound of bells, thunder and lightning, automobiles, airplanes, trees, birds, and

---

[2] Frank Riessman. *Some Suggestions Concerning Psychotherapy with Blue Collar Patients.* Mobilization for Youth and Department of Psychiatry, Columbia University, New York City. Unpublished Mimeographed Paper. 1963. p. 4.

[3] Frank Riessman. *The Culturally Deprived Child.* Harper and Row, New York City. 1962.

their own bodies. Disadvantaged children are no exception; however, their own world may not be the same as their teacher's world. To the teacher, larva, pupa, and butterfly are part of nature; to the pupils these may be meaningless because they may never have seen these things. Skyscrapers, concrete, and alley cats are more meaningful to these children than the Grand Canyon, sedimentary rocks, and protozoa. The culturally deprived child's environment is quite restricted, and we must seek from his environment those elements familiar to him and build our program upon them.

It is also important to enlarge the pupil's environment. This suggests that he be given direct experiences through audio-visual materials. A trip to the farm or zoo where the urban slum child can see and fondle farm animals, a lesson on magnetism where he and his fellow pupils can handle many different magnets, or a film which shows him what makes night and day are all experiences which enlarge the pupil's concepts about his environment.

An Elementary Science Program Must Be Based on Real Problems

Children ask questions about their environment and want answers to their questions. Some of these questions are: How does the school bell ring? What makes the light go on? Why do we want to explore outer space? How can we keep food from spoiling? How does the weatherman forecast weather? How does a telephone work? How can my skates roll more easily? What makes a car stop? Whereas many children frequently obtain the correct answers to their questions from parents or from books, the culturally deprived youngsters generally do not. Their parents are not able to help them and they are not able or motivated to help themselves. They must rely on the school for the correct answer, or else be satisfied with misinformation or no answer. The implications are clear. The teacher must gear her program to help these children find answers to questions about their environment. Indeed, the teacher may need to help the children verbalize questions which their environment has led them to submerge. Questions, such as those listed above, could and should serve as the aims of lessons in elementary science. By basing the aims of her lessons on real problems, the teacher can capitalize on pupils' interest and compensate for the learning they should, but do not, receive at home.

Elementary Science Should Not Depend on Reading or Other Academic Skills

A major weakness of the disadvantaged child is lack of achievement in reading and other academic skills. This lack of achievement in reading probably accounts, in large measure, for lack of success in other curriculum areas which depend on reading. If an elementary science program is to be successful, then the pupils must feel that they can succeed in science. I conceive of elementary science as a truly "democratic" subject—democratic to the extent that every child can participate in, and get a feeling of, achievement and success from it. Therefore, it is important that activities be so chosen that they do not discourage children. One way to do this is to use children's language skills, other than reading, in the elementary science program. Such skills as listening, speaking, reporting, observing, and note-taking (at the pupil's level) should be encouraged.

Teachers should plan lessons which draw on pupils' experiences, and the conclusions to each lesson should be elicited from the class in the pupils' own language. Audio-visual materials should be used extensively to provide basic information and material for research. Children can use filmstrips with individual viewers just as they would use books. The formation of soil and the operation of the water cycle can be demonstrated more effectively by films than by books.

Although the basic science program should not depend on textbooks, children should have contact with many science books at their own reading level. Thus, instead of 30 books of a basic series of texts on one grade level in a class, it might be possible to have 30 books of many series at different levels. Trade books on many topics at varying reading levels should be available. In this way, children could select those books which they are able to read, and which do not frustrate them.

Elementary Science Should Reinforce Basic Academic Skills

Although this may seem contrary to what was previously stated, it it not. Elementary science can and should encourage and motivate growth in reading. As these children get a feeling of success from their science activities, they may be motivated to greater achievement. Thus, they can be encouraged to use some of the trade and textbooks that are to be found in the room. Elementary science can provide even more basic reading experiences. Labelling of specimens, models, and charts provide reading experiences, as do captions on filmstrips. In my own experience, at the end of each lesson I ask the children to tell me what they have learned from that lesson. Their own statements are written on large sheets of paper and the pupils copy these in their notebooks. Many weeks later the pupils are able to read their statements, although they may not be able to read at that level in their basal readers. They are able to read their experience charts because they are motivated to learn to read those statements which arise from their own experience. Elementary science is used to motivate these pupils.

A more formal experiment correlating science and reading is being conducted by Richard Kinney, at Public School No. 188 in Manhattan. In this experiment, reading lessons, based on the children's science experiences, are being prepared on three reading levels. The results so far have been encouraging and point to further study in this area.

Elementary Science Should Afford Children Opportunities to Handle Materials and Equipment

A fundamental concept in teaching elementary science is that all children should have an opportunity to handle materials and equipment. This is especially true for the culturally deprived child since he seems to have greater achievement when tasks are motor-oriented. Teachers, therefore, should provide every opportunity for children to participate in demonstrations and experiments. If possible, there should be enough material so that every child can use the same materials at his seat that his teacher is using at her desk. Kits of materials can be organized which contain, for example, 30 dry cells, 30 switches, 30 bells, and pieces of wire, or 30 sets of different magnets. The materials that are used should be familiar to children. Esoteric and elaborate equipment should be avoided since it may be confusing to children; and assume importance rather than the science concepts being demonstrated. Children should be given recognition for their projects by having their exhibits displayed to other pupils as well as to their parents and to the community at periodic science fairs.

Through proper adaptation of the elementary science curriculum to the needs of this large portion of our children, we may bring about an enrichment of their lives which, in turn, will benefit our entire community. We have, so far, failed to tap America's greatest resources, the creative skills and abilities of all its children. Among these disadvantaged children, there is a large reservoir of future high-level, professional, and skilled personnel, if we learn how to help them realize their potential.

Throughout the country, experimentation with curriculum development for the culturally deprived children, such as the "Higher Horizons Program" and "Mobilization for Youth" in New York City are providing insights into the techniques of teaching such children. Through implementation of our new insights, both society and the child will benefit.

꒰•꒱

Disadvantaged Children and Their Parents

꒰•꒱

JOSEPH C. PAIGE

The Howard University Elementary Science Project (ESP) has been designed to fill some educational gaps of children and their parents that have resulted from economic deprivation. The purposes of ESP are (1) to develop a program of compensatory science experiences for disadvantaged children (K-6) and their parents; (2) to determine whether or not the participation in these experiences by disadvantaged children and their parents can help, in a significant way, to overcome social and personal handicaps which usually attend such privation; and (3) to discover what changes in behavior in both children and parents may result from participation in the project.

The Project, supported by a grant from the Cooperative Research Branch, U. S. Office of Education, grew out of the need to provide innovations to conventional efforts in education that schools in deprived areas either could not or have failed to provide for their students. The program attempts to involve children and their parents simultaneously. Children from kindergarten through sixth grade are given simple instructions for participation in science experiences, to be performed jointly with their parents at school or in their homes.

Project investigation has suggested an urgent need for some drastic reforms in the teaching of science in slum area public schools. ESP research also suggests some basic weaknesses in the teaching of some non-science subjects. Hence, the Project has many implications for school

Reprinted with permission from *Science and Children,* Vol. 2, No. 6, May, 1965. Copyright by the National Science Teachers Association, Washington, D.C. 20036. Dr. Paige is director of the Elementary Science Project at Howard University and helps coordinate the Physical Science Program at the Natural Sciences Program (Honors) in the College of Liberal Arts. In addition, he is Coordinator of the Advanced Education Task Group of the Instructional Systems Division of Litton Industries. A statistical evaluation of the project is currently being made.

systems which have not found adequate means of dealing with these disadvantaged children.

Cooperating Centers

Cooperating centers have been established in Washington, D. C., North Carolina, and New York City. (In Washington, D. C., the Katie C. Lewis School and the New Samaritan Baptist Church serve as centers. In North Carolina, four rural groups comprise one center. In New York, The East River Children's Center of Mills College of Education serves as the center.) Discussions are also under way to use the Project materials in some of the programs of the Howard University Community Service Center and the Model School System of the District of Columbia. More than 300 children and their parents have used the materials in cooperating centers of the Project.

Selection of Participants

When selecting participants for the Project, special consideration is given to persons in the lowest socioeconomic categories. Criteria for family participation in the program includes the following:

1. Residence within the area of a cooperating center;
2. Agreement to attend Saturday sessions by all siblings in grades K-6, and at least one parent or adult member of the household;
3. Free of any physical disability that might impede reasonable participation in program activities;
4. Free of serious behavior problems which the project staff considered undesirable from the point of view of classroom control or teacher effectiveness;
5. Reasonable facility with the English language; and
6. Socioeconomic status of the family within the range generally described as representative of "deprived" or "disadvantaged" circumstances, except in special cases.

Procedure

The operation is divided into four phases. Phase I covered the period of March 1-September 30, 1964; this phase consisted of the development and testing of some materials with respect to their utility. A Summer Writing Conference comprised Phase II. Phase III (still in process) consists of expanded development and testing of materials produced during the Summer Writing Conference of the 1964-65 school year. Phase IV will deal with evaluation of the 1964-65 trial materials, a writing conference, and Project expansion.

Each Project center works with twenty families. Coordinators and interviewers are assigned to explain the Project to the families in home visits. This prepares families for the science experiences to be conducted at home and group meetings, and to establish liaison between the families and the center group. All ESP personnel are readied for this work by an orientation program which includes the following topics: (1) assumptions and aims of the Project, (2) social problems and resources in the local area, (3) problems of communication, (4) methods for approaching, interviewing, and working with disadvantaged persons, (5) group dynamics, and (6) use of the science materials.

Volunteer Assistants

Nonprofessionals comprise the corps of volunteer assistants for the Project. The volunteers are, for the most part, undergraduate college students, high school graduates, and some school dropouts. All volunteers are trained by the Project staff. A volunteer worker has a threefold role. He serves as interviewer, tutor, and aide. As interviewer, he has the responsibility of visiting the homes of a specified number of families to establish necessary rapport, and to collect pertinent data. The volunteer also participates in scheduled periodic interviews usually held by a Project staff member on Saturdays following the science participation session.

As tutor, he visits homes and assists children and their parents in performing their home science experiences. His responsibility as an aide is to assist the teacher-coordinator in all aspects of the science participation program.

Individual histories, reports from interviews, observations of classroom teachers, and other reports of the participating families are made available to the volunteer assistants. This background information enables the assistant to evaluate the progress the entire family is making during their participation in the program.

Home Visits

Home visits by coordinators, interviewers, and volunteer assistants help to effect cooperation among family members in performing the experiences and to prepare them for sharing as families in the programs at the center. Several inter-family projects have been established at the centers.

Supplementary Meetings

Additional sessions for children and adults are scheduled at various homes. These sessions may center around one of the science experiences, a related area, a new science topic, or any area of interest to the group. These sessions are aimed at raising questions of personal and community health and welfare, suggesting relations between science and other areas, and broadening general experiences. In performing the science experiences at home, participants are encouraged to cope with problems in their own way and to follow-up whatever new problems develop.

Small Group Organization

The organization of the centers into small groups has several advantages. It facilitates the coordination of Project operations and observations. Participants seem to develop (1) a sense of individual pride through increased general literacy and scientific literacy in particular, (2) a sense of family pride and harmony through successful interactions in a common experience, (3) the power of articulating needs through science experiences, and (4) a new awareness of the world in which they live.

Design of Experiences

1. *Materials.* Materials for the experiences include science packets, kits, and simple items adapted to the disadvantaged persons. The Project also draws materials from other national science programs, adapting them when necessary to fit into the aims of ESP. To date, the Project has used modifications of material developed by the Elementary Science Study, Educational Services, Inc.; Science Service, Inc.; Science Materials Center, Inc.; and Ward's Natural Science Establishment.

2. *Plan.* The assumption is made that the attention span of our participants is short; discouragement is easy. Hence, the science experiences are designed to be short and simple, yet probing enough to arouse and hold the interest of children and adults. Each experience is designed to allow the participants to make his own discoveries.

3. *Format.* Elementary Science Project kits present wide flexibility with respect to the interests and abilities of family groups. Each kit consists of some simple materials and a work booklet which takes into account the limitations of the participants.

The organizational format of the work booklet provides a minimum set of directions, guiding the children and their parents through the experience by raising questions. Observation and our experience has shown that questions raised by the child- or parent-manipulator and the "trial" and "error" follow-ups, are far more significant than the questions suggested by the materials. The answers to these questions have taken a variety of forms, some have required thought, others have required careful experimentation, and detailed observations.

The design of the science experiences are basically open-ended. Materials have been designed to help the experimenter to develop a logical consistency in his explanation, rather than seeking a correct answer. Understanding of a particular concept or generality is emphasized. "Yes" or "no" answers to questions are discouraged in all Elementary Science Project experiences. Instead, discussions are encouraged whenever questions are raised. In fact, a major provision of the Project plan is that discussion will develop concurrently with the experimentation.

Fifty experience packets have been tested by the Project staff. These materials were the products of the 1964 Summer Writing Conference and cover such diverse topics as: light, color, heat, pressure, friction, nutrition, sensual perception, crystals, metals, magnets, suction cups, and taste. The selection of these topics was somewhat arbitrary, but the staff thought that they would serve to encourage discovery, inference, exploration, observation, and other competencies, attitudes, and skills.

The design of the science experience is to help participants learn (1) how to observe and to keep accurate records of their observations, (2) how to follow directions, (3) how to make accurate measurements, and (4) how to apply some of what they learn to daily living.

One other objective of the Project is the hope that through home and group activities, the subjects might gain experience in (1) meeting unexpected situations, (2) making initial contact with people, (3) arousing interest in problems of mutual concern, and (4) soliciting and utilizing the opinions of others for constructive individual and group action.

Evaluation

At this time, the real value of the Project is difficult to appraise. Parent participants in the Project, rarely, if ever, attended the meetings of the parent-teacher associations, neighborhood clubs, or community civic groups. The children had occasionally attended after-school programs at school, church, or a movie, but seldom, if ever, with their parents. After they had been helped individually in their own homes and at the Saturday sessions, many of these family groups began to relate to each other, to their neighbors, to the community, and to the school. The success of ESP will have to be measured in the positive behavior changes of the children and their parents, as reflected in improved reading and verbal skills, development of scientific attitudes and reasonable competencies, improved human relations practices, and more specifically, in the willingness to share community leadership and work for the solution of community problems.

ഗ•ഗ

Practical Ideas for Building Better Relationships with Parents of the Disadvantaged Kindergarten Learner

ഗ•ഗ

RUBY OSBORNE

Kindergarten classes can become a natural laboratory for extending parent-school experiences on any socioeconomic level. Good communications and involvement of parents are assets for promoting better home-school relationships.

These were some of my personal convictions when I met my first kindergarten class in a disadvantaged area.

My new school was located near a small industrial city of the East Bay in the San Francisco metropolitan area. This school first opened in the fall of 1951 for the purpose of teaching approximately 575 children and serving about 200 families. The majority of the students were Negroes. Very few of them were Spanish-speaking. Thirty kindergarten children were enrolled in my class. Of this number, approximately two had Spanish backgrounds. This composition has remained about the same each year.

I had nearly ten years of experience teaching young children when I accepted this assignment. Yet I was not prepared for the situations which faced me the first day. Maybe I had been living in a "pretend world" too long a time.

Here are some of the situations which were a reality:

1. Kindergarten children who would not tell me their names.
2. Kindergarten children who would not tell me their addresses.

Printed with permission of the author, who teaches kindergarten at Verde School, Richmond, California.

3. Kindergarten children without a telephone in their homes. Those who had them did not know their telephone numbers.

4. Kindergarten children who could not care for their personal needs such as taking off their coats or recognizing their own clothing.

5. Kindergarten children without the knowledge of how to use a handkerchief or cleaning tissue properly.

6. Kindergarten children who refused to go to the toilet alone.

7. Kindergarten children who were too unhappy or angry to say "good morning" in response to their teacher.

It would be wrong for me to report that all members of this class had these "kindergarten learning deficiencies," but the percentage was high enough to register a shocking impression on me!

I felt the need for help from parents more than I ever had in my teaching career. It was because of this real need that I began experimenting with various practical ways of "getting to know" parents better in order to be a more effective teacher. The ideas presented here all seem helpful to me in accomplishing my goal.

Home Visitations. One of the best ways to get acquainted with parents is to meet them in their homes. Maybe it is because the setting is informal. The teacher, I believe, should make the overture. I started visiting parents of the children in my classroom in the year of 1957 and have continued this practice. Many visits are made without the usual social custom of telephoning because some homes have no telephone. Some parents prepare special treats for me if the visit is preceded by a telephone call. Parents receive me with warmth and enthusiasm. Smaller classes or a teacher assistant would permit me to do many more home visits.

Orientation Meetings. Orientation meetings were started in September, 1957. Similar meetings have been held every year since that first one. The meeting is scheduled not more than three weeks after school opens. A fellowship time before the meeting is planned with refreshments. Plans for the year are presented. Parents are told how they can help at home, then questions from parents are encouraged. The number of questions has increased from year to year. The parents are given a booklet published by our county office in order to read more about kindergarten children.

The number of parents attending these meetings has increased progressively. Last year approximately 38 parents attended. (About 50 children were enrolled in both classes.) Many parents who could not attend sent notes or telephoned, giving their regrets.

Individual Conferences. At least one individual conference is scheduled for each child during the school year. For the last three years, the school district has paid a substitute teacher for one day. Conferences are scheduled on that day. Previously, conferences were scheduled between sessions and after school.

Last year, I solicited the help of four "advantaged parents" from this area to make telephone calls the night before the conference day to remind other parents of appointments. The results were exciting!

Parents are encouraged to express themselves while a progress report is evaluated. Sometimes, I need to seek other professional advice in order to answer questions properly.

Letters from the Teacher. During the first week of school in September, a letter is sent home with each child. This letter is intended to reduce the fears and anxieties of parents concerning school. It also requests that each parent, for safety reasons, teach or review with his child his name, address, and telephone number. Thank you letters and other written communication are sent home throughout the year when it seems necessary. These letters suggest a way for parents to communicate with me. This is especially true in homes with no telephone. My "correspondence received" has increased yearly.

Parent Assistants on Study Trips. At least one study trip has been planned each year. As many parents as we can accommodate on a school bus are invited to participate. This invitation is well-received. One time we had more parents than we could accommodate. Our principal suggested that some parents go together in private cars and follow the bus. This idea solved our problem. Parents are a "must" for an effective study trip. Many parents have expressed a greater understanding of my teaching problems after participating in a study trip.

Classroom Visitations during the Regular Day. Parents are encouraged to visit my classroom at any time. These visits are for observations only. The number of parents visiting has increased each year. Last year approximately fifteen parents visited. Some parents remain at school to observe when they bring their children to school.

An Invitational Party in the Classroom. Before the Christmas vacation begins, the children in my class and I plan a party for their parents. Christmas songs and poetry are presented by the children. One year we had a "Sing-Along" and "Read-Along" with parents participating in song and verse. The children serve the parents refreshments. The children are delighted to plan these parties.

Conclusions

It is difficult to evaluate this practical experiment. Many changes have taken place since my first day here in the fall of 1957. For example:

1. A cooperative nursery school opened in this community three years ago.

2. Written communications and home visits have been made by the principal, school nurse, and other teachers.

3. There has been a change of attitudes, both locally and nationally, concerning the disadvantaged learner.

4. This summer a "Head Start Program" was held in this school.

However, with these influencing factors in mind, I still submit the following:

a. A larger percentage of parents have accepted their responsibility in teaching their children the skills they should know before coming to kindergarten.

b. My professional advice is now more often accepted by parents.

c. My reaction to parents is with sincere respect for their helpfulness, practical suggestions, and natural insights. Our relationship seems to be a better one!

ᴄ•ᴄ

Teacher-Parent Communication:
An Approach

ᴄ•ᴄ

Arnette Edwards

Are you pleased with your child's progress? Will he be prepared to take a job that will help him to live a better life in the future or will he be a dropout? How can you help him to have a more successful year in school? Here are some of the questions that were put to the parents of the children in my fourth-grade class when they met one Wednesday evening in the home of my room mother, Mrs. Johnson. There were twenty concerned parents present on this evening, which was a result of some planning by both my room mother and me. At the beginning of and during each school semester, I make it a point to contact each parent by phone to inform him of the school program and to ask for cooperation in helping his child to do better work in school. A visit is made to the homes of those families without telephones. This gives me insight into the child's background and those problems he might be having; I can see him in a different perspective. This also makes for better parent/teacher relationships and eliminates many barriers or fears parents have of teachers and schools. Because of this, school is seen as a friendly place, where there is interest in the welfare of their children. Most parents respond positively to this program. Some need more calling and visiting than others but it is important to keep contacting them. It is also during this contacting that I get a room mother who helps me with parties, field trips, and telephone calls.

Our school, Burnett Elementary School, is in an area frequently referred to as "culturally deprived." The principal, Mr. Don Anderson, is extremely aware of the problems existing within our community and

Printed with permission of the author, who is fourth-grade teacher at Burnett School in San Francisco, California.

is very much concerned. He stresses good school-community relations and thinks of each child as an individual person, not just as a "culturally deprived child." The judgments usually made about this type of school are untrue on the whole. Parents *are* interested in their children, the children *can* learn and achieve, and do so. Every child is not behind. They come to school neatly dressed and many of them have lovely homes. There is great potential within these students, but what is needed is more self-assurance and belief in oneself, more motivation and more sincere teacher interest. The children need to be told by both parents and teachers that they are of worth, that they can achieve.

Within this program I wanted to raise the achievement level of each child, to ask each parent seriously whether he was doing the best he could to help his child in school. Did his child value his education? The parents needed to provide at home a quiet place to study, books for reference and pleasure reading, and encouragement for more use of the library. I needed to reach all the parents together, however, in order to put my point across.

I expressed these thoughts to my room mother one night while we were arranging the night meetings. She was very enthusiastic and volunteered her home for the meetings since the parents would probably feel freer in discussing their problems there.

The letters sent to the parents included a space to be filled in telling whether they could come to the scheduled meeting or not. Each letter was followed by a telephone call to assure the parents of the importance and worth of the meetings. Through this added emphasis, many of those who said initially they could not attend consented to come. Also, they seemed more interested and even requested to be able to invite someone else.

Response was enthusiastic the night of the meeting. Children were brought and fathers came. Car pools were formed for transportation. It was an informal meeting and I was careful to dress simply so that all would feel at ease, no matter how they might be dressed. The seating arrangement in the living room of Mrs. Johnson's home was also informal, in a semi-circle where everyone could easily be heard and seen.

During the meeting I expressed gratitude for the great response of the parents, and afterwards spoke freely about the children being ready and prepared for the future. During this period there was much discussion of sit-ins and bussing. The parents listened intently and then responded. There was much concern about what had been said, and specific ways to help children were requested. I talked to them about making use of the public library, providing magazines and books in their homes, and stressing the value of education and good behavior in school. Concrete suggestions were then given as to how to help with specific reading problems that were mentioned. Dittoed lists of suggestions were also given to the parents.

After the meeting, which lasted but one hour, refreshments were served while parents spoke individually about their own children's problems in school.

As a result of this meeting, a marked change in the attitude and behavior of the children was apparent. School seemed more important now. Study patterns and habits changed so that homework was returned neatly done, signed and checked by their parents. Due to increased help at home and a consistent time and place for studying, work done in the classroom also improved. In addition, more books were read and the children began to bring in many interesting articles to supplement what we were studying. There was respect for school. Some of the parents even got together on weekends and took their children on outings to various sites in our city. Many parents also contacted the principal of our school to express their thoughts about this program and to extend their cooperation in dealing with the children. Some would even come to reading or arithmetic lessons in the classroom in order to learn how to help in reading or arithmetic at home.

Another meeting, at the school, was set for a month later, with the principal present. We talked about some of the results that had taken place in the children since the last meeting and asked that the parents continue with our project. We reviewed ways of helping at home, and some of the aids that were being used to help build skills in the classroom were discussed. A group of the children presented a choral reading program for the parents at which the principal expressed his appreciation for parental interest. A proposed school bond issue of which our school was to be part was also introduced. The final meeting of the year was devoted to discovering ways to help keep the child creatively employed during the summer vacation.

These parent meetings have been scheduled for the past two years now. They have seemed to help the child, the school, and me—the teacher. Other teachers in our school are beginning to initiate similar programs. In reviewing the results of the program I must say that I have enjoyed meeting so many wonderful parents. The cooperation and interest exhibited have been excellent. One meeting, for example, was devoted to explaining the modern math program so that the parents could ask questions about it. Parents have even helped in the preparation of units on Negro history which enlightened the children considerably about the contributions of the Negro throughout history. They felt proud at last of their heritage; it gave them pride in themselves.

Meetings with parents such as those described here have proven to be a great help to any teacher, and more important, to the education of the students. Why not try it? It can really work.

Home Study—Second Grade

LAVERDA HENDERSON

On the second-grade level I made an effort to get parents involved in the reading program. The result was "My Take Home Book" which had its beginning in September, 1964.

With the opening of school of that year came interested parents who wanted their children to further classroom experiences through homework and various other activities.

School had been in session for two weeks when several parents asked me if their children could have homework. Of course their children could have homework! In fact, their children, as well as others in the classroom, had been taking home individual work sheets each day for about a week. However, each day the excuses and explanations were the same. "I forgot mine." "My mother washed mine in my pocket." "I lost mine, but I did it." "My mother put mine in the garbage." It was at this time that I decided to make a weekly assignment book where all papers would be kept together, sent home on Monday, and returned on Friday with each daily assignment completed.

On September 28, 1964, "My Take Home Book" No. 1 was sent home with the following objectives in mind:

1. To build a stronger link between the school, parents, teacher, and child.

2. To help parents become informed of the kind of work the child was engaged in, and to familiarize them with the curriculum.

3. To build the habit of responsibility for daily work.

4. To note the weekly progress of each child and to have evidence of the child's work for parent conferences.

Printed with permission of the author who is third grade teacher at Kensington Elementary School in Richmond, California.

5. To motivate individual studying.

6. To involve parents in helping to broaden the background of the child by seeing what was studied and extending weekend experiences involving the same.

7. To help evaluate children's strengths and weaknesses.

Many of these objectives were accomplished. Most of the children took pride in taking their books home, completing them, and returning them on Friday of each week. An average of twenty-three out of twenty-seven returned their books each week.

As a result of these workbooks, parents showed increased concern about their children's daily assignments. They often called to ask about assignments to make certain their children were doing the work properly. This was especially true when mathematical equations were put in their books. Interestingly, the two very slowest children made a special effort to do each assignment sheet, to return their books to be checked, and to make necessary corrections.

In addition to the above results of this program, many skills were reinforced and developed in reading, spelling, mathematics, and writing. A great deal of art work was also involved in making the covers for these books each week.

When the books were returned on Friday, we took from five to ten minutes to review the assignments and to make necessary corrections. Books were kept at school over a period of six weeks before the pupils took them home to keep. This was done to help evaluate the pupils' strengths and weaknesses and to give additional help in the area where it was most needed.

Using the News to Stimulate Growth in Reading

DONNA C. MACGREGOR

Some children are interested in animals, some in airplanes, some in baseball, but all children are interested in what's real, and what's happening right here and now. It was on this premise that I based my special reading and language program last year.

"Find sixty children in your school who are fairly normal in intelligence but are a year or more retarded in reading. See what you can do to help them." This was the challenge given to me as my city began a compensatory education experiment.

Finding sixty such pupils in grades four, five, and six was easy. In a large school serving a low-income housing project, there are many problems which affect language achievement. Some of the parents are nearly illiterate or poorly educated. In many homes, a language other than English is spoken. Some families have lived six months here, six months there, allowing little continuity in schooling. Health problems are numerous, creating poor attendance records. In spite of the school nurse's efforts, vision and hearing deficiencies are neglected. In about fifty percent of the homes, children are living with only one parent.

For sixty children with reading difficulties there are as many reasons, some easily understood, some defying detection. Test results and teacher judgment soon gave me sixty names—what to do with them was *my* problem.

The children were to be divided into five groups of twelve each to report to my room for approximately fifty minutes a day. Soon I discovered that many of my chosen ones were not overjoyed at the news

Printed with permission of the author, who is teacher of a compensatory class at John McLaren School in San Francisco, California.

that they were to "receive help in reading and language." Four or five years of struggling in the lowest group of every class had turned the words "book" and "reading" into symbols of defeat and discouragement. An extra dose of this was not especially welcome.

The materials selected for use in my class must be stimulating enough to make the children *want* to read. (Primers and preprimers were written for first graders—their content has no appeal for older children.) What could I find that would interest them all and yet be written simply enough to assure the taste of success which they so desperately needed?

After some weeks of trial and error in various fields, I discovered right at hand a continual source of reading material which would capture the attention of most children and which could easily be adapted to their reading levels. It was the newspaper! Here is how I have worked it out for use in my room.

Every morning before I cut from my newspaper twelve simple-to-read headlines and place one on each desk. As the children enter the room they attempt to read them. We take time to work out difficult words and to find many new concepts to add to our vocabulary lists. Frequently the same words will be repeated for several days, giving added reinforcement to the learnings. As the semester progresses, I find I can put out a small clipping instead of a headline, underline two or three key sentences, and have the child read it to the class.

Each day I select from my newspaper two or three articles which should interest my pupils. (I choose the articles myself in order to control the subject matter and I often find items in small print which the children might overlook.) The newspaper offers a wealth of subject matter. Clippings about animals, schools, firemen, policemen, famous people, space, and ships are all topics we can use. Surprisingly often items appear which are closely related to the lives of the children: possibly our school Girl Scouts are pictured; perhaps there was a fire in the neighborhood; maybe Johnny's big brother won third place in the high school track meet (his name may be in small letters, but there it is!)

To introduce a new clipping, I write on the board the headline of the article and then read or tell its content. Discussion follows, bringing out new words to add to vocabularies. Then we summarize the article in two or three simple sentences. (This is merely a cooperative story with adult content.) For the following day I paste the clipping on a sheet of 12 × 18 manila paper and print the news summary beneath it. The presentation of the previous day has prepared most children to read it easily and they do so proudly since this is "grown-up reading."

The stories remain pinned on the front board for several days and are reread each day. New ones, of course, are added daily and some old ones taken down.

From these stories we can develop many reading skills—structural analysis, phonetic skills, dictionary use. Sometimes worksheets are used to follow up the needs, sometimes oral drills, sometimes individual work. The key is to use these techniques while they are of meaning and interest to the child.

Some items are of interest for only a day or two but other stories are chosen to be read over and over again. Whenever a subject seems particularly appealing to children, we explore it further. Now we are ready to utilize other media to learn more about the topic. Various reading materials are used—library books, encyclopedias, magazines, related stories in easy readers, *Weekly Readers,* and perhaps further news clippings on the same subject. Visual aids now become more than mere entertainment. Flat pictures, records, tapes, and films can enrich vocabularies and build new concepts. My favorite is the filmstrip which frequently has simple reading material beneath each picture and which can be moved as slowly as needed. The children also learn to read maps in order to locate places mentioned in the news.

In a large city we often read about local points of interest. Whenever possible, field trips to these places can be invaluable aids to reading and language growth. Occasionally a visitor with information on one of our news topics can be invited to share his experiences (for example, a teacher who has visited a foreign country currently in the news). News topics and related experiences furnish the incentive for creative writing and we have seen considerable growth in ability to express thoughts on paper.

Following is a sample of the development of one center of interest stimulated by news reading:

1. We read several clippings about oceanography and current underwater explorations. The children were fascinated so we searched for more on this theme.

2. The encyclopedia gave us further information on oceans and divers.

3. *National Geographic Magazine* contained excellent pictures and articles of some explorations.

4. One issue of *Weekly Reader* had stories about divers.

5. In our library we found sea adventure tales.

6. Some of our readers contained stories about the ocean.

7. We ordered several related movies and filmstrips from our Visual Aids Department.

8. A skin diver's visit was a highlight. He brought his suit and equipment to show the children.

9. Original stories were written. Since we had previously studied about space, the children chose the topics "ocean" or "space," each telling which he would rather explore.

10. A bulletin board was used to display the work. It was labeled "Be an Explorer—Ocean or Space."

Our old stories are not discarded but saved to put into large books, classified as "News About Animals," "News about Firemen," and the like, for the children to read again and again. Since these are their own stories they never seem to tire of them.

After a few months of activities such as those described, the attitude toward the special class had changed greatly. Most of the pupils were eager to attend and to return to their own classes to share their experiences. Children who previously had little to contribute were able to participate intelligently in their class news period. At the end of the semester we planned a program to be presented to the entire school. We called it our "News Review of the Year" (such as radio reporters put on each December) with each child retelling one news story. This was taped and illustrated with slides from our trips and class work. The writing and rewriting of scripts, reading and rereading of parts on the tape were important and meaningful language experiences. Best of all, perhaps, was the lift in self-confidence which each child felt as reward for his contribution.

Results? A few cases have made spectacular progress. For example, a third-grade girl had been labeled a nonreader. Her group test score listed her I.Q. as 67. Fortunately, her teacher recognized this as an error and asked me to help her. I found her parents were almost illiterate and that the vocabulary was extremely limited. After four months of work of building a meaningful vocabulary, she could read fluently on fourth-reader level.

Of course, not all results have been as rapid as this. Over all, the average child has approximately doubled his expected reading rate; that is, in six months time in the class he has gained one year's growth in reading. Some cases have shown little progress in reading level but have improved greatly in attitude and interest in school work in general. A few very difficult problems have been referred to special reading clinics for further help.

Why has this approach worked so well? The answers, I think, are simple.

1. *It has meaning.* The material in the news is interesting and relevant to each child, whereas the adventures of a middle-class family in a primer may be far removed from reality for him.

2. *It is simple.* The few words from a headline or a three-sentence summary of a news item furnish material which the child can read with success. Thus he is encouraged to try larger hurdles.

3. *It is morale-building.* To be able to read a newspaper is "grown-up" reading as opposed to "baby books." The information gained is something he can use at home and at school in intelligent conversation.

4. *It leads to further learnings.* The variety of activities and skills which can result from a single news clipping is indeed gratifying.

To me, as the teacher, these adventures with the news are a challenging experience. Each day I find myself reading my newspaper through the eyes of a child, eagerly searching for articles which will awaken interest in my pupils. I enjoy trying to foresee what experiences may develop from each item. To be sure, not all these techniques can be used in a classroom of thirty-five pupils but many are adaptable. Were I again to teach in a regular classroom, I know I would make greater use of the news as a means of stimulating growth in reading and language.

꧁ • ꧂

The Learning Center: An Aid to Individualization of Instruction

꧁ • ꧂

WILLIAM F. HENDERSON

The beginning of the school year brought many new and interested faces into my fifth- and sixth-grade classroom. There were twenty-eight fifth graders and ten sixth graders in the following categories: nonreaders, 5; readers at grade level, 13; readers above grade level, 10; and "problem pupils," 10.

My past experiences with a heterogeneous group such as this had provided me with some foresight concerning problems that might arise unless a more practical approach to learning and classroom discipline was formulated. For example, during the regular reading period it was very difficult to have oral reading since both grades had different sets of readers and because of the existing different reading abilities. There were many pupils who resented anyone telling them how to pronounce certain words.

It was very difficult to teach one subject to one class at one time. My approaches therefore immediately began to contain techniques that were geared towards helping each individual pupil.

In an effort to motivate my pupils and impress them with some of the desirable concomitants of education, I decided to use the tape recorder and earphones as a classroom helper. This idea implemented my daily program and accentuated learning. The machine was used in the following areas or subjects.

Spelling. Weekly new words, help in misspelled words, words from other spelling lists, dictation.

Reading. Pronunciation, articulation, phonetic exercises.

Printed with permission of the author, who teaches at Pullman Secondary School in Richmond, California.

Arithmetic. Drills, speed tests, objective-type tests.

Special Reviews. Current events, music, biographical sketches.

In regard to major objectives, the principles of the "learning process" were used as guideposts. For example:

1. Whereas learning takes place as the pupil realizes purposes that are interesting and meaningful to him, it was anticipated that the pupils would enjoy this new experience as they realized main objectives.

2. Whereas learning is a process of growth through active participation, it was anticipated that the pupils would learn by doing and that such learning would be progressive.

3. Whereas learning proceeds best in actual life situations supplemented by books and other sensory instructional materials, efforts were made to transform all vicarious experiences into probable life situations.

4. Whereas learning is more effective as the learner is aware of his own progress toward the goal, pupils were required to record their scores on a progress chart.

The machine, located in a stationary area designed as a learning area or center, was used by both slower and faster groups. Tapes were prepared in advance by me and, in some cases, by pupil committees. For spelling and reading, the words were compiled from the Ayres list, *Success in Spelling* (Grade Six), new words from *Wings to Adventure,* and current events. Such words were selected on the basis of frequency of use as well as phonetic and structural characteristics.

The requirements for admittance to this learning center were, for the slower group, that the pupils had to make less than 50% on weekly tests; and for the faster group, that the pupils had to make 90% and higher on weekly tests. In addition, those pupils qualified to use the machine were to sign up on the pupils' schedule and selected pupils were rotated as "helpers" to assist the teacher while the learning center was in operation.

⚮•⚯

Turning Disadvantages into Advantages

⚮•⚯

Daisy Rivers Mante

In the summer of 1965 I had the privilege of being involved in an NDEA Institute on Disadvantaged Youth. As I began to meet and to talk with other teachers and administrators from all over the country, I became aware that their basic complaints were much the same as those I had heard discussed by teachers working with disadvantaged children in the Berkeley schools.

They simply have not had enough experiences. You have to have experiences to learn to read, and you have to read to succeed in school.

Many people claimed that little could be done because the budget and circumstances would not allow for enough field trips to fill this gap. Others set about vigorously trying to provide experiences, which for their purposes meant nice, big fieldtrips—the assumption being that once this gap was filled, the children could proceed to read as the middle-class children do.

Perhaps these theories are basically true, and all the children have to do is wait until the necessary experiences have been provided. It seems to me, however, that this is an oversimplification and a narrow view of the problem. It is not so much that these children have not had experiences, but rather that they have not had the experiences we demand. We say to them in effect, "This is a middle-class white school—although the enrollment may be 99% Negro, 40% welfare cases, and 20% unemployed—and you are to act like nice middle-class white children. If you are a poor white, a Mexican migrant, or an underprivileged Negro, that's just too bad. Come and prove how stupid you are."

I believe that if we are serious about trying to help the so-called dis-

Printed with permission of the author, who is presently conducting classes for the Trainable Mentally Retarded in Berkeley, California.

advantaged child, we ought to take a good look at him and see what he is really like. One thing is certain, however. The culturally deprived child has had experiences. Thus, in my work with a group of culturally deprived first graders, I set out to capitalize on experiences. I found a six-year-old girl, for instance, who is an expert on fishing—the procedure, the art of, and the laws regarding; a boy who would be a natural for the 1980 Olympics swim team; and a boy who had never been to the zoo but who had made many advanced studies on ants, snails, dragonflies, and other tiny creatures. These children had exciting stories to tell and interesting things to bring to school for us to talk about, write about, and read about. But while these things were very exciting, we could not afford to limit our experiences to the backgrounds of these particular children any more than we could afford to limit the children's experiences to those of the teacher. Moreover, the most exciting thing about the child is his *self*. If a teacher can feel interest and excitement in his being, the child can and will also. In fact, even without the spiritual cooperation of the teacher, the child can feel this excitement unless he is beaten down again and again and finally convinced of his worthlessness. Thus, it was difficult for some children to share life experiences because they had accepted the erroneous belief that only certain kinds of experiences were worthy of being shared.

It became apparent, therefore, that the first objective of the program must be to improve the child's self-concept. In our class discussions, which were not limited in any way, children learned to talk about themselves, their interests and their activities. They learned to become keenly aware of the *self*, of its importance to oneself as well as to others, to grow not by comparison with someone else but with oneself and, moreover, to respect each individual for himself.

Thus this first-grade class was set up on the theory that although culturally deprived children lack many of the experiences associated with middle-class homes and required by middle-class oriented schools, they have many other experiences from which a teacher can draw. Moreover, there are many other experiences which children can be given in the classroom to cause them to be not only ready but also willing.

The classroom environment was carefully prepared so that there were a number of work projects to keep children busy in a constructive way. Each project was simply and carefully planned so that a child could learn many things from it and so that more able or mature children could proceed to the next step. As each new activity was designed and brought into the room, the children were given a demonstration on how to use it in its simplest form. Emphasis was on individual growth. Except for brief periods during which reading lessons were conducted, children were free to choose any project which was not in use or to share another child's project provided the other child did not consider this an intrusion.

Most of the work projects were produced nightly by the teacher's ingenuity, which was created out of dire necessity and desperation at times.

Following is a brief description of some techniques used in teaching subject matter to these young children.

Reading

To stimulate inquiry, two basic approaches were used. 1. In the Active Involvement approach, children first became involved in a discussion of a word such as run or jump. Students talked about the word's meaning and boasted of their ability to perform the action representing the word. When their interest in performing the action reached its peak, they were incited to do so. As each child indicated his comprehension of the word by performing the act, the word was written on the board. The children soon concluded, "I know what she is writing. It's jump (or run . . .)" As a second step, the word was used with each child's name to form an imperative sentence. The children performed the actions enthusiastically as their names appeared on the board. As a third step, the children were asked "What can you do?" As they answered, the teacher printed it on the board. They read it easily and were able to change the sentence to third person by using their own or a classmate's name. They were soon making up their own interrogative sentences as well as complex and compound sentences. The first preprimer vocabulary and many additional words were learned in this way. Children reinforced their reading by writing the words and by forming them and sentences with various types of individual letters.

2. Charts were posted at various intervals. The charts contained large interesting pictures with simple sentences about the children in the classroom. When the children saw their own names they were eager to discover what was being said. The racial content of the pictures represented that of the classroom.

A color chart using plastic spoons was a popular and useful device. Each spoon was glued to a card at the top of which was printed the word "spoon" in black letters. Each spoon fitted into a pocket on which the color name was printed in matching color. The children identified the word "spoon" and learned the color names.

Arithmetic

A number of very simple devices were used. One of the most useful was a set of beads strung on wires. There were ten of the wires, the first containing one bead, the second two, and so on. Each group in the series was the same color except the ten bead. The children were shown the beads and practiced counting them until they became aware of which was the 3, the 6, and the like. They were then introduced to a box which had numbers across the bottom, spaced from 0 to 10. The first step was to lay the correct number of beads beside the printed number. Secondly, some of the children began to add groups of beads and thus were making simple addition problems for themselves. Because the ten was a different color, some children discovered for themselves the tens concept and were able to verbalize "I have one 10 and 2, and that is twelve." These same children made an easy transition when we counted money.

Another simple device was eleven milk cartons opened lengthwise on one side, taped together and numbered 0-10. Children who could count to ten by rote, but did not understand the concepts, learned to start with nothing and to add one each time. If they did not know the numbers, they learned to put the correct concept with the abstract symbol. They used straws for counting and bundled their tens so that some of them learned to count by tens in this manner.

The most popular device was a painted egg carton, numbered 0 to 11, a ping-pong ball, and a carton of large lima beans. The children bounced the ball until it landed in one of the sections. They then read the number and counted out the correct number of beans.

Finally, there was a money board and a carton of change. The board consisted of a quarter, dime, nickel, and penny glued to a piece of heavy cardboard. Next to each coin was a pocket in which children could experiment with finding different ways of producing the same sum or making simple additions. As children worked with this money board they perfected their counting and made it more meaningful.

⊱•⊰

An Approach to the Socially Unmotivated

⊱•⊰

ARTHUR GOLDBERG

From many aspects the crucial problem of public education is that of the socially unmotivated pupil. Certainly from the aspect of dedication to "education for all American youth" this is critical. For certainly education without motivation is a paradox at best and a farce at the worst.

Now let us be clear about this from the start: The socially unmotivated are not the mentally retarded, nor the emotionally disturbed, or simply the economically deprived. They are those whose cultural experience has not predisposed them to value what the school has to offer. In larger numbers than is warranted statistically, the socially unmotivated, by definition, do come from the lower social classes. The key factor here, however, is not that they are economically underprivileged (this may be a doubtful assumption in this day and age) but the system of values to which they give adherence.

No neat characterization can be made of pupils—any more than it can be made of people as a whole. But generalized groupings and trends are necessary for no public policy can be predicated on an individual basis—unless one intends as many policies as there are persons. Sociological studies (e.g., *Yankee City* studies, *Elmtown's Youth, Plainville, Street Corner Society*) have fairly conclusively determined that, among others, anti-authority aggressions, and immediacy of goal satisfactions are characteristics of the value system of those of lower class status.

Again for purposes of broad policy, pupils may be defined motivationally into two categories: those with delayed goals and satisfactions,

From *Teacher Education Quarterly*, Winter, 1962-63. Reprinted by permission of Dr. Bertram Sarason, Chairman, Editorial Board, *Teacher Education Quarterly*, and of the author, principal of The Edwin O. Smith School, Storrs, Connecticut.

and those whose goals are immediate, who will not delay their satisfactions. Consume now, rather than save for later and fuller satisfaction is a familiar manifestation of this value system. For those with delayed goals who will defer their satisfactions for fuller, if later, realizations, schools are ideally suited. Schools are oriented, necessarily so, to deferred goals. Psychologically, schools attempt to provide immediate measures of success. But this is in terms of partial goals as steps in turn to an ultimate goal.

It is these very partial goals which are rejected by those without deferred goals since it is the deferred goal which is the raison d'etre for the partial goal. Schools have attempted to provide immediate goals for students—with rather disastrous results. In most cases it has amounted to little more than a wearing-down of course content on the assumption of the inadequacy of the pupils, or of establishing some sort of therapeutic situation, than which nothing can be more fatal to school and pupil alike.

Still these pupils are valuable per se and as a national resource. Many of them are quite capable. Very many are much better potential students than their achievements would indicate and certainly much brighter than the I.Q. would lead one to believe. Group I.Q. scores on these pupils are rarely reliable as measures of intelligence. It is again the motivational factor which is the key.

If the reasoning to this point is soundly based and logically developed, it would follow that these pupils cannot be motivated through the school's motivational pattern of delayed goals: Study now because it will be helpful later, study now to get into college later, study now to get a better job later, study now to be a better person later. But perhaps we can approach these pupils through their motivational systems but for the school's purposes—implying thereby that these are society's purposes as well.

Certainly nothing meets the criteria of immediacy as well as does money. Money, while not in itself a satisfaction (it can't be eaten or worn), is a claim on satisfactions that our society must honor on demand. This led staff members at the Edwin O. Smith School to consider a work-study program for the socially unmotivated. Work is tied to money, money to the value system of these pupils. If work rewardable in money as well as in marks and praise could be tied to the classroom [would it not be possible to] accomplish more learning in this reduced time than we have been able to accomplish in the past on a full time basis?—this because we have tapped a motivational well-spring.

Characteristic of teenagers of the lower classes, too, is their desire for adult status. They cannot wait to play the adult role. Physically, by the age of sixteen, they are adult. For those with deferred goals this desire to play the adult role (common to all teenagers) is sublimated in study and social activities. The young man or woman who has set his heart on graduate work, research, or medicine defers his fully independent adulthood till very close to the age of thirty. We can scarcely envision the pupils for whom the work-study program has been designed waiting until well into the twenties to assume their adult roles, particularly since their social-cultural heritage predisposes them (to speak euphemistically) to premature sophistication.

This is the first year of operation for the program. Even this early, evidence is appearing that should be recorded.

The Work-Study Program at the Edwin O. Smith School is established on a morning work and afternoon study basis. The reasoning behind this is that the motivation for reporting to the job is greater than for reporting to school. And indeed—to date—there has been no lateness in reporting to the job or to the school in the afternoon. In the one case of a necessary absence, the excuse for it was very carefully arranged prior to the absence. A further reason for the morning-afternoon arrangement was that this would enable the pupils to participate in school activities. Pupils may return to the job after class hours if they wish and if the employer has need of them. Some pupils are doing this. Others have become members of athletic squads, chorus, band, or other groups.

The classroom program is strongly oriented to English-History. Communication skills—or the lack of them—so often label these youngsters, and literature in its varied richness is probably the best carry-over for these pupils. History, centered about the United States, but not exclusive to it, was judged a basic need. The approach to history has been economic: How our economy evolves, its development, money, banking, social security, government regulations, farm problem, international trade and trade policy. Here, too, the response to date has been gratifying.

Of course, weaknesses in specific fields not covered by the program of studies will make themselves evident, notably in mathematics. When the need is identified, teachers will be brought in for specific periods during the week for instruction in these areas. In one instance a girl was to be employed in a drafting office. For several weeks preceding her employment, her morning hours were spent in the mechanical-technical drawing room working on projects under the drafting instructor's guidance to develop her skill in and acquaintance with the demands of her prospective employment.

The program as presently established contains some twenty pupils and is under the direction and instruction of William Paradis. The afternoon hours are spent with him. In the morning hours, he circulates among the employers. Deficiencies on the job become grist for classroom examination and discussion. It is the director's duty, too, to search out job opportunities. Though he makes the initial contact, each pupil must seek an interview with a prospective employer, secure working papers, pass whatever tests may be required of an applicant, and otherwise assume such personal responsibilities as one might when seeking employment. Guidance in this area alone is not the least valuable contribution of the program.

This program might be evaluated in the future through the social adjustment of the pupil, his truancy record, his record as it may reflect his difficulty with civil authority, and his own personal gratification. It is planned to do this but this alone will not justify the program. The learning achievement which is the program's hypothesis, must also be measured. If resistance to school authority is reduced, if through our program we can direct the pupils to goals beyond the immediacy of money itself, then this change in behavior should result in higher achievement. This will be measured.

The evaluation of this program must be based on more than a hunch and socialization. Therefore, these pupils are carefully screened and tested. Before admission to the program each was administered an individual I.Q. test. During the first week of the school year STEP tests were administered so that a record of performance in such areas as reading, listening, mathematics and social studies might be obtained. In June the pupils were retested and their progress in these learning areas is being evaluated. In addition, pupils wrote autobiographically on such topics as "My Fears." Another year projective testing may be employed. Finally, an employer's evaluative criteria check list has been developed.

This program is very much in the experimental stage. The faculty of the Edwin O. Smith School feel that it is based on sound social-psychological theory—and have faith in the manner in which the theory is being put into practice. They are watching attentively and are ready to make alterations, deletions, and additions as the need becomes evident. Experience has been most encouraging. The program may be successful enough to cause its own delimitation. Because of this experience, some of the pupils might return with renewed and increased motivation to a full-time class program. There is some evidence for this hope (for that is all it is) in the number of pupils who, after a year away from school, return to complete the high school program.

It may be well, in conclusion, to re-emphasize that though these pupils tend presently to cluster in the bottom quarter of their rank-in-class, they are not regarded as academically incapable. On individual tests, many have surprisingly high I.Q.'s. They are not shuttled off into a corner nor out of school. The staff is vitally interested and gives its own time to special instruction on a group or individual basis. Nor are these pupils seen as discipline cases—though often they were. They are viewed as people with a motivational pattern not conductive to the learning of the deferred goals of the school. Motivational slight-of-hand in the classroom will not accomplish the school's purpose. Motivation will be aroused by employing (but not ending with) the value system of the pupils themselves. If this means going outside school walls or bringing the real community of work and pay into the school, it will be done. The community will respond and accept its obligations. The student will give a full hour's work for a full hour's pay.

Because of the immediacy of their goals, these pupils do not sublimate their physical maturity nor their desire for adult status to deferred satisfactions. These pupils are given the opportunity to play the adult role under guidance without detriment to learning and with fuller and richer individual development.

꧁•꧂

Saving the Trouble-Prone

꧁•꧂

Nason E. Hall, Jr.

Why is it that even in the highest delinquency areas of a city, a large majority of young boys manage to stay in school, out of trouble, and become law-abiding, productive citizens? Presumably these "good" boys are subject to the same delinquency-producing factors as trouble-prone youth and yet are able to channel their energies into alternative, law-abiding patterns of behavior.

In order to understand this seeming paradox, professors Simon Dinitz and Walter Reckless of Ohio State University collected data through a large number of semistructured, exploratory interviews and questionnaires among "good" boys and "bad" boys residing in high delinquency areas of Columbus, Ohio. The interviews and questionnaires were designed to measure differences in perspectives toward self and others, values, and orientation toward important life areas. The differences, they found, were:

In contrast to boys who stayed out of trouble, boys having difficulty in school and inclined toward delinquent behavior viewed themselves as trouble-makers who were likely to be involved in future difficulty. Furthermore, they had no real desire to avoid future trouble.

Again in contrast to "good" boys, the potential delinquents had poorly formulated or discordant perspectives regarding several life areas: work, school, the family, and law enforcement. That is, either the delinquency-prone boy didn't know what these life areas were all about or if he did have a coherent set of definitions, they were of a type likely to bring him into conflict with employers, school officials, family members, and the police.

From *NEA Journal*, April, 1965. Reprinted by permission of the publisher. The author is assistant professor of sociology; director, Youth Development Project, Ohio State University, Columbus.

Boys headed for trouble tended to belittle their own and their fathers' worth and potential.

These findings and experience gained in two experimental after-school delinquency prevention programs sparked the Youth Development Project*—a three-year, demonstration-research project conducted in cooperation with the Columbus public schools.

The project involves specially designed classes conducted during the regular school day for delinquency-prone seventh grade boys attending eight junior high schools located in high delinquency areas of Columbus. Sixth grade teachers in the forty-four elementary schools which feed these junior high schools select the pupils who participate in the classes.

In May of each year, sixth grade teachers are asked to indicate with regard to each graduating male pupil whether they think it is highly likely, highly unlikely, or uncertain that he will become involved in future difficulty with law enforcement agencies. Each year from 475 to 525 pupils are classed as probable or possible candidates for future difficulties with the law. Candidates are then screened to eliminate those with IQ scores lower than 70 and those with severe emotional difficulties. Half of the remaining delinquency-prone boys are randomly assigned to participate in the project classes while the other half are in the regular curriculum, thus serving as a control group.

The project classes operate as part of the regular class schedule in the Self-Contained Class (SCC). The SCC is normally a three-period time block during which a single teacher instructs in language arts, social studies, and geography. The project classes, although committed to coverage of the regular SCC curriculum, receive additional special units dealing with work, school, the family, and law enforcement. In addition, four periods per week are devoted to remedial reading.

The project teachers are four relatively young male public school teachers selected because of their demonstrated ability to work with pupils of low socioeconomic family status. Interestingly, three of the four teachers are themselves products of slum environments.

In developing a curriculum for these delinquency-prone youngsters, the director and the four teachers were guided by several principles. The central overall aim was to provide the pupils with alternative ways of interpreting and evaluating their environment and their relationship to it.

For example, in the special units, the teachers invite employers,

* The Youth Development Project is part of the ongoing Ohio State University Delinquency Research Program (Walter C. Reckless, director) and is principally financed by a grant from the National Institute of Mental Health.

teachers, policemen, parents, and other adults to talk to the class. Every speaker is asked to give an autobiography and to discuss candidly what he likes and dislikes about his job or family role. In a question period following each talk, the boys ask any questions they wish. (A Catholic nun was asked if she were bald; a juvenile officer was asked if he really enjoyed carrying a gun.)

Throughout the school year, efforts focus upon getting the boys to reassess their stereotyped attitudes about the motivations of significant authority figures. Hopefully, a reassessment of others will lead a boy to a reassessment of the relationship between himself and others and thereby change his self-concept.

A second guiding principle in developing the curriculum was that the materials presented had to be relevant to the prior experience of the pupils. The project is not interested in bringing the world of middle-class norms and values into the slum classroom. Rather, alternative behavior patterns are presented in terms of future consequences for self and others.

Finally, every lesson had to be intrinsically interesting. This commitment led to a broad search for materials and presentation techniques including films, speakers, specially developed stories, tapes, plays, etc. (At the close of the first school year [1963-64], each lesson was reviewed and modified or discarded if necessary. The teachers assisted in this effort by completing an evaluation form for each lesson.)

Any class with twenty-five to thirty boys who have been defined by their former teachers as unmanageable and academically hopeless presents a control problem.

Under the guidance of a child psychiatrist, the project staff developed a means of class control based upon the principle of mutual respect—the pupil can do what he pleases as long as he doesn't infringe upon the teacher's right to teach and other pupils' right to learn. The atmosphere is not permissive, however. Whenever an infringement occurs, the pupil is asked to isolate himself from the class and to think about what he has done. When he feels that he is ready to respect the rights of others, he may return to the class of his own volition.

The decision to avoid such techniques of discipline as corporal punishment, belittlement, and shaming was based upon several things we knew about these boys.

First, as far as corporal punishment is concerned, special project pupils generally have had plenty of it at home and, in some cases, throughout their school career. Obviously this form of discipline hasn't worked.

Second, these boys came to the program considering themselves of little personal worth or potential. One of the crucial problems was to break down this negative self-image and replace it with a more positive self-concept.

Finally, the potential delinquents enrolled in the project generally have a fatalistic outlook; they see themselves as powerless to control or manipulate their environment. The volitional aspects of control by means of mutual respect provides them with an opportunity to shape their own social situation.

After six to eight weeks of orientation to the mutual respect principle, the pupils adapt to the point where all the teacher needs to do when an infringement occurs is to point to the violator. The boy then removes himself, is gone for a while, and returns without a word being said. The teacher need not interrupt his presentation or call undue attention to the problem.

Of course, the boys' interest in the curriculum makes it easier to operate classes on the basis of mutual respect. The boys do not generally desire to leave the class for extended periods of time, if at all. How the principle would work without special curriculum material is another matter.

It became evident early in the program that the pupils were not likely to stay in school (and thereby out of trouble) unless their reading proficiency improved. While, on the average, the boys were reading two-and-a-half years below grade level, their range of abilities was wide —from third through seventh grade. Another problem was that they probably could not be grouped by ability levels and still retain interest and acceptable behavior patterns. Furthermore, the project teachers had little previous training in teaching reading. Finally, and most importantly, the staff had to assume that the boys lacked the motivation to learn to read.

With these problems in mind, the staff, along with a special reading consultant from Ohio State University, sought to develop a systematic and appropriate remedial reading program.

They began by purchasing 240 paperback novels, biographies, and histories, selected for readability and appropriateness of materials. The paperbacks were then placed in each class as a library which could be used at the pupils' discretion, and the teachers noted which books circulated most frequently. By far, the two most popular were H. G. Wells' *The Time Machine* and Don Stanford's *The Red Car*. These were adapted as texts, and exercises were developed covering every four to five pages.

After examining many reading workbooks, the staff selected one series which they thought fitted the project's requirements—the "Turner-Livingston Reading Series." The books in this series deal directly with the project's curriculum topics—work, family, school, law enforcement, and problems of adolescents from low income homes.

The third set of remedial reading materials selected for the project was the *Reader's Digest* "Skill Building Series." These materials have the advantage of skill level grouping which does not require the teacher to work with separate groups. The pupils work on their own, at their individual levels and speeds.

In addition, the reading consultant developed a set of "shotgun" exercises dealing with every type of mechanical reading problem. Each teacher has a set of these exercises and a handbook which notes the reading principle involved and gives suggestions about how to teach the principle. When the teacher finds a commonly shared difficulty, he pulls the appropriate exercise from the file and works at the problem on the spot.

Each class also receives newspapers two days per week from which the boys read orally the articles which interest them.

The remedial reading materials used in the project share several essential characteristics: interest, variety, and adaptability. Each day a different type of learning experience is presented. Although staff members cannot yet assess the effectiveness of remedial reading efforts, they can say that interest and participation are high. All pupils are trying to learn.

Home visits are another important aspect of the delinquency prevention program.

The family of every pupil is visited at least once during the school year, and the families of particularly difficult boys may be visited many times. These visits provide an opportunity for the teacher to observe the nature of the family situation and to gain insights into the dynamics underlying behavioral problems. When sufficient rapport has been established and when the time is appropriate, the teacher may make suggestions to parents regarding their relationship with the pupil.

Along with the home visits, each teacher meets with a child psychiatrist two hours per month to discuss means of handling problem boys. The project recognizes that the problems of school adjustment lie only partly in the attitude of the pupil. Just as important is the perspective of the teacher toward the human being with whom he is in contact.

Whether a one-year program of this type is enough to overcome problems which have been building in these boys for twelve to thirteen years is impossible to say. Nevertheless, the Youth Development Project has demonstrated that delinquency-prone boys can be interested in and can enjoy learning.

The Project has also shown that physical or psychological punitive measures are unnecessary in working with such boys.

Finally, the program does not demand a highly specialized therapeutic staff, the cost of which is prohibitive in most school systems. The regular teacher, properly trained and properly attuned to the needs of his students, is all the direct assistance needed to help these boys recapture their self-esteem—the vital ingredient missing from their lives.

Recommended Readings

Bloom, Benjamin S., Allison Davis, and Robert Hess, *Compensatory Education for Cultural Deprivation*, New York: Holt, Rinehart, and Winston Incorporated, © 1965. This book contains working papers contributed by participants of a conference held at the University of Chicago. An excellent summary of the problems of cultural deprivation is presented as well as suggestions for action. A lengthy bibliography is included.

Englemann, S. E., *Cultural Deprivation—Description and Remedy* (available for 50c from Institute for Research on Exceptional Children, College of Education, University of Illinois, Urbana). An analysis of the language deficit characterizing disadvantaged children, and a recommended approach for overcoming this deficit with pre-school children.

Finocchiaro, Mary, *Teaching English as a Second Language*, New York: Mc-Graw-Hill Company, © 1958. Suggestions for teaching English as a second language based on experience with non-English speaking children and adolescents in New York schools.

Hollbrook, David, *English for the Rejected*, London and New York: Cambridge Press, 1964. Addressed primarily to teachers and administrators, this book is a humane description of the nature and needs of the disadvantaged. Extensive discussion of methods and approaches to be used in training for literacy are included.

Jewett, Arno, *et al.*, *Improving English Skills of Culturally Different Youth*, U.S. Department of Health, Education, and Welfare, Washington D.C., 1964. Papers from a conference on educating the disadvantaged. This includes research reports, descriptions of projects and recommendations for further action.

Programs for the Educationally Disadvantaged, U.S. Department of Health, Education, and Welfare, Office of Education, Bulletin, 1963, No. 17. An excellent survey of current programs designed to assist the disadvantaged learner. Also included are specific instructional approaches and suggestions for needed educational changes.

Rivlin, Harry N., *Teachers for Our Big City Schools*, New York, Anti-Defamation League of B'Nai B'rith, G444, 50c per copy. Dr. Rivlin takes a serious look at the problems facing large city schools and makes a number of worthwhile suggestions.

INDEX

This Index covers all three parts of *The Disadvantaged Learner: Knowing, Understanding, Educating.*

The Contents of
THE DISADVANTAGED LEARNER

PART II: UNDERSTANDING THE EDUCATIONAL PROBLEMS OF THE DISADVANTAGED LEARNER

PART III: EDUCATING THE DISADVANTAGED LEARNER

b

c

d